ALL ABOUT
Chocolate

The Ultimate Resource for the World's Favorite Food

CAROLE BLOOM

MACMILLAN • USA

MACMILLAN
A Simon & Schuster Macmillan Company
1633 Broadway
New York, NY 10019-6785

Macmillan Publishing books may be purchased for business or sales promotional use. For information please write: Special Markets Department, Macmillan Publishing USA, 1633 Broadway, New York, NY 10019.

MACMILLAN is a registered trademark of Macmillan, Inc.

Library of Congress Cataloging-in-Publication Data

Bloom, Carole.
　All about chocolate: the ultimate resource for the world's favorite food / by Carole Bloom.
　　p.　cm.
　Includes bibliographical references and index.
　ISBN 0-02-862283-9 (alk. paper)
　1.　Chocolate.　2.　Cookery (Chocolate)　I. Title.
　TX817.C4B56　1998
　641.3'374—dc21　　　　　　　　　　　　　　　　　　　98-20895
　　　　　　　　　　　　　　　　　　　　　　　　　　　　　CIP

Manufactured in the United States of America

10　9　8　7　6　5　4　3　2　1

Book design by Nick Anderson

The recipe for Chocolate-Espresso Pots de Crème first appeared in an article I wrote for the February 1997 issue of *Bon Appétit* magazine. BON APPÉTIT is a registered trademark of Advance Magazine Publishers Inc., published through its division, The Condé Nast Publications Inc. Copyright © 1997 by The Condé Nast Publications Inc. Reprinted with permission.

Dedicated with love to my husband, Jerry, who eats chocolate every day and to my mother, Florence, the family chocoholic.

This book is also dedicated to chocolate lovers everywhere.

Acknowledgments

Writing a book is a bigger undertaking than most people realize. I'm fortunate to have a great support team and to have received assistance from many people. Thanks to everyone who provided me with information about their products and for sending samples: chocolatiers and confectioners, chocolate manufacturers and distributors, catalog purveyors, equipment manufacturers and suppliers, cooking schools, and others. They were all very enthusiastic and more than willing to share information.

A very special thank you to Sharon Burdick of Pinehill Bed & Breakfast in Oregon, Illinois, who was so willing to help and opened her chocolate research library to me. Thanks also to colleague Liz Clark for putting me in touch with Sharon.

Laura Barton of the Oregon Department of Agriculture provided me with many contacts in Oregon. Thanks to Ginger Johnston, food editor of *The Oregonian*, for her assistance.

Jacques Bergier of Duchateau, Ltd. in New York was very enthusiastic and most gracious in putting me in contact with many people in the world of chocolate. Markus Farbinger, pastry team leader and Dan Budd, teaching chef, both of the Culinary Institute of America in Hyde Park, New York, were helpful in providing contacts and information about chocolate. I especially enjoyed my e-mail correspondence with Markus about the fine points of pralines.

Colleague Elaine Gonzalez gladly shared her knowledge of chocolate and helped with suggestions of who to contact for a variety of information. Toni Allegra, immediate past president of the International Association of Culinary Professionals, and good friend also helped with contacts and good suggestions. Thanks also to colleague Sue Zelickson, food reporter for WCCO Radio in Minneapolis, Minnesota, for her assistance. My thanks to Susan S. Smith of the Chocolate Manufacturers Association in McLean, Virginia, who helped me ferret out information on some events and birth dates of many popular American candy bars.

A big thank you to Gilles Renusson, founder of the U.S. Pastry Alliance, and teaching chef at Grand Rapids Community College in Grand Rapids, Michigan. Gilles spoke to me at great length about professional competitions and generously shared his vast knowledge and experience as team captain of the United States pastry team, who competed at the World Pastry Cup in Lyons, France and as coach of the team when they won a silver medal at the competition in 1997. Thanks to Kelley Regan of *Food Arts* magazine for helping me ferret out information about chocolate competitions and to David Kee at Classic Gourmet in Atlanta, Georgia, for so enthusiastically sharing information about chocolate and professional competitions.

I was delighted to make contact with Sarah and Gary Legon of Estate Films in Los Angeles, California, who shared with me their experiences in the world of chocolate and their recent documentary film, *Chocolate*. Phillipe Laurier of Paris Gourmet Patisfrance graciously shared his vast knowledge of chocolate. Rick and Rena Pocrass of Chocolates à la Carte were also helpful in providing information.

Many thanks to the reference librarians at the Carlsbad City Library, in particular Karen Mitchell at the La Costa Branch, for their assistance in tracking down many obscure works on chocolate. Thanks also to Lauren Lessing, research librarian at the Ryerson and Burnham Libraries, The Art Institute of Chicago, for help in locating works of art depicting chocolate and information about them.

Larry Beezley, staff curator at Quail Botanical Gardens in Encinitas, California, was very helpful with information about the technical aspects of cacao cultivation and generously lent me books from his personal library. Daniele Piomele, researcher at The Neurosciences Institute in San Diego, California gave a most entertaining lecture on the psychopharmacology of chocolate and helped me understand more fully the technical reasons why chocolate makes us feel so good.

Thank you to my good friend and colleague Kitty Morse for help with French translation and chocolate tasting, for being so enthusiastic and supportive, and for ferreting out some interesting chocolate sources. Thanks also to my good friend Janet MacWilliams for finding sources for me during her world travels. Friend and colleague Sara Jayne-Stanes in London generously shared her knowledge of chocolate history and sources for chocolate and equipment in England, and provided me with her delicious truffles. And many thanks to my other personal friends and colleagues who provided moral support and were most willing to help in tasting the many chocolate samples sent from around the world: Betz Collins, Bonnie Jo Bechtold, Lesa Heebner, Susie Hostetter, and Mindy Tremblay. A special thank you to Susie for keeping me gliding and on the right edge through this process by making sure I kept up with my ice skating.

My agent, Jane Dystel, provided savvy and sage advice and, as always, was there for me when I needed her. My editor, Jennifer Griffin, was a pleasure to work with and I appreciate her insightful editing. Thanks also to Jim Willhite, Jennifer's assistant, for not missing a beat and for guiding this book through the publishing process. Thanks to everyone at Macmillan who worked on this book and saw it through its many phases.

My kittens Tiger and Casanova, also known as "the yummy tummy boys," gave me hours of entertainment with their antics and provided lots of good vibrations by sleeping in my lap and on my desk as I worked. And last, but far from least, my husband, Jerry Olivas, who is truly my hero, was there through it all helping in every way possible with ideas, searching the World Wide Web late at night and finding things most of us would never even think about, eating lots of chocolate (after all, someone has to do it), keeping my computer working, making many trips to the library, providing moral support, washing dishes, planning a well-deserved vacation, and most importantly, making me laugh. Without his unwavering support and help this book would have taken much longer to complete.

Contents

CONTENTS

Introduction

"All I really need is love, but a little chocolate now and then doesn't hurt!"
—Lucy Van Pelt in Charles M. Schulz's *Peanuts*

"Chocolate . . . is the secret drug of happiness."
—Jonathan Ott, *The Cacahuatl Eater: Ruminations of an Unabashed Chocolate Addict*, 1985

How can you get the most out of your experience with chocolate? The answer is, of course, eat more chocolate. But there is another answer, find out more about chocolate. This way you will be better able to explore and discover all the various forms of chocolate with the ultimate goal of finding what's just right for you.

In this book you will learn practically everything there is to know about chocolate. It is more than a dictionary of chocolate terms with some recipes and techniques. This book is a guide to the whole world of chocolate.

If you are new to the world of chocolate you will be introduced to a wide variety of exciting information. If you want to know the history of chocolate or learn some chocolate vocabulary, such as what is meant by chocolate bloom or tempering, it's in this book. For chocolate aficionados there is some great information for you, too. You will learn where the very best chocolate shops in the world are and where to go to school to refine your chocolate making skills. Also, for both novice and professional cooks there are twenty-five fabulous, easy-to-prepare chocolate recipes that are both my personal favorites and favorites of my students.

I've been eating chocolate for as long as I can remember. Like most people, I started out with chocolate chip cookies. Eating the batter before it reached the oven was more fun than eating the finished cookies, although they were yummy, too. Chocolate in just about any form was fine with me. When I grew up and began to learn more about food, my interest in chocolate expanded and I discovered that not only do I love to eat chocolate, but love to work with it.

It was in Europe, Switzerland mostly, where I became aware of the vast world of chocolate. I loved chocolate before I went to Europe, but after tasting all (almost all) the great chocolates my consciousness expanded greatly. For example, my preference went from milk to dark chocolate and I began to like white chocolate and chocolate with hazelnuts. Also, chocolate truffles became my favorite, especially ones with fruit and liqueur fillings. Raspberry truffles remain one of my passions.

When I studied pastry making in Europe I could see that chocolate held a special place in the pastry kitchen. That became even more apparent when I was working as a pastry chef in Europe and the United States. It wasn't that chocolate was more difficult to work with than other ingredients, but that chocolate was so well liked by everyone, including the kitchen staff. Every day, at least two desserts were made with chocolate and there were always chocolate ice cream and sauces that were freshly made.

These days there appears to be a chocolate revival. Good-quality chocolate is readily available and there are many chocolatiers who are eager to share their unique creations with the world. Also, chocolate manufacturers are creating chocolates based on a single type of cocoa bean or from beans that are grown in one area of the world. The amount of cocoa components in fine-quality chocolate is increasing. People's palates are becoming more educated and their quest for premium-quality chocolate is expanding.

Chocolate is part of our lives in many more ways than simply something good to eat. It has spurred the establishment of several industries. There are cacao growers, chocolate manufacturers, equipment manufacturers and suppliers, confectioners and shops, catalogs for mail-order sources for bulk chocolate, equipment, and chocolate bonbons, and chocolate web sites. And there are chocolate schools, museums, factory tours, and festivals springing up throughout the world that celebrate chocolate.

Often people get mixed up between chocolate manufacturers and confectioners. This happens because sometimes the names are the same, such as

Lindt-Sprüngli, which both manufactures chocolate and makes confections. Also, most people purchase the finished product through a confectioner or shop, such as See's Candies or Fannie May. It's easy to think that the chocolate is made by the confectioner. But it is the confectioner who uses the chocolate to make candies and confections, which are called chocolates. Chocolate manufacturers make chocolate couverture that is sold to confectioners. I encourage people to ask confectioners, pastry shops, and restaurants what chocolate they use, so they can become more familiar with the many different brands. In this book you will find a list of the major chocolate manufacturers, as well as a separate list of confectioners and shops.

For years I have thought about writing a book that was all about chocolate with only a few select recipes. A book that could answer practically any question about chocolate or at least direct people to where they could easily get the answer. It would be less of a "how-to" book and more fun and educational. I envisioned a book that would be the ultimate resource for chocolate lovers. This is it.

In this book you will find "Chocolate Lexicon," from A to Z, of terms about and relating to chocolate. This includes types of chocolate and chocolate products, the names of well-known chocolate desserts, pastries, and confections, techniques, equipment, and tools for working with chocolate, and well-known names of people in the world of chocolate. Within the "Chocolate Lexicon" are twenty-five "to-live-for" chocolate recipes. You will also learn about chocolate's fascinating history in the "Chronology of Chocolate History" and discover how chocolate is made in the section titled "From the Bean to the Bar." There is a section on "Tasting Chocolate" and "Chocolate Tips" for working with chocolate, including how to store and serve it. Several other sections are included covering health, lore, cocoa futures, festivals and events, museums and tours, themes parks, competitions, organizations, associations and clubs, chocolate schools, World Wide Web sites, chocolate shops worldwide, manufacturers and factories, sources for chocolate, and for chocolate equipment, utensils, and tools, and an appendix listing chocolate publications, literature, movies and videos, and chocolate in visual art and the theater. The book also has a bibliography of significant chocolate books for those who wish to explore the field in more depth.

You can use this book in various ways. First, it is a good reference that can be opened to any section to find the information you seek. Second, you can work your way through the book by reading the various sections in any order. Start with whatever section you would like, then choose another. You can also read through the book from start to finish. This will assure that you don't miss anything and also allow you to bookmark information that is of particular interest. You don't have to follow any particular order for the recipes either. Just go for whatever appeals to you.

Why do we like chocolate so much? The simple answer is that it tastes wonderful and makes us feel good. Just thinking about eating a luscious chocolate dessert makes us happy. Chocolate is an incredible substance with many, many facets. The more I learn about it, the more I am intrigued and fascinated. My hope is that this book will heighten your interest in chocolate. That you will not only want more chocolate, but what's just right for you—what gives you the most pleasure. Chocolate, above all else, is a pleasure food.

PART I

Knowing All About Chocolate

$\mathscr{C}$HOCOLATE
LEXICON

"Now, Watson, there's cocoa ready in the next room. I must beg you to hurry, for we have a great day before us."
— Sherlock Holmes to Dr. Watson in "The Adventure of the Priory School," by Sir Arthur Conan Doyle, in *The Return of Sherlock Holmes*

A

ADM Cocoa   Established over one hundred years ago, ADM Cocoa is currently the world's largest producer of cocoa-related products. The company manufactures coating chocolates made to exact specifications for clients in block or liquid form, compound coatings, and a wide variety of cocoa powders. ADM markets its products to industrial food producers. In 1997 ADM Cocoa acquired Grace Cocoa, one of the world's largest chocolate products companies, which owned Cacao De Zaan, a well-known Dutch company. Ambrosia and Merckens chocolates are also part of this group. ADM has offices in the United States and several other countries including Canada, the Netherlands, France, Germany, and Singapore. *See also* **couverture**.

Almond Joy   A popular, classic American candy bar introduced by Peter Paul in 1947. In 1988 Hershey Foods Corporation acquired Peter Paul and currently manufactures the candy bar, whose motto is "Indescribably Delicious." The bar is composed of two $2^1/_2$-inch long, 1-inch wide, $^1/_2$-inch thick, oval-shaped sections of corn syrup–sweetened coconut that are each topped with two whole, unblanched almonds. The bar is completely coated with milk chocolate. The two sections are considered to be one serving with a caloric content of 240.

Alprose   A Swiss chocolate company founded in 1957 in Caslano, near Lugano. The company merged with the German chocolate company Stollwerck in 1975. A museum was opened to the public in 1991 and shows the Swiss chocolate tradition and the process of making chocolate. *See also* "Chocolate Museums, Attractions, Theme Parks, and Factory Tours."

amenolado   A variety of the ubiquitous forastero cacao bean, cultivated in Ecuador, that produces the arriba bean. Amenolado cocoa is the only variety of forastero cacao that is delicate and mild-flavored, rather than harsh and bitter. Its flavor is equal to some of the world's best cacao. *See also* **arriba; forastero**.

arriba   The name for a variety of forastero cacao bean cultivated in Ecuador that produces a delicate, mild-flavored cocoa, considered to be one of the world's best. *See also* **amenolado; forastero; nacional**.

B

Baby Ruth   A popular American candy bar that has been manufactured in Chicago since 1921 and whose motto is "Official Candy Bar of the NBA." The candy bar is named after the daughter of President Grover Cleveland, not the baseball star. It is an enduring favorite with a $^1/_2$-inch-thick center of nougat, topped by a layer of roasted peanuts enclosed in caramel, which is completely covered with milk chocolate. Each 2.1-ounce bar measures $4^3/_4$ inches long, $1^1/_4$ inches wide, and $^3/_4$ inch thick and is considered to be one serving with a caloric content of 280.

Baci   The Italian word for kiss, Baci are candies made in Perugia, Italy, by Perugina. They are shaped like a dome and wrapped in silver foil covered with blue stars with Baci written across the top in the same blue. Each wrapping carries a hidden message inside because legend maintains that the first Baci were passed to the sweetheart of the man who created them and inside the wrapping he wrote love notes to her. The bite-size candy has an outer coating of dark chocolate that encloses a whole toasted hazelnut surrounded by finely chopped hazelnuts mixed with dark chocolate ganache. Baci are world famous and have been made by the same company since 1922. *See also* "Chronology of Chocolate History."

Bahia   A province in eastern Brazil that gives its name to a hybrid of the forastero cacao bean grown there. Bahia beans have a strong flavor that is favored for blending with other beans. *See also* **forastero**.

bain marie   The French term for water bath. A bain marie or double boiler is used to melt chocolate gently over warm water so it will not burn from exposure to too much heat. *See also* **double boiler.**

Baker's   The brand name for chocolate made by the Walter Baker company, which was established in 1764 in Dorchester, Massachusetts, by James Baker, a physician, and John Hannon, an Irish-American chocolate maker.

baking chocolate   This chocolate is pure, unsweetened chocolate liquor, pressed from the cacao bean during processing. Baking chocolate usually has lecithin added, which acts as an emulsifier, and vanilla, for flavoring. Baking chocolate is also called unsweetened and/or bitter chocolate. It is used in many American-style baked goods, such as brownies and cakes, for icings and sauces, and in candy making. It comes in packages of eight individually wrapped 1-ounce blocks. *See also* "From the Bean to the Bar."

balao malacha   A hybrid of the forastero cacao bean cultivated in Ecuador. Balao malacha beans are used for blending with other beans because their flavor is not considered to be fine enough to produce an unblended cocoa. *See also* **Bahia; forastero.**

ballotin   The French word for a small, elegant box of chocolates. The ballotin was created in 1912 by Louise Agostini, wife of the grandson of the founder of Neuhaus Chocolates. It was designed to hold chocolates so they would not damage each other as they do when packed in a cone. The ballotin became recognized throughout the world as the symbol of Belgian chocolates and was adopted by all top-quality chocolate makers.

banana cream pie   A well-known variation of Boston cream pie. This dessert is composed of two layers of sponge cake that enclose a filling of creamy, thick vanilla pastry cream and sliced bananas. The cake is completely covered with a shiny dark chocolate glaze. *See also* **Boston cream pie**.

Barry Callebaut   In 1997 two major chocolate manufacturing companies, Barry of France, producer of high-quality Cacao Barry chocolate since 1842, and Callebaut of Belgium, the largest Belgian manufacturer of fine-quality coating chocolate since 1925, merged to become one company. The new company plans to continue to manufacture both brands and maintain the distinction between them. Cacao Barry and Callebaut chocolates are used by professional confectioners and pastry makers throughout the world.

basler brunsli   These are a traditional specialty type cookie from Basel, Switzerland, made with chocolate, almonds, and spices. The cookies' dark color and city of origin led to the creation of their name. These cookies are available in variations made with either cocoa powder or finely chopped chocolate. The flourless dough is a combination of sugar, finely ground almonds, cocoa powder or chocolate, cinnamon, cloves, and egg whites. It is mixed and pressed into the traditional tiny flower-shaped molds and air-dried before baking. Alternatively, the dough is hand-rolled into balls or rolled out and cut into flower shapes using one-inch cutters. The cookies are traditionally served with afternoon tea or coffee.

Baumkuchenschnitten   This is the homemade version of Baumkuchen, the classic Austrian and German "tree cake," that is sold in bakeries during the Christmas holiday season. The cake is broiled in successive layers on a rod that rotates over a hot grill, forming concentric rings of cake resembling the cross section of a tree, hence its name. It is made by professional pastry cooks and is only available in pastry shops. The homemade version is broiled in a square cake pan, cut into strips, and glazed with dark chocolate. After the glaze sets, the strips are cut into bite-size squares.

belle hélène   A traditional French cold dessert of poached pears served over vanilla ice cream, topped with chocolate sauce.

Bensdorp   A Dutch manufacturer of high-quality cocoa powder.

Bicerin   A unique paste that is a blend of cocoa, bitter chocolate, hazelnuts, and honey, manufactured exclusively by Peyrano of Turin, Italy. Bicerin paste comes in pots and is used to sweeten coffee.

bittersweet chocolate   Chocolate liquor, pressed from the cacao bean during processing, with the addition of cocoa butter, a small amount of sugar, vanilla, and usually lecithin. Bittersweet chocolate has a deep, strong flavor that is both piquant and slightly sweet. It is used for making all types of desserts, pastries, and confections and is excellent for eating out of hand. Bittersweet chocolate is also made as couverture (coating) chocolate, which has more cocoa butter than regular chocolate, and is used by professionals to produce thin outer coatings on dipped candies and truffles. Couverture chocolate must be tempered before use to stabilize the cocoa butter. Bittersweet chocolate can be easily interchanged with semisweet chocolate without having to alter the other ingredients in a recipe. It will keep for a few years if stored under optimal conditions. *See also* **baking chocolate; couverture; extra-bittersweet chocolate; semisweet chocolate;** "Chocolate Tips"; "From the Bean to the Bar."

black bottom pie   This American dessert takes its name from its bottom layer of dark chocolate custard, which is topped by rum or vanilla-flavored custard, followed by a top layer of sweetened whipped cream. Shaved dark chocolate is sprinkled over the top of the pie as a final decoration.

Black Forest cherry torte   A classic German cake composed of three layers of chocolate génoise that are moistened with kirsch-flavored sugar syrup, then filled with sweetened whipped cream and cherries. The cake is iced with whipped cream, covered with shaved dark chocolate, and decorated with cherries. It takes its name from the Black Forest region in southern Germany, which produces the best quality kirschwasser (cherry brandy).

Bloomer   An American manufacturer of a full spectrum of Dutch-processed cocoa powder and chocolate products including couverture, compound coatings, and chocolate chips for the industry.

bonbon   The French word for sweets, referring to a small candy or confection.

boeri   The name of an Italian specialty candy of dark chocolate logs filled with whole brandied cherries.

Boston cream pie   A classic American dessert that is really a cake, not a pie at all. Two layers of sponge cake enclose a filling of creamy, thick vanilla pastry cream. The cake is completely covered with a shiny dark chocolate glaze. *See also* **banana cream pie; chocolate glaze.**

Brach's   Based in Chicago, Illinois, Brach & Brock Confections is a wholesale manufacturer of a large variety of candies such as peanut clusters, malted milk balls, chocolate-covered raisins, and chocolate-dipped peanuts. Brach's candies are found in supermarkets and drugstores throughout the United States.

brownies   A true American confection, brownies are a cross between a cake and a cookie. They almost always are made with chocolate and often with nuts, usually walnuts. Brownies come in different textures, such as chewy, dense, and fudgy, or cakelike and moist. They are usually cut into squares or rectangles and are often eaten out of hand. Brownies are typically not frosted, but are often dusted with powdered sugar and/or cocoa powder.

CHOCOLATE FUDGE BROWNIES

These classic brownies have a potent chocolate flavor and a very fudgy texture. The perfect accompaniment is a very cold glass of milk or a steaming cup of coffee.

Makes twenty-five 1¹/₂-inch-square brownies

- 1 tablespoon unsalted butter, for the pan
- 2 teaspoons all-purpose flour, for the pan
- 7 ounces bittersweet or semisweet chocolate, finely chopped
- 6 ounces (1¹/₂ sticks) unsalted butter, cut into small pieces
- 4 large eggs, at room temperature
- 1 cup sugar
- 1 teaspoon pure vanilla extract
- 1 teaspoon dark rum
- 1 teaspoon instant espresso powder dissolved in 1 teaspoon water
- ¹/₃ cup all-purpose flour
  - Pinch of salt
- 1 cup walnuts, finely chopped

1 Use the tablespoon of butter to generously butter the inside of an 8-inch-square baking pan. Dust the inside of the pan with the 2 teaspoons flour, then shake out the excess. Center a rack in the oven and preheat to 350°F.

2 Place the chocolate and butter together in the top of a double boiler over hot, not simmering, water. Stir frequently with a rubber spatula so they melt evenly.

3 In the bowl of an electric stand mixer using the wire whip attachment or in a mixing bowl using a hand-held mixer, beat the eggs and sugar together until they are very thick, pale colored, and hold a ribbon when the beaters are lifted, about 5 minutes. Blend in the vanilla, rum, and espresso.

4 Combine the flour with the salt and add slowly to the egg mixture with the mixer at low speed. Stop and scrape down the sides of the bowl with a rubber spatula and mix again.

(continues)

5 Take the double boiler off of the heat, remove the top pan from the water, and wipe it dry. Pour the melted chocolate and butter into the mixture and blend thoroughly. Then add the nuts and mix briefly to blend.

6 Pour the batter into the prepared pan. Bake the brownies in the preheated oven for 30 to 35 minutes, or until a toothpick inserted 2 inches in from the edge still has moist crumbs clinging to it. The center will be very moist. Remove the pan from the oven and cool completely on a rack.

7 Cut the brownies into $1^1/_2$-inch squares, 5 rows in each direction, using a knife dipped in hot water and dried. The brownies will last for 3 days at room temperature stored in an airtight container, or 1 week in a well-covered container in the refrigerator. If refrigerated they will firm up slightly, but still remain very fudgy.

Butterfinger   A popular American candy bar manufactured by the Nestlé Company, a 130-year-old Swiss company based in Lausanne. Nestlé established its chocolate production branch in 1929 with the acquisition of the Swiss chocolate company Peter, Cailler, Kohler. It has a crisp and crunchy peanuty brittlelike center completely covered with milk chocolate. Each 2.1-ounce rectangular bar measures $5^1/_2$ inches long, $1^1/_4$ inches wide, and $^1/_2$ inch thick and is considered to be one serving with a caloric content of 280. Butterfinger bars are also available in miniature size.

C

cacahuatl   The Aztec word for cacao bean from which the word *chocolate* derives.

cacao   The tropical evergreen tree and its dried and partially fermented beans that are processed to make chocolate, cocoa powder, and cocoa butter. *See also* **cocoa butter; cocoa powder.**

Cacao Barry Founded by the Englishman Charles Barry in 1842 this company began to produce chocolate products in Meulan, France, in the early twentieth century. Originally the company produced plain chocolate that was sold in grocery stores, but it soon became famous for its cocoa powder. In 1952 the company shifted its focus to producing top-quality chocolate and couvertures. Today Cacao Barry has the distinction of being the French company that processes the most cacao beans. Cacao Barry chocolate is available in specialty food stores, cookware shops, and some mail-order catalogs. In the United States the chocolate sold by he company is called Cocoa Barry. In 1997 the Barry company merged with the Belgian company, Callebaut to become Barry Callebaut. *See also* **Callebaut.**

cacao mothers Tall trees grown on plantations next to cacao trees to shade them from the sun. These trees are banana, rubber, or coconut palms depending on the location of the plantation. *See also* **cacao; cacao walks.**

cacao walks Large groves or orchards of cacao trees.

Cacao De Zaan Founded in 1911, the Dutch company De Zaan produces cocoa powder that is considered to be one of the best quality brands in the world. In 1964 the company was bought by W. R. Grace Company but retained its name. In 1997 the company was acquired by ADM and renamed ADM Zaan. *See also* **cocoa powder.**

Cadbury A brand of chocolate produced in England since 1824, when John Cadbury opened his shop in Birmingham where he sold coffee, tea, and chocolate to drink. He was one of the early British chocolate manufacturers who transformed chocolate from a luxury item affordable only by the wealthy to a widely available product. In 1866 Cadbury began to use the machinery invented by the Dutchman Coenraad Van Houten, which pressed all remaining traces of cocoa butter from cocoa powder, creating pure, unadulterated powder. This was the first "pure" cocoa powder available in Britain. Cadbury's sons, George and Richard, founded the company village of Bournville in 1879, where all of their workers were provided with housing, education, and health care. As Quakers, the

Cadburys were concerned with working conditions not only at their facility, but at the Portuguese cacao plantations on the African islands of Príncipe and São Tomé from whom they bought their cacao beans. They spoke out against slavery and in 1909, refusing to buy cacao from slave plantations until the working conditions were improved. Today Cadbury is the biggest British chocolate manufacturer, producing myriad products. Cadbury chocolate is known around the world. Some of the most popular Cadbury products are the Dairy Milk Bar, Fruit and Nut Bar, Bournville Bar (plain chocolate), and the Chocolate Orange. *See also* **Van Houten, Coenraad**.

Cadbury's Caramello A popular candy bar originally manufactured by the English company Cadbury and currently by Hershey's Chocolate U.S.A. through a franchise arrangement between the two companies. Each rectangular bar is $4^1/_2$ inches long by $1^1/_4$ inches wide and is divided into four pieces that can be easily broken apart. Each piece has a creamy caramel filling that is completely surrounded by milk chocolate formed into a flat-topped, $3/_4$-inch tall pyramid. Each bar is considered to be one serving with a caloric content of 220.

Caffarel This chocolate firm is based in Turin, Italy, and was established in 1826. It has been making their famous chocolate-hazelnut candy bar, Gianduiotti, using the flavorful locally grown hazelnuts, since 1865. Caffarel invented gianduia, chocolate made with hazelnuts, a delicacy that has become world famous. The Swiss chocolate pioneer, François-Louis Cailler, worked for Caffarel in the late eighteenth century where he learned the art of chocolate making. *See also* **Cailler, François-Louis; gianduia**.

Cailler, François-Louis One of the pioneers of the modern chocolate industry, François-Louis Cailler became a master chocolate maker by studying this art form at the Caffarel factory in Turin, Italy, in the late eighteenth century. In 1819 in Corsier, Switzerland, near Lausanne, he opened the first Swiss chocolate factory with machinery he had invented. The machines were used to manufacture the world's first chocolate in blocks that were meant for eating out of hand. Prior to that chocolate came only as a powder. The company he founded specialized in producing chocolate fondant or paste, which was used to make many chocolate products, including candies. *See also* **fondant chocolate**.

Callebaut   A well-known brand of Belgian chocolate widely used by pastry chefs and confectioners throughout the world. In the late 1940s Charles Callebaut conceived the idea of supplying other producers of chocolate candies and pralines with chocolate in its hot liquid form, rather than in a dried cake. This innovation created an entire new dimension in chocolate production, allowing companies to have their couverture custom made to order. The company was sold to Suchard Tobler in the early 1980s. At that time Bernard Callebaut, Charles's grandson, emigrated to Calgary, Canada, and began to manufacture high-quality European-style pralines and candies. Bernard Callebaut chocolates are well known throughout Canada and the United States. *See also* **pralinés**.

Camille Bloch   A Swiss manufacturer of high-quality chocolate couverture and a full line of chocolate bars and pralinés for the consumer. The company was established in Bern, Switzerland, in 1929.

caraque   A name given by the Spanish to the criollo variety of cacao bean when it was first brought to Europe. *See also* **criollo**.

Carma   A Swiss brand of top-quality chocolate couverture and other chocolate products, used primarily by professional bakeries and pastry shops. Carma has been produced in Dübendorf, Switzerland, near Zurich for sixty-five years. *See also* **couverture**.

charlotte mold   The classic French charlotte mold is deep and cylindrical with tapered sides and a handle on each side. It is made of tinned steel and is available in graduated sizes from 6 ounces to 2 quarts. Brioche pans, cake pans, soufflé dishes, rounded glass bowls, or any other container with either straight or flared sides can be used to mold charlottes.

checkerboard cookies   Also called black-and-white cookies, these are made from chocolate and white butter cookie dough. The two doughs are shaped into a variety of different designs that display their contrasting colors, such as chessboards, snails, peacock's eyes, pig's ears, and marbled rounds. Each dough design is wrapped on the outside with chocolate dough that forms a border.

chocoholic   A word coined in the 1980s signifying one who constantly craves chocolate.

chocolate bar(s)   Liquid chocolate molded into rectangular shapes, often flavored and filled with other ingredients, such as nuts, dried fruits, coffee, essences, and liqueurs. Chocolate bars were a breakthrough when they first came on the market in the early twentieth century because they were an inexpensive way to make chocolate widely available. There are many types of chocolate bars and many well-known brands on the market including Hershey, Cadbury, and Toblerone bars. A chocolate bar is often the first experience many people have of the wonders of chocolate. *See also* names of individual candy bars.

The United States candy bar business blossomed after World War I because the returning soldiers had developed a fondness for the chocolate bars they had eaten as part of their field rations and wanted to have more of the same on a regular basis. During the 1920s close to forty thousand different kinds of candy bars were made in the United States.

chocolate bark   A popular, irregularly shaped, flat chocolate candy that is broken into pieces and eaten out of hand. Bark often contains toasted nuts and/or chopped dried fruits such as raisins or cherries. Bark is made from all types of chocolate. The name derives from its appearance, which is reminiscent of the rough outer layer of a tree.

chocolate bloom   This is a condition that occurs when the cocoa butter in chocolate separates out from the other ingredients, floats to the top, and crystallizes. It appears as white dots and streaks or as a dull, gray film on the chocolate. This is only a cosmetic effect and does not mean that the chocolate is spoiled. The cocoa butter will blend in when the chocolate is melted. This condition is also called fat bloom. *See also* **cocoa butter**.

chocolate caramel   The chocolate version of the popular creamy, chewy candy made with sugar, corn syrup or honey, butter, and milk or cream.

chocolate charlotte   A molded dessert of French origin assembled in a deep, flared round or cylindrical pan that is lined with ladyfingers, madeleines, sponge cake, or coils of jam-filled jelly-roll cake, formed in an attractive pattern or design. The filling is a light chocolate mousse, custard, or Bavarian cream. The dessert is unmolded and cut into slices for serving. *See also* **charlotte mold**.

chocolate chestnut torte   Known by the name Kastanientorte in Austria where it originated, this torte is made with cake layers flavored with semisweet chocolate and chestnut puree, then assembled and decorated with chocolate and chestnut-flavored whipped cream.

chocolate chip   Chocolate manufactured in tiny pieces ranging in diameter from $1/8$ to $1/2$ inch. Chocolate chips are available in many flavors including semisweet, milk chocolate, and white chocolate. They are used primarily to make cookies and brownies. They tolerate high heat without burning and maintain their flavor and texture after baking. Because of their composition, chocolate chips do not melt to a smooth and fluid consistency like bulk chocolate and should not be substituted for chocolate in other recipes. Also do not substitute chopped chocolate for chocolate chips as it may burn and its texture change during baking.

chocolate chip cookie   A popular American cookie made with sugar, brown sugar, butter, flour, eggs, vanilla, and chocolate chips. The original chocolate chip cookies were called Toll House after the name of the Whitman, Massachusetts, restaurant where they were created by the proprietress, Ruth Wakefield, in the 1930s.

CHOCOLATE CHIP COOKIES

These are the quintessential American chocolate chip cookies. Chilling the cookies before baking keeps them from spreading too much in the oven.

Makes sixty 3-inch cookies

$2^1/_2$ cups all-purpose flour
   1 teaspoon baking soda
  $^1/_2$ teaspoon salt
   8 ounces (2 sticks) unsalted butter, softened
   1 cup firmly packed light brown sugar
  $^3/_4$ cup granulated sugar
   2 teaspoons pure vanilla extract
   2 large eggs, at room temperature
   2 cups chocolate chips
   1 cup roughly chopped walnuts or other nuts

1 Combine the flour, baking soda, and salt in a mixing bowl and set aside.

2 Place the butter in the bowl of a stand mixer and beat until fluffy, about 2 minutes. Add the brown sugar, granulated sugar, and vanilla and cream together until well blended.

3 Add the eggs one at a time, stopping to scrape down the sides of the bowl with a rubber spatula after each addition.

4 Blend in the flour mixture in three stages, blending well after each addition. Stir in the chips and nuts. Cover the bowl tightly with plastic wrap and chill for 30 minutes.

5 Line four cookie sheets with parchment paper. Use a small ice-cream scoop or two teaspoons to scoop out walnut-size mounds of the cookie dough and place on the cookie sheets, leaving 2 inches between them. Chill the cookies for 30 minutes.

6 Meanwhile, adjust the oven racks to the upper and lower thirds and preheat the oven to 375°F. Bake the cookies for 5 minutes, then switch the pans. Bake until golden, another 5 to 7 minutes. Transfer cookies to racks to cool. Store in an airtight container at room temperature for up to a week.

chocolate-covered almonds Whole unblanched toasted almonds completely coated in bittersweet chocolate, then dredged in a mixture of cocoa powder and powdered sugar. Hazelnuts may be similarly chocolate covered.

chocolate crème brûlée A rich, creamy, cold chocolate custard sprinkled with granulated or brown sugar that is caramelized in the broiler, with a propane torch, or with a salamander just before serving. This makes the sugar topping crisp and brittle, creating the dessert's renowned textural contrast. Chocolate is a variation on the traditional vanilla flavor of this dessert.

chocolate decadence The name given to a spectacular chocolate dessert composed of a dense, moist, very chocolaty cake with a texture similar to that of a chocolate truffle. The dessert is traditionally served with sweetened whipped cream and a tart raspberry sauce. For a more glamorous presentation, the cake is completely iced and decorated with whipped cream and served with raspberry sauce on the side.

chocolate decorations Many different decorations fashioned out of chocolate are used to adorn desserts, pastries, and confections. In order for the decorations to last several months stored at room temperature use tempered chocolate. In most cases it is easier to make the decorations from tempered chocolate. If they are made from untempered chocolate they must be kept in the refrigerator until served because they discolor when exposed to the air for very long. Butterflies, cigarettes, circles, curls, dots, fans, leaves, pipings, ribbons, roses, ruffles, squares, shavings, and triangles are examples of the decorations that can be made from chocolate. Chocolate decorations can be made from any type of chocolate: milk, dark, white, and couverture.

CHOCOLATE LEAVES

Use any type of waxy leaf as a guide for making these leaves. Camellia leaves work very well. Be sure to wash and thoroughly dry the leaves before using them.

1 Chop 8 ounces of chocolate into very tiny pieces. Melt and temper the chocolate (see pages 92–94). Line a baking sheet with parchment or waxed paper.

2 Use a spoon to coat the underside of the leaves with a thin layer of chocolate. Be careful not to drip chocolate onto the top side of the leaf. Let the excess drip off. Place the leaves on the lined baking sheet, chocolate side up. Chill the sheet in the refrigerator until the chocolate is set, about 15 minutes.

3 Let the leaves stand at room temperature for a few minutes, then carefully peel the real leaf from the chocolate. Handle the chocolate side of the leaves as little as possible so you don't leave finger marks.

4 The chocolate leaves will keep for several weeks stored at room temperature in a tightly covered container.

CHOCOLATE CIGARETTE CURLS

Once made, chocolate cigarette curls will keep for several months in an airtight container at room temperature. They instantly dress up any dessert.

1 Melt 8 to 10 ounces of chocolate in the top of a double boiler over hot water, stirring often with a rubber spatula. Do not overheat the chocolate. Remove the top pan and wipe it completely dry.

2 Pour the chocolate onto a marble board or the back of a baking sheet that has been warmed to body temperature. Use an offset spatula to spread the chocolate out into a large rectangle. Gently work the spatula over the chocolate in a side-to-side motion until the chocolate begins to loose its gloss and set up.

3 Use a chef's knife or the edge of the spatula to form the cigarettes. Hold the blade at a 45-degree angle to the board or pan and to yourself. Working from the upper right-hand corner toward the center, hold the blade with both hands and pull toward yourself for a couple of inches. The chocolate will curl over itself. If the chocolate splinters, it is too cold. If this happens melt it and reuse. Gently lift the cigarette curls from the board or pan with an offset spatula and place on waxed or parchment paper.

4 Two-tone or marbled chocolate cigarette curls are created using the same method as above. Melt a small quantity of another contrasting chocolate (about one quarter the amount of the first chocolate). As an example, use white chocolate over dark or milk chocolate, or milk chocolate over dark chocolate. When the first chocolate has started to set very lightly, pour or pipe lines or designs of the second chocolate over it and work the two together with the offset spatula. Then proceed as above to shape curls.

5 Another method for creating two-tone chocolate is to spread the first chocolate until it is almost set. Use a pastry comb or a fork to scrape lines through the chocolate. Then pour the second chocolate over the first and work with the offset spatula until it is set. Proceed to shape the cigarette curls.

CHOCOLATE CUTOUTS

As with Chocolate Leaves and Cigarette Curls, any chocolate can be used to make cutouts. They can also be made two-tone or marbled, following the same techniques as for Chocolate Cigarette Curls. These are great to have on hand to decorate all types of desserts.

1 Line a baking sheet with waxed paper. Melt and temper (see pages 92–94) 8 to 10 ounces of chocolate. Spread the chocolate onto the paper. Holding opposite corners of the paper, gently shake it to release any air bubbles. Chill in the refrigerator for 15 minutes to set the chocolate, then rest at room temperature for 3 to 4 minutes.

(continues)

2 Use any type of cutter or template and a sharp knife to shape the cutouts. Gently lift them from the paper with a small offset spatula and place on waxed or parchment paper. Store them without touching between layers of waxed paper in an airtight container at room temperature for several months.

chocolate-dipped   A confection such as a truffle or other candy that has been partially or completely coated with chocolate by being immersed into fluid, usually tempered, chocolate.

chocolate dipping forks   These European hand tools are designed to hold truffles and candies for dipping into chocolate. They are also called truffle dippers and candy dippers. There are a variety of shapes and sizes available: oval, round, spiral, grid, and various long-tined forks. Each shape is used for a particular candy, which is determined by the candy's shape and size. These dippers are made of a 3-inch-long round, thin, stainless steel strip with the shape at the top end. The metal strip is attached to a $3^1/_2$-inch-long wooden handle. Dipping forks are available singly or in sets, ranging from six to ten pieces. There are also plastic dipping tools available. If these tools are not available, a dipping fork can be made from a plastic fork by breaking out the two middle tines. *See also* **chocolate truffle**.

chocolate extract   A liquid flavoring ingredient made from a blend of roasted cacao beans, water, and alcohol. Chocolate extract has a rich, deep chocolate flavor and aroma. It is used like vanilla or other extracts, to enhance the chocolate flavor of desserts, pastries, and confections.

chocolate fondue   A dessert that consists of a rich mixture of melted chocolate and heavy cream, often flavored with liqueurs or extracts. Chocolate fondue is accompanied by a variety of sliced fruits and small pieces of cake that are dipped into the mixture with individual long forks. Fondue is kept liquid and warm in a specially designed pot that sits over a warming candle. Chocolate fondue is made with dark, milk, or white chocolate.

chocolate frappé   Chocolate-flavored liquid, usually a water ice, that is partially frozen, then beaten to break up the crystals and form a slushy consistency. Frappés are of French origin. It is served either as a drink or as a dessert.

chocolate gelato   The Italian version of chocolate ice cream, gelato is denser, creamier, and richer than American ice cream because it contains less air.

chocolate glaze   A mixture of melted chocolate and cream or butter used to coat cakes, pastries, and confections. The mixture is fluid enough so that it pours smoothly and coats evenly, but not so thin that it runs off without adhering to the cake or pastry. Chocolate glaze gives the cake, pastry, or confection a smooth, shiny surface. Occasionally corn syrup is added to help keep the glaze shiny, or sugar is added to increase the sweetness. A mocha flavor can be made by adding instant espresso powder dissolved in a small amount of water. When using a glaze, it should be poured quickly working from the center to the outside edge. A flexible blade spatula is helpful to even out the glaze. Only make one or two passes over the top or the glaze will begin to set and show the spatula marks.

chocolate ice cream   A smooth frozen dessert of milk and/or cream, sugar, eggs, and chocolate. Chocolate ice cream is made either with a cooked custard base, like the French-style ice cream, or with an uncooked version, which is most common in the United States. Either style is blended, cooled, and processed in an ice-cream maker until it reaches the desired consistency.

CHOCOLATE ICE CREAM

This ice cream is smooth and creamy with deep chocolate flavor. Although it's wonderful on its own, with the addition of hot fudge sauce it's spectacular. Try it as an accompaniment to French Chocolate Macaroons (page 24), Chocolate Pound Cake (page 29), Cocoa Angel Food Cake (page 40), or Chocolate Fudge Brownies (page 9).

Makes 1 quart

10 ounces bittersweet or semisweet chocolate, finely chopped
2 cups milk
2 cups heavy cream
1 vanilla bean
8 large egg yolks, at room temperature
³/₄ cup sugar

1 Place the chocolate in the top of a double boiler over low heat. Stir often with a rubber spatula until completely melted and smooth.

2 Place the milk and cream in a 3-quart heavy-bottomed saucepan. Using a sharp knife split the vanilla bean lengthwise, scrape out the seeds, and add both the vanilla bean and seeds to the liquid. Heat the mixture over medium heat until bubbles begin to form around the edge, just before the boiling point.

3 In the bowl of a stand mixer using the wire whip attachment or in a mixing bowl using a hand-held mixer, whip the egg yolks and sugar together until they are pale yellow colored and hold a slowly dissolving ribbon when the beater is lifted, about 5 minutes.

4 Reduce the mixer speed to low and slowly pour 1 cup of the hot liquid into the egg and sugar mixture. Stir to blend well, then return the mixture to the saucepan. Reduce the heat to low and stir the mixture constantly with a wooden spoon until the mixture reaches 185°F on a candy thermometer, about 10 to 15 minutes. At this point the mixture will thicken and when a line is drawn through the custard on the back of the spoon it leaves a clearly defined path.

5 Remove the saucepan from the heat. Strain the mixture through a fine sieve into a bowl. Take the double boiler off the heat. Take the top pan off the water and wipe the bottom and sides of it dry. Pour the melted chocolate into the ice cream mixture, then blend thoroughly. Cover the mixture tightly with plastic wrap, cool to room temperature, then chill in the refrigerator for several hours or overnight. Process the mixture in an ice-cream maker according to the manufacturer's instructions.

6 Store the ice cream in a covered container in the freezer for up to a month. If it is frozen solid, soften it in the refrigerator for a few hours before serving.

chocolate leaves   *See* **chocolate decorations**.

chocolate liquor   After cacao beans are roasted and the outer hulls removed, the remaining inner nibs are ground. This produces a thick, dark, nonalcoholic liquid, called chocolate liquor, which is the basis of all chocolate. Chocolate liquor occasionally is also called chocolate paste. *See also* "From the Bean to the Bar"; **nibs**.

chocolate macaroons   In the United States, chocolate macaroons are small, chewy cookies made with almond paste or ground almonds, egg whites, sugar, and chocolate or cocoa. French chocolate macaroons are made from two small, round almond cookies sandwiched together with ganache or chocolate buttercream.

23

FRENCH CHOCOLATE MACAROONS

These are the classic chocolate macaroons found in fine French pastry shops. They are a perfect accompaniment for afternoon coffee or tea.

Makes 30 assembled cookies

MACAROONS
- 4 large egg whites, at room temperature
- $^1/_4$ teaspoon cream of tartar
- $1^1/_3$ cups powdered sugar, sifted
- Pinch of salt
- $^1/_4$ cup unsweetened Dutch-processed cocoa powder, sifted
- $1^1/_2$ cups finely ground almonds or almond flour
- 1 teaspoon pure vanilla extract

GANACHE
- 4 ounces bittersweet or semisweet chocolate, very finely chopped
- $^1/_2$ cup heavy cream

1 Adjust the oven racks to the upper and lower thirds and preheat the oven to 350°F. Line two baking sheets with aluminum foil, shiny side up.

2 Place the egg whites in the bowl of a stand mixer or in a mixing bowl. Using the wire whip attachment or a hand-held mixer, whip on medium speed until frothy. Add the cream of tartar and continue to whip. Slowly add the sugar and whip until the whites hold firm, but not dry, peaks.

3 Add the salt to the cocoa powder and fold into the egg whites along with the finely ground almonds, then blend in the vanilla.

4 Fit a 14-inch pastry bag with a pastry tip with a $^1/_2$-inch plain round opening. Holding the pastry bag 1 inch above the lined baking sheets pipe out 1-inch mounds.

5 Bake the macaroons for 7 minutes, then switch the baking sheets, and bake until set, another 7 to 8 minutes. Remove from the oven and place on racks. Immediately lift up a corner of the foil and carefully pour $^1/_4$ cup water under the foil. This creates steam and makes it very easy to remove the macaroons from the foil. Leave to cool. Then lift the macaroons from the foil.

6 For the ganache, melt the chocolate in the top of a double boiler over low heat, stirring often with a rubber spatula. Scald the cream in a separate small saucepan over medium heat. Remove the top of the double boiler and wipe dry. Pour the cream into the chocolate and stir to blend thoroughly. Transfer the mixture to another bowl, cover tightly with plastic wrap, and cool to room temperature. Refrigerate until thick, but not stiff, 1 to 2 hours.

7 Transfer the ganache the bowl of a stand mixer or to a mixing bowl. Use the flat beater attachment or a hand-held mixer and whip until the filling holds soft peaks, about 1 minute. Fit a 14-inch pastry bag with a pastry tube with a $1/2$-inch plain round opening. Pipe a small mound of filling on half of the macaroons. Top each with another macaroon, pressing together lightly so they stick together. If not serving the macaroons immediately, store in the refrigerator, tightly covered, for up to 2 days. They will soften slightly, but retain their delicious flavor.

chocolate madeleines   A chocolate version of the famous seashell-shaped little cakes that were immortalized by the French novelist Marcel Proust. Madeleines are delicate, classic sponge-type cakes baked in ribbed, scallop-shell, oval molds, which gives them their special shape. They are eaten more like cookies than cakes. Chocolate madeleines are made with either melted chocolate or cocoa powder, butter, flour, eggs, and sugar. They are best eaten within a day or two of baking as they tend to become crisp and dry if kept longer.

chocolate meringue   A mixture of egg whites and sugar whipped together until firm, then flavored with sifted cocoa powder. Meringues are dried in a low oven until set. Chocolate meringues are used in concord cake, created by French pastry chef Gaston Lenôtre, and as a component in other pastries. *See also* **concord cake.**

chocolate modeling paste   This pliable decorating paste is made from a mixture of chocolate and corn syrup. It has a malleable texture, similar to marzipan. It is also called chocolate plastic and is used to wrap around the outside of cakes and confections. A variety of designs and shapes, such as ribbons, ruffles, various flowers, leaves, and stems can be cut and fashioned from thinly rolled out chocolate modeling paste and used for decorating desserts, pastries, and confections. Chocolate modeling paste can be made with dark, white, or milk chocolate.

chocolate mold   There are two types of chocolate molds—shallow molds that are used for solid molding and two-part molds that are used for both hollow molding and filled chocolates. The shallow, flat molds are generally made of plastic and are very flexible. Each mold is for a particular shape or design with twelve to eighteen cavities in the mold, depending on its size. There are a host of designs available, ranging from mini to large size. Tempered chocolate is piped into the cavities up to the top edge. The molds are chilled briefly to set the chocolate, then the candies are turned out of the mold. The two-part molds are made of either metal or sturdy plastic and are available in many shapes and sizes, such as rabbits and Santas. They are filled with tempered chocolate, left to set very briefly, then the chocolate is poured out, leaving a thin coating of chocolate on the mold. If the chocolates are to be filled, the filling is inserted at this point. In either case, the pieces of the mold are clipped together and left to set completely. Chocolate molds should be handled with care. If they are scratched, chocolate will not release from them. To avoid this, wash the molds in warm, soapy water and dry them with a soft towel. Do not use abrasive cleansers or cleaning pads, which will scratch the molds. The molds should be stored in a cool, dry place and be completely dry before they are used. *See also* **classic tempering.**

chocolate mousse   An airy, soft, creamy dessert of melted chocolate lightened with beaten egg whites and/or whipped cream. Chocolate mousse is served cold. Some chocolate mousses contain butter and egg yolks, which gives them a firmer consistency, while retaining a velvety texture. The firm texture makes this type of mousse ideal to use as a filling in a cake or tart.

Henri de Toulouse-Lautrec, the French painter, is credited with creating chocolate mousse, which was originally called chocolate mayonnaise.

SPICED CHOCOLATE MOUSSE

This is a classic chocolate mousse—airy, soft, and creamy—spiced up with cassia cinnamon and nutmeg. It's delicious on its own or as the filling in another dessert.

Makes 1¹/₂ quarts

  8 ounces bittersweet or semisweet chocolate, finely chopped
  2 cups heavy cream
  2 teaspoons pure vanilla extract
¹/₂ teaspoon cassia cinnamon
¹/₄ teaspoon freshly grated nutmeg
  3 large egg whites, at room temperature
¹/₂ cup plus 1 tablespoon granulated sugar
  1 tablespoon unsweetened Dutch-processed cocoa powder
  1 teaspoon pure vanilla extract for whipped cream garnish
  2 tablespoons shaved bittersweet or semisweet chocolate for garnish

1 Melt the chocolate in the top of a double boiler over hot, not simmering, water. Stir frequently with a rubber spatula to ensure even melting.

2 In a separate small saucepan heat ¹/₂ cup of the cream to the boiling point. Remove the top pan of the double boiler, wipe it dry, pour the hot cream into the chocolate, and stir together until thoroughly blended. Transfer the mixture to a 2-quart mixing bowl. Blend in the vanilla, cinnamon, and nutmeg.

3 In a chilled mixing bowl with chilled beaters whip 1 cup of the cream to soft peaks and fold it into the chocolate mixture in four stages, blending thoroughly after each addition. In a separate grease-free mixing bowl

(continues)

with grease-free beaters, whip the egg whites until frothy. Slowly add the sugar and continue whipping the egg whites until they hold firm, but not stiff, peaks, about 4 minutes. Fold the whipped egg whites into the chocolate mixture in three stages, blending thoroughly after each addition. Sprinkle on the cocoa powder and fold in completely. Pour the mousse into a $1^1/_2$-quart soufflé dish or other serving bowl, or into individual serving bowls or glasses, and smooth the top. Cover the mousse with plastic wrap and chill in the refrigerator for at least 2 hours, until set.

4 In a chilled mixing bowl with chilled beaters whip the remaining $^1/_2$ cup of cream until frothy. Add the teaspoon of vanilla extract and continue to whip the cream until it holds soft peaks. Fit a pastry bag with a number 3 large, closed star tip and fill the bag partway with the whipped cream.

5 Decorate the top of the mousse with an outside border of piped shells or rosettes. Sprinkle the shaved chocolate over the whipped cream decorations and the top of the mousse. The mousse is best served within 6 hours of preparation.

chocolate mousse cake A rich, flourless chocolate cake with a soft, creamy texture, similar to chocolate mousse, baked in a water bath. Chocolate mousse cake is also sometimes made by molding chocolate mousse between two layers or on top of a layer of chocolate sponge cake, in a springform pan or flan ring. The cake is chilled, then unmolded, and decorated before serving.

chocolate parfait In the United States this is a dessert of chocolate ice cream layered with whipped cream and chocolate sauce in a cylindrical footed glass. It is decorated with whipped cream, nuts, and occasionally a maraschino cherry. In France a chocolate parfait is a molded frozen custard that is light and creamy. It is sliced or cut into a variety of shapes and served decorated with whipped cream, nuts, and candied fruit.

chocolate pound cake   This is a chocolate version of the classic cake that takes its name from the original recipe which was a pound each of eggs, butter, sugar, and flour. It is a creamed cake, meaning that the butter and sugar are creamed together before the other ingredients are added. In French, pound cake is called *quatre-quarts*, which means four quarters, referring to the four main ingredients. Today's pound cakes use the same ingredients but in different proportions, which makes them less dense and heavy. Also, modern pound cakes usually use baking powder, and occasionally milk, to lighten the batter. Pound cake is typically baked in a loaf shape. Pound cake came to America with the British settlers in the seventeenth century and has become a classic American cake. Pound cake is often accompanied by fresh fruit, ice cream, or fruit sauces such as lemon or raspberry. It is generally served for afternoon tea or dessert. Pound cake keeps for several days at room temperature if well wrapped in aluminum foil, or it can be frozen.

CHOCOLATE POUND CAKE

Although this cake is delicious on its own, try it accompanied by a scoop of chocolate ice cream, chocolate sorbet, or hot fudge sauce. For variety try a fruit sauce or fresh fruit. It is perfect for afternoon coffee or tea and packs well for a picnic.

Makes one 9 × 5-inch loaf

1	tablespoon unsalted butter, for the pan
1	tablespoon cake flour, for the pan
$^1/_3$	cup unsweetened Dutch-processed cocoa powder
4	tablespoons hot water
2	teaspoons pure vanilla extract
$1^2/_3$	cups cake flour
1	teaspoon baking powder
$^1/_4$	teaspoon salt
8	ounces (2 sticks) unsalted butter, softened
$1^1/_2$	cups superfine sugar
4	large eggs, at room temperature

(continues)

1 Center a rack in the oven and preheat the oven to 325°F. With the table-spoon of butter, generously butter the inside of a 9 × 5 × 3-inch loaf pan. Dust the inside of the pan with the tablespoon of cake flour, then tap out the excess. Set the pan aside briefly while preparing the batter.

2 Place the cocoa powder in a small mixing bowl. Add the hot water and stir until it is a smooth paste. Blend in the vanilla.

3 Sift together the cake flour, baking powder, and salt.

4 In the bowl of an electric stand mixer using the flat beater attachment or in a mixing bowl using a hand-held beater, beat the butter until it is fluffy, about 2 minutes. Gradually add the sugar and continue beating to cream the two ingredients together, about 2 more minutes. Occasionally stop and scrape down the sides of the bowl with a rubber spatula.

5 Add the eggs one at a time, beating well to blend after each addition. Then add the cocoa mixture and blend well.

6 With the mixer on low speed, slowly add the dry ingredients to the bat-ter. Stop and scrape down the sides of the bowl with a rubber spatula occasionally as the batter is mixing. When the batter is thoroughly blended, transfer it to the prepared loaf pan. Use the rubber spatula to smooth the top.

7 Bake the pound cake in the preheated oven until the top is risen and the cake is set, about 1 hour and 10 minutes. When a cake tester is inserted into the center it will come out clean. Remove the cake from the oven and cool on a rack for 15 minutes. Run a thin-bladed knife around the inside rim of the loaf pan to loosen the cake. Turn the cake out of the pan, then turn it right side up. Leave the cake to cool com-pletely on the rack.

8 Well wrapped in aluminum foil, pound cake will keep for 4 days at room temperature or it can be frozen. If frozen, defrost it in the refrigerator for 24 hours before serving.

chocolate pudding   A soft, thick, creamy chocolate dessert made with eggs, milk, and sugar. Chocolate pudding cooked in a water bath in the oven produces a firmer consistency than when cooked in a double boiler on the stovetop. It is served either warm or cold and is often decorated with whipped cream. A fresh fruit or chocolate sauce can accompany the pudding.

chocolate sauce   A fluid, pourable mixture of melted chocolate and cream or butter, often sweetened and flavored with an extract or a liqueur. Chocolate sauce is used to garnish and accompany desserts and pastries. It is best known for its use in a chocolate sundae. Chocolate sauce can be made with dark, milk, or white chocolate. *See also* **chocolate sundae.**

chocolate sorbet   A blend of water, sugar, melted chocolate, and dissolved cocoa that are briefly cooked together, cooled, and frozen. Chocolate sorbet usually has a soft, smooth texture. Since it has no fat it does not become as firm as ice cream. It is served as a dessert and often accompanied by cookies.

CHOCOLATE SORBET

This is a smooth and intensely chocolate sorbet that is excellent on its own, but superb with Chocolate Pound Cake (page 29), Cocoa Angel Food Cake (page 40), Chocolate Nut Biscotti (page 38), or fresh fruit.

Makes 1 pint

   $1^1/_4$ cups water
   $^3/_4$ cup superfine sugar
   $^1/_3$ cup unsweetened Dutch-processed cocoa powder, sifted
   4 ounces bittersweet or semisweet chocolate, finely chopped

1 Combine the water and sugar in a 2-quart saucepan and bring to a boil over medium heat to dissolve the sugar.

2 Add the cocoa powder and stir until it is dissolved and smooth. Remove the pan from the heat and add the chopped chocolate. Stir until it is completely melted.

(continues)

3 Strain the mixture into a bowl. Cover tightly with plastic wrap and cool to room temperature. Chill for several hours or overnight, then process in an ice-cream maker according to the manufacturer's instructions.

chocolate soufflé A dense yet airy chocolate dessert based on a sweet egg custard that rises as it bakes due to the air whipped into the egg whites in the custard. As the soufflé is heated, air and steam are trapped inside the structure, causing it to rise to almost double in size. Chocolate soufflé must be served as soon as it is removed from the oven or it will collapse. Chocolate soufflé is baked in a straight-sided round dish coated with butter and sugar, which form a crust on the outside. When a spoon punctures the soufflé it deflates and releases the creamy center.

chocolate sundae An ice-cream dessert assembled in either a tall, cylindrical dish or in a shallow, round dish. A chocolate sundae has two or three scoops of chocolate ice cream topped with chocolate sauce, chocolate syrup, or hot fudge. Nuts, candied cherries or other fruits, and whipped cream are also occasionally included.

chocolate syrup A specially formulated mixture of sugar, water, cocoa extracts, and flavorings used to flavor drinks, ice cream, and desserts. Monin is the brand name of a well-known French syrup company.

chocolate thermometer This specially designed thermometer is used primarily during the process of tempering chocolate when extreme accuracy is necessary. It is an essential tool for anyone who works with chocolate. The slim, glass mercury thermometer has distinct markings and reads in 1-degree gradations in the range of 40°F to 130°F. This thermometer should be handled very carefully and stored where it will not be jostled by other utensils. *See also* **tempering**.

chocolate truffle This rich, elegant, and highly treasured confection is considered to be the ultimate in chocolate candy. Chocolate truffles are made up of about 80 percent chocolate. Their centers are composed of ganache, a mixture of chocolate and cream, which is shaped into balls.

Chocolate truffles have countless variations that can be made with the addition of butter, liqueurs, extracts, coffee, nuts, fruit purees, or candied fruit. The centers have an outer coating of tempered chocolate, cocoa powder, powdered sugar, shredded coconut, or finely chopped nuts. Classic chocolate truffles are generally small and should literally melt in your mouth. They take their name from the much-sought-after similarly shaped fungi that grow around the roots of trees in France and Italy. *See also* **chocolate dipping forks; classic tempering; cocoa powder; ganache**.

SWISS WHITE CHOCOLATE TRUFFLES

Following the classic Swiss tradition, these truffles are dipped in chocolate twice, then tapped with toothpicks or a fork to create a slightly rough texture. Be sure to use the best quality white chocolate you can buy.

Makes 30 truffles

8 ounces premium quality white chocolate, finely chopped
$^1/_3$ cup heavy cream
1 tablespoon cognac
Powdered sugar to roll truffles
1 pound premium quality white chocolate, tempered

1 Melt the chopped chocolate in the top of a double boiler over hot water over very low heat. Stir often with a rubber spatula to ensure even melting.

2 In a separate small saucepan, scald the cream over medium heat. Remove the top from the double boiler and wipe the bottom very dry. Pour the cream into the chocolate and stir until the mixture is smooth and completely blended. Add the cognac and blend well. Cover the mixture tightly with plastic wrap, cool to room temperature, then chill until thick.

3 Line a baking sheet with waxed paper. Transfer the truffle mixture to the bowl of a electric stand mixer or a mixing bowl. Use the flat beater attachment or a hand-held mixer and whip the mixture until it holds firm peaks, about 2 minutes.

(continues)

4 Fit a pastry bag with a pastry tip with a $^1/_2$-inch plain round opening and fill partway with the truffle mixture. Pipe out 1-inch mounds onto the baking sheet. Chill until firm. Dust your hands with powdered sugar and roll the mounds into balls. Cover and chill again until firm.

5 Temper the remaining white chocolate using whatever method you prefer (see pages 92–94). Dip each truffle into the chocolate and remove using a dipping tool or fork. Let the excess drip off and turn the truffle out onto a lined baking sheet. Repeat, then chill the truffles briefly to set the coating.

6 Dip the truffles again. Turn them out onto a lined baking sheet. Use toothpicks or a fork to tap the coating while soft to create a rough texture. Chill to set completely. Place each truffle in a paper candy cup.

7 Store the truffles between sheets of waxed paper in a tightly sealed container in the refrigerator for up to 3 weeks. Bring the truffles to room temperature before serving.

chocolate truffle tart   A shallow, sweet pastry shell is baked then filled with dense chocolate ganache truffle cream. The tart is chilled until the filling is firm and served with a dollop of whipped cream. Chocolate truffle tart can be made in a variety of sizes and shapes.

chocolate tuiles   Tempered chocolate is spread into disks on parchment paper then draped over a rolling pin to form a shape that resembles the red tiles used in roofs in the south of France, from which these confections take their name. Chocolate tuiles can be flavored with ground toasted hazelnuts or other nuts, or toasted coconut. They are often served as part of an assortment of candies and confections and are divine accompanied with coffee and brandy.

chocolatier   A professional specializing in making fine quality chocolate and chocolate confections who has trained extensively and studied the art of working with chocolate under master chocolate makers.

chocolatine   An individual French pastry consisting of two round almond meringue shells that hold a filling of dark chocolate mousse. The pastry is sprinkled with a mixture of cocoa powder and powdered sugar.

Chocovic   A brand of high-quality couvertures produced in Barcelona, Spain. Chocovic makes a line of three dark couverture varietals, each produced from single-origin fine-grade cacao beans labeled "Origen Unico," as well as blended couvertures.

chuao   An isolated plantation in Venezuela created in the seventeenth century that produces one of the world's most highly prized, flavorful varieties of the criollo cacao bean. The beans are rare and are always blended with other beans before they are shipped to the market. *See also* **criollo**.

Clark Bar   An American classic candy bar made by Clark Bar America in Pittsburgh, Pennsylvania, since 1917. The candy bar has a crumbly peanut butter center topped with a rich milk chocolate coating. Clark Dark has dark chocolate on the outside and Winter Clark has a white chocolate coating. Clark Bars are available in 1.75-ounce, 3-ounce (king size), and $1/2$-ounce miniatures, dubbed Clark Jrs. Each 1.75-ounce bar measures 5 inches long, 1 inch wide, and $1/2$ inch thick and is considered to be one serving with a caloric content of 240. Clark Bars are available at grocery and drugstores and mass merchants throughout the United States.

classic tempering   A method of stabilizing the cocoa butter in chocolate so the chocolate has a shiny, even appearance and smooth texture, allowing it to set quickly so it will release easily from molds and form an even coating on dipped candies and truffles. To temper chocolate: Melt the chocolate until it is completely smooth and fluid. Pour two thirds of it onto a marble slab and spread from one side to the other with an offset spatula. Then gather the chocolate into the center. Repeat this several times until the chocolate noticeably thickens. Use a chocolate thermometer to take its temperature, which should be at about 78°F to 80°F. Return this chocolate to the remaining one third liquid chocolate and stir together for a couple of minutes until thoroughly blended. The final temperature should be 89°F to 91°F for dark chocolate and 85°F to 88°F for milk and white chocolate. If the temperature is below this, reheat carefully until it reaches the correct point. When the chocolate is tempered it is ready to be used for dipping candies and truffles and for molding.

cocoa butter   Extracted during the process of producing chocolate and cocoa powder, cocoa butter is the ivory-colored, naturally occurring fat in cacao beans. It is extracted from chocolate liquor during the processing of chocolate, but is added back to the resulting cocoa cake to give chocolate its smooth texture and rich flavor. Cocoa butter is the basis of white chocolate. *See also* **cocoa powder; white chocolate;** "From the Bean to the Bar."

cocoa cake   Also called presscake, cocoa cake is a fairly dry, solid cake, which is the result of hydraulic presses extracting the cocoa butter from chocolate liquor during the processing of chocolate. Cocoa cakes are crushed, ground, and sifted to produce cocoa powder.

cocoa dance   In Trinidad and some regions of South America when cacao beans spread out to dry are ready to be turned, the women shuffle through them. This ritual ensures the beans will dry evenly. It also removes extra particles and polishes the beans. The cocoa dance is performed twice a year after the cacao beans are harvested, when they are being processed before shipment to chocolate factories for processing.

cocoa liquor   *See* **chocolate liquor.**

cocoa painting   A technique of painting and drawing on marzipan or pastillage with unsweetened cocoa powder diluted with water in varying amounts to produce different shades. The addition of clear liquor, such as vodka or gin, creates very light tones. Cocoa paint is applied with artists' brushes using the same techniques as with paint.

cocoa paste   *See* **chocolate liquor.**

cocoa powder   A product of the cacao bean, which grows on the tropical evergreen tree *Theobroma cacao*. The cacao beans are removed from large pods that grow on the trunk of the tree, then they are fermented and dried. The beans are sent to chocolate factories where they are roasted, the outer hulls removed, and the inner nibs ground to produce chocolate liquor. Most of the cocoa butter is extracted from the chocolate liquor, leaving a dry paste, which is further dried and processed to become unsweetened cocoa powder. The cocoa is called Dutch-processed if it is treated with alkali to produce a dark, mellow-flavored powder. *See also* **Dutch-processed cocoa.**

CHOCOLATE COINS

Cocoa, cinnamon, and vanilla are a delicious combination that's brought together in these cookies, made from a classic refrigerator dough. All you need to do is slice and bake just before the kids come home from school or company arrives.

Makes $4^1/_2$ dozen $2^3/_4$-inch cookies

$2^1/_4$ cups all-purpose flour
  1 cup sugar
  $^1/_3$ cup unsweetened Dutch-processed cocoa powder
  $^1/_2$ teaspoon baking powder
$1^1/_4$ teaspoons cinnamon
  8 ounces (2 sticks) unsalted butter, cold
  1 large egg, at room temperature
  2 teaspoons pure vanilla extract
  4 ounces bittersweet or semisweet chocolate, finely chopped
  2 tablespoons crystal sugar (optional)

1 Combine the flour, sugar, cocoa powder, baking powder, and cinnamon in the work bowl of a food processor fitted with the steel blade. Pulse briefly to blend.

2 Cut the butter into small pieces and add to the mixture. Pulse, using on-off turns, until the butter is cut into tiny pieces, about 2 minutes.

3 Lightly beat the egg with the vanilla and add. Pulse until the dough is well blended. Add the chocolate and pulse to blend well.

4 Divide the dough in half and place each half on a large sheet of waxed paper. Use the waxed paper to shape each into a log about 8 inches long and 2 inches wide. Wrap the logs in the waxed paper and chill in the freezer for about 40 minutes.

5 Adjust the oven racks to the upper and lower thirds of the oven and pre-heat the oven to 350°F. Line three cookie sheets with parchment paper. Slice the dough rolls into $1/4$-inch-thick coins and place on the cookie sheets, leaving 2 inches between them. Sprinkle the top of each cookie with a few grains of crystal sugar, if using.

6 Bake the cookies for 5 minutes, then switch the pans. Bake until set, another 5 to 6 minutes. Transfer the cookies to racks to cool. Store in an airtight container at room temperature for up to 1 week.

CHOCOLATE NUT BISCOTTI

These scrumptious cookies are perfect for dipping in hot chocolate or coffee. They keep well, so you can have them on hand for a spur of the moment coffee klatch.

Makes 3 dozen

  $1^1/_2$ cups all-purpose flour
   $^1/_2$ cup unsweetened Dutch-processed cocoa powder
   2 teaspoons baking soda
     Pinch of salt
   $^1/_2$ cup granulated sugar
   $^1/_3$ cup firmly packed light brown sugar
   3 large eggs, at room temperature
  $1^1/_2$ teaspoons pure vanilla extract
   $^1/_2$ teaspoon chocolate extract
   2 ounces bittersweet or semisweet chocolate chopped into
     small chunks
  $1^1/_2$ cups sliced almonds

1 Center a rack in the oven and preheat the oven to 350°F. Line a baking sheet with parchment paper.

2 Sift together the flour, cocoa, baking soda, and salt and transfer to the bowl of a stand mixer. Blend in the granulated and brown sugars.

3 Whisk the eggs with the vanilla and chocolate extracts and add to the dry ingredients. Blend the mixture on low speed until thoroughly combined. Stop and scrape down the sides of the bowl with a rubber spatula as needed.

4 Add the chopped chocolate and almonds and blend thoroughly.

5 Divide the dough into two equal pieces. Shape each into a log about 10 inches long, 2 inches wide, and $^3/_4$ inch high. Place on the baking sheet leaving 2 inches between them.

6 Bake until set, about 20 minutes. Remove the baking sheet from the oven and rest for 10 minutes. Lower the oven temperature to 325°F.

7 Cut the logs on the diagonal into $^1/_2$-inch-thick slices and place the slices on their sides. Bake until firm, 15 to 20 minutes. Transfer the biscotti to racks to cool. Store in an airtight container at room temperature for up to 2 weeks.

COCOA ANGEL FOOD CAKE

Cocoa adds an extra flavor dimension to a classic angel food cake. Serve this accompanied with a scoop of Chocolate Ice Cream (page 22), Chocolate Sorbet (page 31), or drizzled with Hot Fudge Sauce (page 71). Fresh fruit is also a good accompaniment. The cake travels well, too, so pack some slices in with your next picnic.

Makes one 10 × 3½-inch cake, 14 to 16 servings

> 1 cup sifted cake flour
> 3 tablespoons unsweetened natural cocoa powder, sifted
> ¼ teaspoon salt
> 1½ cups superfine sugar
> 12 large egg whites, at room temperature
> 1 teaspoon cream of tartar
> 1 tablespoon pure vanilla extract

1 Position a rack in the center of the oven and preheat the oven to 325°F.

2 In a 1-quart bowl, thoroughly blend the flour with the cocoa powder, salt, and ¾ cup of the superfine sugar. Set this mixture aside. Place the remaining ¾ cup superfine sugar in a measuring cup near the mixer.

3 In the grease-free bowl of an electric stand mixer using the wire whip or in a mixing bowl using a hand-held mixer, whip the egg whites on low speed until they are slightly frothy. Add the cream of tartar and whip the egg whites until they begin to mound. While the egg whites are whipping on medium speed, slowly sprinkle on the remaining ¾ cup of superfine sugar, 2 tablespoons at a time, then continue whipping the whites until they are firm, but not dry. Blend in the vanilla, then remove the bowl from the mixer.

4 Sprinkle the dry ingredients over the whipped egg whites, 3 tablespoons at a time and gently fold them into the whites, using a long-handled rubber spatula.

5 Turn the batter into a 10 × 4-inch tube pan, preferably with a removable bottom. Use the rubber spatula to smooth and even the top. Tap the pan on the countertop gently a few times to eliminate any air bubbles.

6 Bake the cake in the preheated oven until it is golden brown, springs back when lightly touched, and a cake tester inserted near the center comes out clean, about 40 minutes. Remove the pan from the oven and immediately invert it onto its feet, or hang it by the center tube over a funnel or the neck of a bottle. Leave the cake to hang for several hours, until it is completely cool.

7 To remove the cake from the pan, run a thin-bladed knife around the inside of the pan and around the tube. Gently loosen the cake from the edges and push the bottom of the pan up, away from the sides. Run the knife between the bottom of the cake and the bottom of the pan and invert the cake onto a plate, then reinvert, so it is right side up. Angel food cake is best cut with a serrated knife using a sawing motion.

8 The cake will keep at room temperature, well wrapped in plastic, for 3 days, or it can be frozen for up to 3 weeks. If frozen, defrost in the refrigerator for 24 hours before serving.

Cocoa Tree   One of the famous early chocolate houses in London, established in the late seventeenth century. These establishments were gathering places, similar to coffeehouses. Members of the Tory party frequented the Cocoa Tree, which closed soon after the end of the nineteenth century. *See also* **White's**.

compound chocolate   *See* **confectionery coating**.

conch and conching   The machine and the technique for stirring liquid chocolate during the final stages of the manufacturing process to make it extremely smooth and palatable. The liquid chocolate is poured into a deep container, then a heavy roller moves back and forth over the liquid mixture continuously to break down any particles and thoroughly blend the ingredients. The result is velvety smooth, melt-in-the-mouth chocolate. Conching can take place for up to seventy-two hours. The longer the time, the smoother the resulting chocolate will be. The technique and the machine were developed by the pioneer Swiss chocolate manufacturer Rodolphe Lindt in the late nineteenth century. The name comes from the Spanish word for shell, *concha*, whose shape the first conching troughs resembled.

concord cake   Created by modern French pastry chef Gaston Lenôtre, this cake is made from three round or oval-shaped chocolate meringues that are filled with chocolate mousse. The cake is completely covered with a decoration of irregular pieces of chocolate meringue. *See also* **chocolate meringue.**

concord sundae   An ice-cream dessert composed of two scoops of dark chocolate ice cream garnished with orange sauce and decorated with irregular pieces of chocolate meringue or with shaved dark chocolate.

confectionery coating   Also called summer coating and compound chocolate, confectionery coating is a substitute for pure chocolate. It is made with a vegetable fat other than cocoa butter. It also contains sugar, milk solids, and a variety of flavorings. One of the advantages to using confectionery coating is that because it does not contain cocoa butter it does not need to be tempered. However, some consider this to be a drawback because without cocoa butter it doesn't taste like chocolate. Confectionery coating is used for dipping candies and for molding, not for cooking. *See also* **cocoa butter; tempering.**

Cortés, Hernán   The leader of the Spanish conquest of the Aztecs in the sixteenth century. Cortés was warmly welcomed by the Aztec ruler, Montezuma, who believed Cortés was the legendary god Quetzalcoatl returning to earth from "where the sun rises." Cortés used this opportunity and the Aztecs' trust in him to bring about their enslavement and the destruction of their civilization. Cortés quickly recognized the value the Aztecs placed on cacao beans and was the first to bring some of the cacao beans and utensils for preparing them back to Spain upon his return in 1528. (It's ironic that the word *cortés* translates from Spanish as courteous or polite, which Cortés was definitely not.)

couverture Chocolate that contains at least 32 percent cocoa butter, which is a higher percentage than regular chocolate. This makes the chocolate the correct consistency to create the thin, smooth, and shiny coatings on dipped truffles and candies. Because of its high cocoa butter content, couverture must be tempered before use. Couverture is used for coating by professional confectioners. In addition to coating candies and truffles, couverture is used for molding, baking, dessert making, candy making, pastry making, and eating out of hand. *See also* **cocoa butter; tempering**.

cremino *See* **Fiat Cremino.**

criollo Criollo, which means native of America in Spanish, was the name given to the cacao tree when the Spanish conquered the Aztecs in the sixteenth century. The criollo tree was the original cacao tree cultivated by the Mayas. Today criollo trees are grown primarily in Central and South America, where they originated. The criollo tree produces the finest and most flavorful cacao bean. Criollo is one of the three main varieties of cacao beans used to produce chocolate. It is a delicate tree that is difficult to grow and produces small yields, so its beans are usually combined with other types of cacao beans. The criollo bean is highly prized by chocolate manufacturers and is used primarily by manufacturers of top-quality chocolate. The criollo bean is also called caraque, a name given it by the Spanish when it was brought to the old world. *See also* **caraque, forastero, trinitario.**

crostata di cioccolata An Italian bittersweet chocolate and hazelnut tart with a flaky crust and a dense, chewy filling.

"Venice is like eating an entire box of chocolate liqueurs in one go."
—Truman Capote

CROSTATA DI CIOCCOLATA

CHOCOLATE AND HAZELNUT TART

The combination of chocolate and hazelnut is a delicious blend of flavors that works perfectly in this tart. The crust is a delicate cookie dough that makes a superb foil for the rich, chewy filling.

Makes one 11-inch tart, 16 servings

PASTRY
- 1³/₄ cups all-purpose flour
- ¹/₂ teaspoon baking powder
- Pinch of salt
- ¹/₃ cup plus 1 teaspoon granulated sugar
- Zest of half an orange, finely minced
- 5 ounces (1 stick plus 2 tablespoons) unsalted butter, chilled
- 1 teaspoon pure vanilla extract

FILLING
- 1³/₄ cups raw hazelnuts
- 2 tablespoons granulated sugar
- 3 ounces (6 tablespoons) unsalted butter, softened
- ³/₄ cup granulated sugar
- 2 large eggs, at room temperature, lightly beaten
- Zest of half an orange, finely minced
- 1 tablespoon all-purpose flour
- 3 ounces bittersweet chocolate, finely chopped
- 1 teaspoon pure vanilla extract
- 2 teaspoons orange liqueur

GARNISH
- 1 cup heavy cream
- 1 teaspoon orange liqueur
- 1 teaspoon pure vanilla extract

1 For the pastry dough: Place the flour, baking powder, salt, sugar, and orange zest in the bowl of a food processor fitted with the steel blade. Cut the butter into small pieces and add. Pulse the mixture until the butter is cut into tiny pieces and the dough is crumbly, about 1 minute. Add the vanilla and pulse the mixture until the pastry wraps itself around the blade, about 1 minute.

2 Roll out the pastry dough on a lightly floured, smooth work surface into a 14-inch circle, about $^1/_8$-inch thick. Gently drape the pastry around the rolling pin and unroll it into an 11-inch fluted edge, removable bottom tart pan. Carefully lift up the sides of the pastry and fit it into the bottom and against the sides of the tart pan. Trim off the excess pastry at the top of the pan leaving a $^1/_2$-inch border. Turn this into the inside, doubling the outside edge of the pastry. Pierce the bottom of the pastry and chill the shell for at least 30 minutes.

3 For the filling: Center a rack in the oven and preheat the oven to 350°F. Place the hazelnuts on a jelly-roll pan or in a cake pan and toast until they turn golden brown and the skins split away from the nuts, 15 to 18 minutes. Remove the pan from the oven and wrap the nuts in a kitchen towel. Allow them to steam for a minute or two, then rub them in the towel to remove most of the skins. Place the hazelnuts in the work bowl of a food processor fitted with the steel blade. Add the 2 tablespoons sugar and pulse until the nuts are very finely ground, about 1 minute. Increase the oven temperature to 375°F.

4 In the bowl of an electric stand mixer or in a mixing bowl using the flat beater attachment or a hand-held mixer, beat the butter for several minutes until it is light and fluffy. Add the sugar and continue to beat to cream the mixture. Add the eggs and orange zest and blend well. Stop occasionally and scrape down the sides of the bowl with a rubber spatula. Add the flour, hazelnuts, and chocolate and blend thoroughly. Add in the vanilla and orange liqueur and blend the mixture well.

(continues)

5 Place the tart pan on a jelly-roll pan and pour the filling into the pastry shell. Bake until the filling is puffed, golden colored, and set, about 30 minutes. Remove from the oven and cool on a rack.

6 For the garnish: In the bowl of an electric stand mixer or in a mixing bowl, use the wire whip attachment or a hand-held mixer to whip the cream until it is frothy. Add the orange liqueur and vanilla, and continue to whip the cream until it holds soft peaks.

7 Serve slices of the tart with a dollop of whipped cream. The tart will keep at room temperature tightly covered with aluminum foil for up to 3 days.

cru   The French word for growth, this refers to cacao beans from a specific plantation.

crystallization   Sugar crystals are formed during the process of cooking sugar when the particles stick together because the liquid they are mixed with is saturated to its fullest point and cannot absorb any more sugar. Whether fudge has a grainy or smooth texture is determined by controlling the sugar crystallization. If the mixture is stirred while warm, large crystals form and produce a grainy texture. If it is stirred when cool, small crystals form, resulting in a smooth texture. Sugar crystallization also occurs when moisture accumulates on the surface of chocolate and the sugar is drawn up. This condition is called sugar bloom, which is visible as white streaks and dots and grainy texture. It is not the same as chocolate bloom. *See also* **chocolate bloom**.

cupuaçu   A relative of cacao, cupuaçu is the fruit of the tree of the same name that is native to the Amazon rain forest of Brazil. Its Latin name is *Theobroma grandiflorum*. A cupuaçu pod is about the size and shape of a football, with skin that resembles the skin of a kiwi fruit. The seeds are buried in the moist pulp of the fruit inside the pods. The seeds are dried, then processed like cacao beans to produce a light-colored chocolate that has a mellow, mild bittersweet flavor with fruity undertones. Cocoa butter is present in cupuaçu as it is in chocolate. Cupuaçu is processed into both powder and bars and is used in the same way as cocoa powder and chocolate. *See also* **cacao; cocoa butter; cocoa powder.**

cuvée A blend of different types of cacao beans.

D

dacquoise au chocolat A classic French cake composed of two or three disks of crisp hazelnut or almond meringue filled and decorated with chocolate buttercream. The top of the cake is heavily dusted with powdered sugar and the sides are covered with either shaved chocolate or ground toasted hazelnuts or finely chopped toasted almonds. Dacquoise is made both in a large size as a cake and as an individual pastry. There are also variations made with mocha buttercream.

DACQUOISE AU CHOCOLAT

Making this classic cake is easier than it seems because you can make the meringues in advance and put the dessert together several hours before serving. Make it for your next dinner party or special occasion and watch your guests' eyes light up.

Makes one 9-inch round cake, 10 to 12 servings

CHOCOLATE HAZELNUT MERINGUES
- 5 large egg whites ($^3/_4$ cup), at room temperature
- $^1/_2$ teaspoon cream of tartar
- $^3/_4$ cup granulated sugar
- 1 tablespoon cornstarch
- 3 tablespoons unsweetened Dutch-processed cocoa powder
- 1 cup toasted, skinned, and finely ground hazelnuts
- 3 tablespoons granulated sugar

BITTERSWEET CHOCOLATE GANACHE   Makes 3$^1/_2$ cups
- 1 pound bittersweet chocolate, very finely chopped
- 2 cups heavy cream

(continues)

47

ASSEMBLY

    1 cup shaved bittersweet chocolate
       Powdered sugar for garnish

1 For the meringues: Cut three pieces of aluminum foil to fit three baking sheets. Using a 9-inch cardboard circle as a guide, trace a circle onto the dull side of each sheet of foil with a pencil and place the foil (pencil side down) onto the baking sheets. The pencil will indent the circle onto the foil so that you can follow its line while avoiding the risk of eating lead. Adjust the oven racks to the upper and lower thirds of the oven. Preheat the oven to 200°F.

2 Place the egg whites and cream of tartar in the bowl of an electric stand mixer or in a mixing bowl and use the wire whip attachment or a hand-held mixer to beat until the whites become frothy. Slowly add $1/2$ cup of the sugar while beating. Beat the whites until they hold firm, but not stiff peaks, 3 to 4 minutes. Just before taking the whites off the mixer, sprinkle on the remaining $1/4$ cup sugar.

3 While the egg whites are beating, sift together the cornstarch and cocoa powder and combine with the ground hazelnuts and 3 tablespoons sugar. Toss to blend well.

4 Remove the egg whites from the mixer and use a long-handled rubber spatula to fold in the nut mixture until well blended. Fit a 14-inch pastry bag with a number 4 plain $1/2$-inch round pastry tip and fill with the meringue mixture.

5 Use the traced circles as a guide and pipe concentric circles onto the foil very close together, or spread the mixture to fill in the lines of the guide. The meringues should be about $1/4$ inch high.

6 Place the baking sheets in the oven for 2 hours. Then turn off the oven and leave the meringues to set until the oven is cool. Remove the pans from the oven and very carefully peel the foil off the back of the meringues. Store the meringues at room temperature in foil or brown paper. They will last for several days, although they are subject to humidity and may soften if it is too humid or damp.

7 For the ganache: Melt the chocolate in the top of a double boiler set over warm water. Stir the chocolate frequently as it is melting with a rubber spatula. At the same time, scald the cream in a separate saucepan.

8 Remove the top pan of the double boiler and wipe the bottom and sides very dry. Pour the hot cream into the melted chocolate and stir together until thoroughly blended.

9 Pour the ganache into a mixing bowl, cover with plastic wrap and refrigerate until thick, but not stiff, about 3 hours.

10 Place the ganache in the bowl of an electric stand mixer or in a mixing bowl. Use the flat beater attachment or a hand-held mixer and beat on medium speed until it becomes fluffy, about 1 minute. Do this step carefully because the ganache will curdle if it is overbeaten.

11 To assemble the pastry: Trim the edges of the meringues gently so that they are even. Place one meringue layer on a 9-inch cardboard cake circle and spread with one quarter of the ganache, using a flexible blade spatula.

12 Place a second meringue layer on top of the ganache, positioning it evenly. Spread this layer with a second quarter of the ganache. Turn the third meringue layer up side down and place on top of the ganache, positioning it evenly.

13 Use a flexible blade spatula to spread the top of the cake with another quarter of the ganache and fill in the sides of the cake with the remaining ganache, smoothly and evenly.

14 Spread the shaved chocolate on a sheet of waxed or parchment paper. Use the flexible blade spatula to gently lift the cake up and place one of your hands underneath it. With your other hand gently press the shaved

(continues)

chocolate into the ganache on the side of the cake so that it will stick. The excess shaved chocolate will fall off. Carefully place the cake down on waxed or parchment paper. Sprinkle the top of the cake with shaved chocolate covering it completely. Lightly dust the top of the cake with powdered sugar.

15 Place the cake on a serving plate and refrigerate for at least 2 hours before serving. Remove the cake from the refrigerator 30 to 45 minutes before serving so the ganache can warm up to room temperature. Use a sharp serrated knife, dipped in warm water and dried, to cut the cake into serving pieces.

dark chocolate   Made from chocolate liquor pressed from the cacao bean during processing, with the addition of cocoa butter, sugar, vanilla, and usually lecithin to act as an emulsifier. Semisweet, bittersweet, and extra bittersweet chocolates are all dark chocolates. The only difference is the amount of sugar added when they are processed. Semisweet chocolate has the largest amount of sugar, bittersweet has less, and extra bittersweet has the least. Dark chocolates are also available as couvertures, which have more cocoa butter than regular chocolate, and are used by professionals. Dark chocolates can be successfully interchanged for each other in recipes without having to alter the other ingredients. Use whichever chocolate you want based on the flavor you prefer. Dark chocolate is used to make myriad desserts, pastries, and confections and is excellent for eating out of hand. Dark chocolate will keep for a few years if stored under optimal conditions. *See also* **bittersweet chocolate; couverture; extra-bittersweet chocolate; semisweet chocolate;** "Chocolate Tips"; "From the Bean to the Bar."

death by chocolate   The whimsical name given to a spectacular chocolate cake composed of layers of chocolate brownie, mocha mousse, cocoa meringue, and ganache. The cake is assembled in a springform pan, chilled, and then completely covered with a poured ganache glaze. Mocha mousse is piped with a star tip to form a decorative border on top. Mocha rum sauce is served as an accompaniment to the cake. *See also* **brownies; ganache.**

Debauve & Gallais A celebrated French chocolate shop located at 30 rue des Saint-Pères, dating from 1819, that retains the atmosphere of the old-fashioned apothecary it once was. The shop has tall mirrored walls and a beautiful curved carved wood counter topped with glistening glass jars. The firm was founded in 1800 and originally produced medicinal chocolates. Today they still manufacture some chocolates considered to be historical examples and many other exquisite chocolates by hand, giving them the distinction of being the oldest firm to do so.

devil's food cake This classic American cake is a rich, moist, very chocolaty two-layer cake filled and iced with fudgy, rich chocolate frosting. The name comes from its dark reddish-brown color, which occurs when the baking soda neutralizes the acid of the natural cocoa powder. Also, this dark color is the opposite of the snowy whiteness of angel food cake.

DEVIL'S FOOD CAKE WITH MOCHA BUTTERCREAM

Be sure to use natural, not Dutch-processed, cocoa powder, which provides deeper flavor and darker color to this classic American cake. The frosting is a matter of personal choice. In this recipe I use a French-style buttercream, but you can use any chocolate frosting you like.

Makes one 9-inch round cake, 12 to 14 servings

CAKE

- 1 tablespoon unsalted butter, melted, for the cake pans
- 1 tablespoon all-purpose flour, for the cake pans
- 2 cups cake flour, sifted
- 1 teaspoon baking soda
- 1/4 teaspoon salt
- 1/2 cup unsweetened natural cocoa powder, sifted
- 1/2 cup hot water
- 1 cup buttermilk
- 1 1/2 teaspoons pure vanilla extract
- 4 ounces (1 stick) unsalted butter, softened
- 1 1/2 cups firmly packed light brown sugar
- 1/2 cup granulated sugar
- 2 large eggs, at room temperature

(continues)

BUTTERCREAM   **Makes 4 cups**

- 2 large eggs, at room temperature
- 2 large egg yolks, at room temperature
- 1 cup plus 2 tablespoons granulated sugar
- $^1/_2$ cup water
- $^1/_4$ heaping teaspoon cream of tartar
- 14 ounces ($3^1/_2$ sticks) unsalted butter, softened
- 6 ounces bittersweet chocolate, melted and cooled
- 2 teaspoons instant espresso powder dissolved in 1 tablespoon water

ASSEMBLY

- 1 cup toasted and finely chopped or ground nuts (walnuts, hazelnuts, almonds, or pecans)

1 For the cake: Center a rack in the oven and preheat the oven to 350°F. Brush the insides of two 9 × 2-inch cake pans with melted butter, then dust with flour and shake out the excess. Cut two rounds of parchment paper to fit the bottoms of the cake pans and place in the pans. Brush the parchment rounds with butter.

2 Sift together the flour, baking soda, and salt.

3 Place the cocoa powder in a mixing bowl and add the hot water. Stir together until the cocoa is dissolved and there are no lumps. Combine the buttermilk and vanilla in a measuring cup.

4 Place the butter in the bowl of an electric stand mixer or in a mixing bowl. Use the flat beater attachment or a hand-held mixer to beat the butter until it is light and fluffy, about 2 minutes. Add the sugars and beat until the mixture is light and fluffy, about 8 minutes. Stop occasionally and scrape down the sides of the bowl with a rubber spatula.

5 Beat the eggs lightly with a fork, then add slowly to the mixture. Continue beating until smooth and well blended, stopping as needed to scrape down the sides of the bowl. Alternately, add the dry ingredients and buttermilk in four stages. Blend thoroughly after each addition.

6 Divide the batter equally between the prepared pans. Use the rubber spatula to smooth and even the tops. Bake the cakes until a toothpick inserted in the center comes out clean, about 30 to 35 minutes.

7 Remove the cakes from the oven and cool on racks for 15 minutes. Place a 9-inch cardboard cake circle over the top of each cake pan and invert. Peel off the parchment paper from the back of the cakes. Place another cardboard cake circle over the back of each cake and invert again, so the top is facing up. Leave to cool completely. Fill and frost immediately or cover the cakes with plastic wrap and hold at room temperature for no longer than 2 days. The cakes can be frozen to keep longer.

8 For the buttercream: Combine the eggs and yolks in the bowl of an elec-tric stand mixer or in a mixing bowl. Use the wire whip attachment or a hand-held mixer and beat on medium-high speed until very pale col-ored and the mixture holds a slowly dissolving ribbon when the beater is lifted, about 5 to 8 minutes.

9 At the same time, combine the sugar, water, and cream of tartar in a 2-quart heavy-duty saucepan and bring to a boil over high heat. Cook the mixture until it reaches 242°F on a candy thermometer. Wash down the inside of the pan with a pastry brush dipped in warm water two or three times as the mixture is cooking, to prevent crystals from forming.

10 When the sugar is at the correct temperature, turn the mixer speed to low and pour the sugar syrup into the egg mixture in a slow, steady stream. Then turn the mixer speed up to medium-high and beat the mixture until the bowl is cool to the touch, 5 to 8 minutes. Beat in the softened butter 2 tablespoons at a time and continue to beat the but-tercream until it becomes fluffy and homogenous, 2 to 3 minutes.

11 Stop the mixer and add the melted chocolate. Blend well, then add the liquid espresso. Beat together, stopping to scrape down the sides of the bowl with a rubber spatula, until the mixture is thoroughly blended.

(continues)

12 This buttercream can be prepared in advance of use and kept refrigerated, covered, for 3 days, or frozen for up to 4 months. If frozen, defrost in the refrigerator for 24 hours before using. To rebeat the buttercream, place chunks of it in the bowl of a mixer and place the bowl in a saucepan of warm water. When the buttercream begins to melt around the bottom and sides of the bowl, remove the bowl from the water, wipe it dry, and beat the buttercream with the flat beater of an electric stand mixer or with a hand-held mixer on medium speed until it is fluffy, 2 to 3 minutes.

13 To assemble the cake: Cut each layer in half horizontally. Place one bottom layer, on the cardboard cake circle, on a cake decorating turntable or a countertop. Spread some of the buttercream evenly over the cake layer. Position another layer of cake on top of the buttercream and spread more buttercream over this layer, evenly and smoothly. Repeat with the remaining two cake layers. Spread the remaining buttercream over the sides and top of the cake. Use the flexible blade spatula to smooth and even the top.

14 Sprinkle the nuts onto a sheet of waxed paper. Use the flexible blade spatula to carefully lift the cake from the bottom and wedge your hand under it, lifting it up. With your other hand press the nuts into the sides of the cake up to the top. Excess nuts will fall back onto the waxed paper.

15 Carefully place the cake onto a serving plate and sprinkle any remaining nuts over the top. Serve the cake immediately or cover carefully and refrigerate until 30 minutes before serving.

De Zaan   *See* **Cacao De Zaan**.

dipping methods   There are two main methods for dipping items into chocolate, by hand and with hand-held tools. Dipping by hand involves dropping a candy center into a pool of tempered chocolate, swirling it to coat completely, and retrieving it by letting it balance between the first two fingers of the hand. This allows excess chocolate to drip off of the center, which is then turned out onto a lined cookie sheet or other pan. As the hand is lifted there is a thread of chocolate that clings to the finger. This is used to form a design on top of the candy. Dipping with tools is similar, but specially designed tools are used to scoop the candy center from the pool of chocolate and to allow the excess chocolate to drip off. It's important for excess chocolate to drip off or it will form an unattractive puddle, called a foot, under the candies after they are turned out. Industrially manufactured candies and confections are usually coated with chocolate by enrobing machines. *See also* **chocolate dipping forks; enrobe.**

Dobos torte, Dobosch torte   A world-famous, classic Hungarian torte that takes its name from its creator, Josef Karl Dobos. He won top honors for his specialty, created in 1884 for the Hungarian National Exhibition. The cake is composed of at least seven very thin, round layers of chocolate sponge cake or génoise that are filled and frosted with rich chocolate buttercream. The top of the cake is covered with a layer of crisp, shiny caramel scored into serving pieces.

double boiler   Two pans that fit snugly together with the top pan sitting partway down the bottom one. The bottom pan holds a shallow amount of water that is warmed to gently heat the ingredient in the top pan. A secure fit is important so no water or steam escapes and mixes with the ingredient in the top pan. A double boiler insulates and provides a continuous source of heat to evenly melt ingredients such as chocolate and butter, and to cook delicate custards and sauces without burning or curdling.

double chocolate raspberry tart   This yummy tart has a delicate, buttery pastry dough that holds three distinct layers. First is a seedless raspberry puree filling, topped by a luscious whipped white chocolate buttercream, and crowned with a glistening dark chocolate glaze. For a final flourish the tart is decorated with piped white chocolate buttercream rosettes that are each topped with a fresh raspberry.

double-dip   To dip twice in chocolate. This technique is used when a heavier outer coating of chocolate is desired on various truffles, candies, and cookies. In some cases a second coat is applied so the item can be rolled over a grate to form a rough texture, as in the outer finish of classic Swiss chocolate truffles.

Dove   A popular American candy bar manufactured by Mars, Inc. The bar is pure high-quality sweetened chocolate and is available in both milk chocolate and dark chocolate. Each 1.3-ounce bar measures 5 inches long, $1^1/_4$ inches wide, and $^1/_2$ inch thick and is separated into five sections that easily break apart. Each bar is considered to be one serving with a caloric content of 200. Ice cream bars are also made under the Dove label.

drinking chocolate   Chocolate was originally consumed as a liquid by the Aztecs, who ground it finely and added a variety of spices, including vanilla, to make the drink more palatable. The mixture was stirred until frothy or poured from a great height from one container to another to aerate it, which formed foam on top. Occasionally, cornmeal was added to the concoction to absorb some of the cocoa butter that floated to the surface. When chocolate traveled to Europe in the sixteenth century, the Spanish mixed it with sugar and formed it into tablets that could be carried with them as they traveled. These tablets were dissolved in water to make a chocolate drink. Coenraad Van Houten irrevocably changed chocolate in 1828 with his invention of a machine that extracts most of the cocoa butter from chocolate liquor and leaves behind cocoa cake that is processed into cocoa powder. Today drinking chocolate is a prepared mixture of cocoa and sugar that is manufactured to be dissolved in water or milk (usually warm) to form a drink. Many chocolate companies make these mixtures. *See also* **hot chocolate.**

Droste   A Dutch chocolate firm, known for their pastilles (chocolate drop candies) and for their cocoa powder.

Dubuisson   A French inventor who developed a technological breakthrough in the processing of cacao beans in 1732. He invented a table for grinding chocolate that was heated from underneath by charcoal. This allowed the workers to stand up while grinding the beans, thereby making the operation more productive. Previous to this invention the workers kneeled in front of a small stone to grind the cacao beans, the same as the Aztecs had done. By being able to stand up the workers would not tire as fast and could reach a larger surface to process more cacao beans at a time.

Duchess of Parma torte   An elaborate Italian cake created in 1985 to honor the winners of Parma's international prize for journalism. The cake is composed of layers of hazelnut meringue alternated with buttercream fillings of marsala-flavored zabaglione and dark chocolate accented with rum and espresso. The cake is covered with a shiny chocolate glaze.

Dutch-processed cocoa   Cocoa powder that has been treated with an alkaline solution during its processing. This reduces the naturally present acid and results in a more mellow flavor. The alkaline treatment also makes the color of the cocoa powder darker and makes it easier to dissolve in liquid. The process was invented in the early nineteenth century by Coenraad Van Houten, who was Dutch, thereby spawning its name.

E

Elite   An Israeli manufacturer of chocolate and confectionery products established in 1933 by a group of Latvian immigrants.

El Rey   Established in 1973, El Rey is a manufacturer of premium-quality chocolate couvertures and derivatives such as cocoa butter and cocoa powder from the flavorful criollo cacao beans grown in particular regions, such as Carenero, in Venezuela.

enrobe   The process of coating candies and confections with chocolate in a specially designed machine.

enrober   A machine that coats candies and confections with chocolate as they sit on a conveyor belt and pass under a shower of liquid chocolate. Excess chocolate flows through the mesh conveyor belt on which the confections sit so their bottoms don't sit in a pool of chocolate and form a "foot."

Esprezzo A line of chocolate candy bars marketed by Esprezzo Confectioners of Mill Valley, California. The bars are made with high-quality dark chocolate and roasted espresso coffee beans in a variety of combinations, some of which include hazelnuts and/or almonds. Each bar weighs 2.25 ounces and is marked in seven pieces that easily break apart. The bars each measure $5^3/_4$ inches long, $1^1/_2$ inches wide, and $^5/_8$ inch high and are considered to be one serving with a caloric content of 310.

Ethel M Chocolates This company produces premium chocolates created by Forrest Mars, former owner of Mars, Inc. He named this line of chocolates after his mother, Ethel, who used to make high-quality chocolates when Forrest was a young boy. Mr. Mars developed Ethel M Chocolates when he retired to Las Vegas, Nevada. The company began production in 1980.

extra-bittersweet chocolate Chocolate liquor with the addition of cocoa butter, a very small amount of sugar, lecithin, and vanilla. Extra-bittersweet chocolate has a deep, pronounced, slightly bitter flavor with a hint of sweetness. It's flavor takes some getting used to, but once the taste for it is acquired, it is preferred by many. It is used for making all types of desserts, pastries, and confections and is excellent for eating out of hand. Extra-bittersweet chocolate can also be couverture chocolate, which has more cocoa butter than regular chocolate, and is used by professionals. It will keep for several years if stored under optimal conditions. *See also* **baking chocolate; bittersweet chocolate; couverture; semisweet chocolate;** "Chocolate Tips."

extrude To push with force, press, or shape by forcing with pressure, referring to shaping chocolate or chocolate mixtures through a pastry bag or with equipment in an industrial factory setting.

F

Felchlin, Max A Swiss manufacturer of high-quality chocolate couvertures and products for the confectionery industry. His plant was established in 1908 in Schwyz, Switzerland.

Ferrero This Italian chocolate manufacturing firm is one of the world's largest with a wide variety of products. They are famous for Rochers, the most popular Italian chocolate candy in the world. Rochers have a toasted hazelnut paste center dipped in chocolate. They are similar in size to Baci candies. Ferrero also produces Mon Cherí candies, cherry liquor–filled chocolates, and Nutella, a popular cocoa-hazelnut spread.

Fiat Cremino A candy created by the Italian chocolate company Majani in 1911 in honor of the new car introduced by the Fiat company, Fiat Tipo 4. The small candy square is wrapped in white paper with gold trim and gold writing. The delicacy is composed of two layers of exquisite dark chocolate mixed with almonds that alternate with two layers of melt-in-the-mouth milk chocolate mixed with hazelnuts.

5th Avenue A popular American candy bar first manufactured in 1936 by William H. Luden of Reading, Pennsylvania, but now made by Hershey Chocolate U.S.A. The bar has a crunchy peanut center completely covered by milk chocolate. Each 3.4-ounce king size bar measures $5^3/_4$ inches long, $1^1/_2$ inches wide, and $^1/_2$ inch thick and is considered to be two servings, each with a caloric content of 230.

florentines A classic confection that is a cross between a candy and a cookie. Florentines are made with a mixture of butter, sugar, cream, honey, almonds, and flour that are first cooked, then baked in round shapes. The underside of the confection is spread with tempered chocolate and a pastry comb is run through it to create a wavy design.

fondant chocolate Chocolate that is extremely smooth and palatable. The invention of the conching machine by Rodolphe Lindt in 1879 and his experiments with adding cocoa butter to chocolate liquor created chocolate with a velvety smooth, fluid texture that has no trace of bitterness. Fondant chocolate has become the standard for modern, high-quality chocolate.

forastero One of the three main types of cacao beans used to make chocolate, forastero beans originated in the upper Amazon. Forastero cacao is hearty and produces high yields, which account for approximately 90 percent of the world's crop. Forastero cacao is widely grown in Africa, the West Indies, and Central and South America. Because its flavor is strong and bitter it is most often used to blend with other beans. As with the other two main types of cacao beans, forastero beans have several hybrids and varieties, many of which are named by their places of origin. *See also* **amenolado; Bahia; balao malacha; chuao; criollo; Guayaquil; trinitario.**

Frango   These chocolate candies are touted as "The Original Frederick & Nelson Frango." They are made and distributed by The Bon Marché department stores in Seattle, Washington. The candies come in a variety of flavors such as mint, ebony dark mint, moka, rum, latté, toffee crunch, raspberry, and almond. Each piece is 1 inch long, $^3/_4$ inch wide, and $^1/_2$ inch thick and is solid flavored milk chocolate.

Frangomints   These legendary candies were made popular by the Chicago, Illinois, department store, Marshall Field. They have a dark chocolate-mint–flavored center completely coated with milk chocolate. Each piece measures 1 inch long, $^5/_8$ inch wide, and 1 inch high.

J. S. Fry & Sons   English chocolate producing pioneers who were the first to grind cacao beans by steam power in 1795. The Frys also were among the first to use Van Houten's cocoa press to produce pure cocoa that dissolved easily in water to make drinking chocolate. The Frys were one of the English Quaker families who chose to deal in cocoa after being barred from attending Cambridge and Oxford universities and, as a consequence, from most professions due to their faith. They saw cocoa as a healthy alternative to gin and hoped to persuade the poor to stop drinking gin in favor of cocoa. The Frys, along with the other English Quaker families in the cocoa business, the Cadburys, Rowntrees, and Terrys, built model villages to house their workers where they were provided with free education and healthcare. *See also* **Cadbury; Rowntree; Terry.**

fudge   A classic American candy, fudge is traditionally semisoft and creamy, made from a combination of butter, cream, and sugar cooked together to a set temperature (usually soft-ball stage, 234° to 240°F). Chocolate is the most popular and most often made flavor. Fudge often contains nuts, such as walnuts. The texture of fudge can be either smooth or grainy, depending on whether it is beaten when cool or while hot. The temperature of the mixture when beaten will cause either small or large crystals to form, which affect the texture. When fudge is set it is cut into squares.

CHOCOLATE NUT FUDGE

This classic fudge is soft, creamy, and richly flavored. It's perfect to pack in a lunch or to serve at your next casual gathering.

Makes thirty-six 1$^1/_4$-inch squares

2	tablespoons unsalted butter, softened
1	cup granulated sugar
1	cup firmly packed light brown sugar
	Pinch of salt
$^1/_2$	teaspoon cream of tartar
$^1/_4$	cup light corn syrup
$^3/_4$	cup heavy cream
7	ounces bittersweet or semisweet chocolate, very finely chopped
2	teaspoons pure vanilla extract
$1^1/_2$	cups roughly chopped walnuts or other nuts

1 Line an 8-inch-square baking pan with aluminum foil so that it extends over the sides. Use $^1/_2$ tablespoon of butter to coat the bottom and sides of the foil. Cut the remaining butter into small pieces. Rinse a jelly-roll pan with cold water, shake off the excess, and set the pan on the countertop near the stove.

2 In a heavy-bottomed 3-quart saucepan combine the granulated sugar, brown sugar, salt, cream of tartar, corn syrup, and cream. Cook over medium heat, stirring continuously with a long-handled wooden spoon to dissolve the sugar, about 3 minutes. Brush down the sides of the pan with a pastry brush dipped in warm water to prevent crystallization.

3 Take the pan off the heat and stir in the chocolate in three to four stages, making sure each addition is melted before adding the next. This will

(continues)

take 1 to 2 minutes. Return the pan to medium heat and position a candy thermometer in the pan. Let the mixture cook, without stirring, until it registers 238°F on the candy thermometer, 20 to 25 minutes.

4 Remove the pan from the heat and quickly stir in the remaining butter and the vanilla, then immediately turn the mixture out onto the jelly-roll pan. Do not scrape out the bottom of the pan. Let the mixture cool, undisturbed, until it registers 110°F on the candy thermometer, 10 to 15 minutes.

5 Transfer the mixture to a mixing bowl or the bowl of an electric stand mixer using a plastic bowl scraper. Using either a hand-held mixer or an electric stand mixer with the flat beater attachment, beat the mixture on low speed until it thickens and loses its sheen, 5 to 10 minutes. Stop and scrape down the sides of the bowl 2 or 3 times as it is beating. When the fudge reaches the right point it will thicken, lighten in color, and form peaks. Add the chopped walnuts and beat another minute or two to blend.

6 Turn the fudge out into the foil-lined pan. Use your fingertips to push it into the corners of the pan and to even the top. Set the pan on a cooling rack and let firm at room temperature for 1 to 2 hours.

7 Remove the fudge from the pan by lifting out the aluminum foil. Gently peel the foil off of the back of the fudge. Cut the fudge into six rows across, then cut each row into six pieces. Store the fudge between layers of waxed paper in an airtight container at room temperature for up to 10 days.

G

ganache   A mixture of chocolate and cream with a velvety smooth texture. Ganache is made with varying proportions of chocolate and cream, depending on the desired final texture and the use for which it is intended. More chocolate than cream yields a firm ganache, whereas more cream than chocolate makes a softer mixture. Ganache is very versatile and is used for many items of confectionery, such as the center for truffles, as the filling for cakes and tarts, and in its liquid state it is poured over cakes and pastries for a glaze. Ganache can be flavored with liqueurs and extracts. It can be combined with soft, beaten butter to create ganache beurre that is used like buttercream. *See also* **ganache beurre**.

LEMON GANACHE SQUARES

Lemon adds lively fresh flavor to these rich chocolate ganache squares. They are typical of the type of ganache bonbons found in the best European confectionery shops.

Makes sixty-four 1-inch squares

12 ounces bittersweet chocolate, finely chopped
1 cup heavy cream
3 large lemons
1 pound bittersweet chocolate, finely chopped, to temper
2 ounces milk chocolate, finely chopped, to temper

1 Line an 8-inch square baking pan with waxed paper so that it extends over the sides.

2 Melt the chocolate in the top of a double boiler over low heat, stirring often with a rubber spatula. In a separate small saucepan, scald the cream over medium heat. Take the top pan off the double boiler and wipe it very dry. Pour the cream into the chocolate and blend with a rubber spatula until the mixture is smooth. Finely grate the zest of the lemons into the ganache. (Be careful not to grate any of the bitter white pith under the zest.) Stir to blend well. Pour the mixture into the lined pan and cover tightly with plastic wrap. Refrigerate until firm, about 3 hours.

3 Remove the pan from the refrigerator. Lift the edges of the waxed paper to remove the mixture from the pan and gently peel off the waxed paper.

(continues)

4 Line a baking sheet with waxed paper. Dip a sharp-bladed knife in hot water and dry it, then cut the chocolate into 1-inch-wide squares. Transfer the squares to the baking sheet, cover loosely with waxed paper, then tightly with plastic wrap and chill in the refrigerator until firm.

5 Temper the remaining bittersweet chocolate using whatever method you prefer (see pages 92–94). Dip each square into the chocolate and remove using a dipping fork. Let the excess chocolate drip off and slide the square onto a lined baking sheet. Repeat with all the squares, then chill briefly to set the coating.

6 Temper the milk chocolate and pour into a paper pastry cone. Fold down the top tightly and snip off a tiny hole at the point. Using a side-to-side motion, pipe lines of chocolate over the coating in a random pattern. Let the decoration set briefly, then place each square in a paper candy cup.

7 Store the squares between sheets of waxed paper in a tightly sealed container in the refrigerator for up to 3 weeks. Bring them to room temperature before serving.

ganache beurre   Also called ganache soufflé, this is ganache with the addition of butter beaten until light and fluffy. It is used in the same way as buttercream, to fill and frost cakes, and as a filling for tarts and other pastries. *See also* **ganache**.

gâteau l'opéra   This classic French cake is named in honor of the Paris Opera. It is composed of three rectangular layers of almond génoise or biscuit, moistened with sugar syrup, that are alternated with layers of coffee buttercream and ganache. The sides of the cake are left open. The cake is topped with a chocolate plaque that has "L'Opéra" written on it with piping chocolate. Often, flecks of edible gold leaf decorate the chocolate plaque. The cake is cut across the width, into strips, for serving. *See also* **ganache**.

Così *Fan Tutte* is an opera by Wolfgang Amadeus Mozart, in the first scene of which the maid Despina sings of how much work it is to beat the chocolate for her mistress. After a taste she declares it to be delicious, and presumably worth the effort.

The Chocolate Soldier is an operetta by Oscar Straus.

gelato *See* **chocolate gelato.**

Gerkens A Dutch manufacturer of high-quality cocoa powder, cocoa liquor, and cocoa butter for use by the industry.

German's chocolate Baking chocolate with milk, vanilla, and a large amount of sugar added. The chocolate takes its name from its creator, Samuel German, who thought it would be more convenient for bakers to have sugar already added to their chocolate. Baker's chocolate company manufacturers German's chocolate in a 4-ounce bar. It is readily available in most grocery stores throughout the United States.

German chocolate cake An American two-layer cake made with German's sweet chocolate that has a cooked coconut-pecan filling and frosting. The name comes from the chocolate used to make it, German's Sweet Chocolate, created by Samuel German. The cake became wildly popular in the late 1950s when the recipe was published in a Dallas, Texas, newspaper. *See also* **German's chocolate.**

Ghirardelli An American manufacturer of chocolate and cocoa products, established in 1852 in San Francisco, California, by Domingo Ghirardelli, an Italian immigrant. Ghirardelli produces a wide range of chocolate and cocoa products for the consumer.

gianduia A type of chocolate, gianduia is a commercially blended mixture of roasted hazelnuts and chocolate with a velvety smooth texture. Often, roasted almonds are used in place of the hazelnuts or in combination with them. Although milk chocolate is most commonly used to make modern gianduia, it was originally made with cocoa powder. It is also occasionally made with dark chocolate. Gianduia is one of the true wonders of the world. Once tasted, it is impossible to forget. Its flavor is so subtle that it is practically impossible to pick out the separate ingredients. Gianduia is used in the same way as chocolate, to flavor a wide variety of desserts, pastries, and confections, including ice cream. Gianduia is also the name for the flavor combination of hazelnuts and chocolate and the name given to a group of candies and confections made with a combination of hazelnuts and chocolate. Gianduia was originally created in Turin, in the Piedmont region of Italy, the home of Italian hazelnuts. *See also* **gianduiotti**.

GIANDUIA CHOCOLATE SQUARES

In these delectable candies the superb flavor of gianduia is created by combining praline paste with chocolate.

Makes sixty-four 1-inch squares

5 ounces bittersweet or semisweet chocolate, finely chopped
3 ounces milk chocolate, finely chopped
1 cup praline paste, at room temperature (page 86)

1 Line an 8-inch-square baking pan with waxed paper so that it extends over the sides.

2 Melt the bittersweet and milk chocolates together in the top of a double boiler over low heat. Stir often with a rubber spatula. Remove the top pan of the double boiler and wipe it very dry. Add the praline paste and stir until well blended.

3 Transfer the mixture to the lined pan and cover tightly with plastic wrap. Refrigerate until firm, about 2 hours.

4 Remove the pan from the refrigerator. Lift the edges of the waxed paper to remove the mixture from the pan and gently peel off the waxed paper.

5 Line a baking sheet with waxed paper. Dip a sharp-bladed knife in hot water and dry it, then cut the chocolate into 1-inch-wide squares. Place each square in a paper candy cup.

6 Store the squares between sheets of waxed paper in a tightly sealed container in the refrigerator for up to 3 weeks. Bring them to room temperature before serving.

gianduiotti A gianduia candy created by the Italian chocolate manufacturer Caffarel in 1865 to honor the World's Fair. Gianduiotti is a small triangular-shaped candy made with the renowned chocolate and hazelnut paste. Traditionally the candies are wrapped in gold paper. Legend tells that the name *gianduia* was given to the candy in honor of a beloved character from Turin in the Italian commedia dell'arte, who symbolized the Piedmontese people during their struggle for freedom and independence in 1799. Considered by many to be a special delicacy, gianduiotti was the official chocolate chosen by Prince Rainier and Princess Grace for their wedding in 1956. *See also* **Caffarel**.

Goo Goo Cluster A popular American candy first produced in 1912 by Standard Candy Company of Nashville, Tennessee. Goo Goo Cluster was the first candy bar to combine milk chocolate, caramel, marshmallow, and peanuts. Each 1.5-ounce bar is a $2^1/_2$-inch round patty that is $^1/_4$ inch thick. It is considered to be one serving with a caloric content of 190. Because of heat and humidity, this candy is not available during the summer.

Green & Black's An English company that manufactures high-quality organic chocolate from cacao beans grown in Belize and Togo. The company philosophy concerns fair trade and it believes that paying a fair price for the cacao directly to the growers allows the farmers to live a better quality life and in turn, enables them to keep producing high-quality organic cacao.

Guayaquil   A region in western Ecuador that gives its name to a variety of the trinitario cacao bean grown there. Guayaquil beans have a sweet flavor that blends well with other beans. *See also* **trinitario**.

Guittard   An American manufacturer of a wide range of chocolate and cocoa products for both the consumer and the industry. The company was established in San Francisco, California, by Etienne Guittard in 1868. Today the company is still managed by members of the founding family.

H

Hawaiian Vintage Chocolate   Established in 1986 by Jim Walsh, a former advertising executive, this is the first company to successfully grow cacao beans in the United States. Hawaiian Vintage Chocolate produces high-quality couverture from cacao grown on the Big Island of Hawaii, which is then processed to bring out its best qualities.

haystacks   A popular two-bite–size candy cluster made with toasted coconut and tempered chocolate. Haystacks are made in milk chocolate and dark chocolate versions.

Heath Bar   A popular American candy bar, whose recipe has been a well-kept company secret for over eighty years, was introduced and manufactured in 1928 by L. S. Heath & Sons, Inc., of Robinson, Illinois, who launched their business in 1914. Currently, Hershey Chocolate U.S.A. produces the Heath Bar. The candy bar has an English toffee center completely coated in milk chocolate. Each 1.4-ounce bar has two pieces, each measuring $2^5/_8$ inches long, 1 inch wide, and $^1/_4$ inch thick. It is considered to be one serving with a caloric content of 210.

Hershey, Milton S.   Hershey was one of the American chocolate manufacturing pioneers and he is credited as the creator of the candy bar in 1894. He established his chocolate company in the Pennsylvania countryside and set up a village to house and care for his workers, modeled after the Cadbury village of Bournville in England. The town was eventually named after him to recognize his generosity. Today, the company that bears his name, based in Hershey, Pennsylvania, is one of the world's largest manufacturers of chocolate, making myriad well-known and loved products and candy bars, such as Hershey's Milk Chocolate with Almonds.

hot chocolate   A hot drink of chocolate and milk or cream served with a topping of whipped cream or marshmallows. *See also* **drinking chocolate**.

"Hot Chocolate" is a pas de deux from the ballet *The Nutcracker*.

PARISIAN HOT CHOCOLATE

This unusual rich and creamy hot chocolate is comparable to the one served at Angelina, the famous tea salon in Paris. It is meant to be sipped slowly and savored.

Makes 3 cups, 6 servings

2   cups milk
$1/2$ cup heavy cream
$1/4$ cup unsweetened Dutch-processed cocoa powder
6   ounces bittersweet or semisweet chocolate, very finely chopped
1   teaspoon pure vanilla extract

GARNISH
$1/4$ cup heavy cream
1   teaspoon superfine sugar

1 In a medium-size heavy-bottomed saucepan, combine the milk, cream, and cocoa powder. Warm over medium heat, stirring to dissolve the cocoa. Add the chopped chocolate and stir until it melts completely. Bring the mixture to a simmer, but do not boil. Return the heat to medium and cook for 5 minutes, stirring occasionally.

2 Remove the saucepan from the heat and stir in the vanilla. Stir the mixture to cool briefly, then ladle into serving cups.

(continues)

3 In the bowl of a stand mixer using the wire whip attachment or in a mixing bowl using a hand-held mixer, whip the cream until frothy. Add the sugar and continue to whip until the cream holds soft peaks. Place a dollop of cream on top of each serving of hot chocolate.

THE FIRST CHOCOLATE DRINKS

The drink the Aztecs consumed was far different than what is known today as hot chocolate. They drank a bitter liquid flavored with chile peppers. In much the same way as is done today, the cacao beans were sun dried, roasted, and then ground on a metate with a small amount of water. Often vanilla was added along with maize and achiote (annatto), for color. A paste was produced, which was shaped into little cakes that could be stored until needed. To make the beverage *chocolatl*, they broke off a piece of cocoa cake and mixed it with water. Then they transferred this liquid back and forth between two gourd vessels, to make it frothy and light.

When Cortés brought chocolate to Spain in 1530, it was much too bitter for the Spanish taste. They added sugar and spices that they were familiar with, such as cinnamon, black pepper, and anise to the cocoa paste, which made it much more palatable and widely accepted. Occasionally a variety of other flavorings were added to the mixture, such as achiote, almonds, hazelnuts, ambergris, and orange flower water or powdered roses. The chocolate paste was mixed with warm rather than cool water and frothed by beating with a molinillo. The Spanish liked their chocolate so well that they tried to keep it a secret from the rest of Europe, and succeeded for close to a hundred years.

hot fudge   A thick, rich topping of dark chocolate, butter, and sugar that is used hot to top ice cream and desserts.

HOT FUDGE SAUCE

This delicious sauce has many uses. Try it over ice cream to make a terrific sundae.

Makes 1¹/₂ cups

- ¹/₂ cup water
- 4 tablespoons unsalted butter, cut into small pieces
- 2 tablespoons unsweetened Dutch-processed cocoa powder, sifted
- 4 ounces bittersweet chocolate, very finely chopped
- ¹/₄ cup light corn syrup
- ¹/₄ cup firmly packed light brown sugar
- ¹/₄ cup granulated sugar
- 1 teaspoon pure vanilla extract

1 Combine the water and butter in a 2-quart saucepan. Bring to a simmer over medium heat.

2 Add the cocoa powder and stir with a wooden spoon until it is completely blended. Remove the saucepan from the heat and add the chocolate. Stir until completely melted and smooth.

3 Add the corn syrup and sugars. Return the saucepan to the heat and bring to a simmer over medium heat. Cook for 5 minutes, stirring frequently.

4 Remove from the heat and stir to cool for 2 minutes. Blend in the vanilla thoroughly. Serve the sauce while warm or store in a tightly covered container in the refrigerator for up to 2 weeks. Warm the sauce in a double boiler or the microwave oven before using.

I

Ibarra chocolate   A brand of Mexican sweet chocolate used primarily for making hot chocolate. The chocolate is sold in the form of 3-inch round tablets that are ⁵/₈ inch high. It is packaged in octagon-shaped, cylindrical, bright yellow and red cardboard boxes. Each 18.6-ounce box holds six tablets. Ibarra chocolate is available in the imported food section in many supermarkets and in specialty food shops. *See also* **Mexican chocolate.**

imperial torte   One of the treasures of classic Viennese pastry, this torte has five layers of marzipan that alternate with layers of rich chocolate cake and chocolate buttercream. The torte is covered with a smooth chocolate glaze. It is served cut into individual slices or squares. Imperial torte was created by a pastry chef at the court of Emperor Franz Joseph in the mid-nineteenth century. Today this torte is shipped to customers around the world in specially designed wooden boxes.

Indianerkrapfen   A classic Austrian pastry that consists of a small vanilla-flavored sponge cake. The cake is hollowed out and filled with sweetened whipped cream, then covered with a shiny, smooth chocolate glaze.

K

Kit Kat   A popular confection bar of crisp wafers coated with milk chocolate. Each 1.5-ounce bar has four chocolate-covered wafers that break apart at horizontal seams. The bar measures $3^3/_4$ inches long, $2^1/_2$ inches wide, and $^1/_2$ inch high. It is considered to be one serving with a caloric content of 220. Kit Kat is made by H. B. Reese Candy Co., a division of Hershey Foods Corporation.

Kohler, Charles-Amédée   A Swiss pioneer chocolate manufacturer who began producing his own chocolate in 1830. He added hazelnuts to his chocolate to distinguish it from other brands. Kohler and his son manufactured their chocolate in Lausanne, Switzerland, until their company was bought out by the firm of Daniel Peter on January 11, 1904.

L

lecithin   An emulsifier often added to chocolate during the manufacturing process to help give it a smooth, fluid consistency. Lecithin stabilizes fat drops and keeps them from congealing and separating. The majority of lecithin used in chocolate manufacture is derived from soybeans, although it also occurs naturally in egg yolks and some vegetables.

Lindt, Rodolphe   Lindt was one of the Swiss chocolate pioneers. In 1879 his invention of the conch and the method for continuous stirring of chocolate in its final production stages revolutionized the manufacture of chocolate and created the first fondant or melting chocolate. Lindt was also the first to add extra cocoa butter to the chocolate mixture, which added extra smoothness to its texture. In 1899 the company merged with Sprüngli and the name became Lindt & Sprüngli.

M

M & M's   A very popular American candy introduced in the 1940s, M & M's are bite-size, $1/2$-inch-round candies coated with milk chocolate. M & M's are available in both plain and peanut types. The candies are known for their bright coatings in such colors as red, apple green, lemon yellow, and Day-Glo blue. They come in various size packages; the 1.74-ounce package is considered to be one serving with a caloric content of 120.

magra   A hand tool used by inspectors on plantations in Africa to open cacao pods lengthwise so the cacao beans can be classified into various grades by their appearance. The magra has a blade that is suspended in a frame which drops swiftly to open the pods.

maragnan   A Brazilian-grown variety of the forastero cacao bean. Maragnan beans have a strong flavor that is favored for blending with other beans. *See also* **forastero**.

marbelized chocolate   This effect is created when one or two chocolates are drizzled over another chocolate (white over dark or milk chocolate), then a knife or toothpick is drawn through them in an abstract design. For marbelized chocolate decorations such as cigarette curls, drizzle one chocolate onto a marble board or the back of a baking sheet. Pour another chocolate over this and spread it out with a spatula so it covers the first chocolate. Let the chocolates firm up, then use a flexible-blade spatula to scrape the mixture from the marble or pan to form the curls. *See also* **chocolate decorations.**

marjolaine   A classic French cake developed by the legendary twentieth-century chef Ferdinand Point at his restaurant La Pyramid in Vienne, France. This cake was originally composed of rectangular layers of almond and hazelnut light sponge cake. Today these are replaced by layers of crisp hazelnut and almond meringue. Three different cream fillings of chocolate, buttercream, and praline are alternated between the layers. The sides and ends of the cake are covered with ground toasted hazelnuts or dark chocolate shavings and the top is decorated with buttercream or with piping chocolate. Marjolaine is similar to dacquoise. *See also* **dacquoise.**

marquise au chocolat   A delicate, molded, chilled chocolate dessert with a soft texture similar to a mousse or a parfait. Marquise is composed of chocolate, cream and/or butter, sugar, and eggs. The mold for the marquise is lined with a delicate baked good such as génoise, ladyfingers, or madeleines before the mixture is added. The dessert is chilled to set, then turned out of its mold and accompanied with a sauce such as crème anglaise or crème fraîche.

Mars   An American chocolate company founded by Frank and Ethel Mars in 1911 in Tacoma, Washington. The company is one of the world's largest candy manufacturers, producing such popular candy bars as Snickers, 3 Musketeers, and Mars Bar. Forrest Mars, creator of Ethel M Chocolates, a division of Mars, Inc., and M & M's was Frank and Ethel's son. *See also* **Ethel M Chocolates; M & M's; Snickers; 3 Musketeers.**

Maya   The pre-Columbian people who planted and cultivated the first cacao plantations in the Yucatan region of Mexico about 600 A.D. These plantations made them wealthy and established them as significant traders.

Menier, Emile-Justine   One of the early pioneer families of the French chocolate manufacturing industry. In the mid-nineteenth century, Emile-Justine Menier propelled the company into becoming the largest chocolate manufacturer in the world. He bought cacao plantations in Nicaragua so the company could control the entire process of the production of chocolate. Menier Company was famous for its cocoa powder. Emile-Justine Menier himself was the first industrialist to build a village to house his chocolate factory workers and to offer remarkable benefits, such as free healthcare and education. It became the model for those villages built in England by the Cadburys and in the United States by Milton Hershey. Today Menier is owned by Nestlé-France.

metate   The concave curved stone slab used by the Aztecs to grind shelled cacao beans to paste. The same method was used in Europe until the late nineteenth century.

Mexican chocolate   Sweet chocolate used primarily for making hot chocolate. It has a distinctive flavor because of its unique combination of ingredients: sugar, cacao nibs, almonds, cinnamon, and lecithin. These ingredients are similar to those used by the Aztecs to create their chocolate drinks. The texture of Mexican chocolate is grainier than that of other chocolates. Mexican chocolate is available in supermarkets and Mexican food markets.

midge   The tiny insect that pollinates the flowers on cacao trees. They are prevalent in the tropical climates where cacao is grown.

milk chocolate   Made from chocolate liquor, pressed from the cacao bean during processing, with the addition of sugar, cocoa butter, powdered milk solids, vanilla, and usually lecithin to act as an emulsifier. Milk chocolate is also available as couverture, which has more cocoa butter than regular chocolate, and is used by professionals. Milk chocolate cannot be interchanged for other types of chocolate in recipes. Milk chocolate is used to make many desserts, pastries, and confections and is excellent for eating out of hand. Milk chocolate will keep for up to ten months if stored under optimal conditions. *See also* **couverture;** "Chocolate Tips"; "From the Bean to the Bar."

Milk Duds   A popular American candy developed in 1926 by the Holloway Company of Chicago, Illinois, and currently made by Hershey

Chocolate U.S.A. Milk Duds are milk chocolate–covered caramels. Each bite-size piece measures slightly over $^1/_2$ inch and is shaped like a large drop. A 1.85-ounce box is considered to be one serving with a caloric content of 230.

Milky Way A very popular classic American candy bar introduced by Frank Mars in 1923. It is composed of a $^1/_2$-inch-thick layer of vanilla nougat topped with a layer of creamy caramel. The entire bar is covered with either milk chocolate or dark chocolate. Each rectangular bar is 4 inches long, $1^1/_4$ inches wide, and $^5/_8$ inch thick and is considered to be one serving with a caloric content of 220. Milky Way bars are also available in miniature size.

mocha A scrumptious flavor made by combining chocolate and coffee that is used extensively in desserts, pastries, and confections.

modeling chocolate *See* **chocolate modeling paste.**

mole poblano A classic Mexican dish composed of turkey in a spicy, savory chocolate sauce. It is reputed to have been invented by the nuns of Puebla near Mexico City.

molinillo Also called molinet, this is a long-handled wooden tool for stirring chocolate drinks. At one end is it fat and round with several deep carved grooves. The molinet is twisted in the hands in a back-and-forth motion that beats the chocolate drink to make it frothy. It was developed by the Spanish in the sixteenth century. When the French created chocolate pots in the seventeenth century, the lid was made with a center hole to hold a molinillo to stir the chocolate.

molten chocolate cake A cake with a soft center that oozes out when cut into, making its own sauce. This cake is sometimes called a soufflé cake because its delicate texture is similar to a soufflé.

MOLTEN CHOCOLATE CAKES

Use the very best quality chocolate for this cake so it can realize its full flavor potential. It is wonderful accompanied by fresh raspberries or strawberries.

Makes six 4½-inch round cakes

- 1 tablespoon unsalted butter, melted, for pans
- 8 ounces bittersweet chocolate, finely chopped
- 4 ounces (1 stick) unsalted butter, cut into pieces
- 1½ teaspoons instant espresso powder
  Pinch of salt
- 6 large egg yolks, at room temperature
- ⅓ cup superfine sugar
- 1 teaspoon pure vanilla extract
- ½ teaspoon chocolate extract
- 2 large egg whites, at room temperature
- ⅛ teaspoon cream of tartar

GARNISH
- ½ cup heavy cream
- 1 teaspoon powdered sugar
- ¼ teaspoon pure vanilla extract
- 1 cup fresh berries (optional)

1 Butter the insides of six 4½-inch tart pans with removable bottoms. Place the tart pans on a baking sheet.

2 Melt the chocolate and butter together in the top of a double boiler set over hot water. Stir frequently with a rubber spatula. Stir in the espresso powder and salt and blend thoroughly. Remove the top pan from the water and wipe dry. Cool briefly.

3 Place the egg yolks and sugar in the bowl of an electric stand mixer or in a mixing bowl. Use the wire whip attachment or a hand-held mixer and whip until they are pale yellow colored and hold a ribbon as the beater is lifted, about 5 minutes. Blend in the vanilla and chocolate extracts.

(continues)

Fold one quarter of this into the chocolate mixture, then fold the chocolate mixture into the egg yolks.

4 In a separate grease-free mixing bowl whip the egg whites until frothy. Add the cream of tartar and whip until they hold soft peaks. Fold into the chocolate mixture.

5 Evenly divide the mixture among the tart pans, filling them three quarters full. Cover tightly with plastic wrap and chill at least 1 hour. The cakes can be chilled up to 4 hours before baking.

6 Center a rack in the oven and preheat the oven to 400°F. Bake the cakes until the edges look set and the centers are still soft and shaky, about 10 to 11 minutes. Remove and cool on a rack for 2 minutes. If needed, run a thin-bladed knife carefully around the rim of the pans, then gently remove the sides and slide the cakes off of the bottoms onto individual serving plates.

7 Whip the cream in the bowl of an electric stand mixer using the wire whip attachment or in a mixing bowl using a hand-held mixer until frothy. Add the powdered sugar and vanilla and whip until the cream holds soft peaks. Top each cake with a scoop of whipped cream and scatter fresh berries over the top and onto the plate.

8 The cakes are best eaten warm. They can be covered with plastic wrap and refrigerated, but the texture will become denser.

Monin   The name of a French manufacturer of flavored syrups used for drinks, ice cream, and desserts. *See also* **chocolate syrup**.

Montezuma   The Aztec ruler in sixteenth-century Mexico who welcomed Hernán Cortés, thinking him to be the returned god, Quetzalcoatl. Cortés turned out to be the exact opposite and eventually enslaved Montezuma and murdered him. During the height of his power, Montezuma drank as many as fifty cups of chocolate a day, usually before visiting his harem. He could well be considered the world's first chocoholic.

Mound's   This popular American candy bar introduced in 1922 by Peter Paul is now manufactured by Hershey Chocolate U.S.A. The bar called "Indescribably Delicious," has a filling of corn syrup–sweetened coconut that is completely covered with dark chocolate. Each bar contains two $2^1/_2$-inch-long, $1^1/_8$-inch-wide, and $^1/_2$-inch-thick oval pieces, which are considered to be one serving with a caloric content of 250. Mound's bars are also available in miniature size.

Mr. Goodbar   A popular American candy bar introduced in 1925 and manufactured by Hershey Chocolate U.S.A. The bar is composed of roasted peanuts completely covered with milk chocolate. Each 1.75-ounce bar measures $5^1/_2$ inches long, $2^1/_4$ inches wide, and $^3/_8$ inch thick. It is marked into twelve separate sections that easily break apart and each is imprinted with "Hershey's" on top. Each bar is considered to be one serving with a caloric content of 270.

mud pie   An American dessert composed of a cookie crust that holds a gooey, fudgy chocolate filling that is topped with whipped cream and shaved chocolate. Occasionally mud pie is made with an ice cream filling.

N

nacional   The name for a variety of forastero cacao bean cultivated in Ecuador that produces a light-seeded, delicate, and flavorful cocoa, considered to be as good as the world's best. This cocoa is also called arriba. *See also* **arriba; forastero.**

négresco gâteau   An elaborate cake composed of a base layer of a chocolate meringue disk, covered with chocolate buttercream, followed by a layer of savarin (a rich yeast cake) baked in a cake pan, topped by a layer of chocolate buttercream. A second chocolate meringue disk is placed on top, then the sides and top of the cake are spread with chocolate buttercream and chilled. The entire cake is covered with poured chocolate glaze. The top is decorated with chocolate buttercream and "Négresco" is written with royal icing.

Nestlé   In 1867 Henri Nestlé began a small food company in Vevey, Switzerland. It was with Nestlé's condensed milk that another Swiss, Daniel Peter, was successful in creating the first milk chocolate. Since the company's beginnings it has diversified into a multinational food corporation with chocolate and chocolate products one of its largest focuses. Nestlé is a household word throughout the world and produces a wide range of chocolate bars, including its world-famous Nestlé Crunch, Butterfinger, Baby Ruth, and Kit Kat. *See also* **Baby Ruth; Butterfinger; Nestlé Crunch; Peter.**

Nestlé Crunch   A classic American candy bar composed of crisped, sweetened rice completely covered with milk chocolate. Each 1.55-ounce bar measures $5^1/_2$ inches long, $2^1/_4$ inches wide, and $^3/_4$ inch high. Each bar is considered to be one serving with a caloric content of 230.

Newman's Own Organics   This company, a division of Newman's Own, produces chocolate bars made entirely from organically grown cacao and other ingredients. The company philosophy is based on supporting sustainable agriculture and does this by working with farmers who grow the cacao in the rain forests of Costa Rica. The company also donates all of its after-tax profits to a variety of educational and charitable causes.

nibs   The inner almond-shaped seed of the cacao bean. The nibs are exposed after the outer shells of the cacao bean have been removed. Nibs are roasted, then ground to produce chocolate liquor, from which all chocolate products are made.

O

Omanhene Cocoa Bean Company   Manufacturer of the only chocolate and cocoa grown and processed in Ghana in a joint venture between the Ghanaian government and a U.S. businessman. Established in 1991, the company currently produces a dark milk chocolate and a hot cocoa drink. The name *Omanhene* comes from the title bestowed on the local chief who has moral and legal authority over his people.

Othellos   This pastry takes its name from Shakespeare's character. Two 3-inch-round, delicate, sponge cake–like biscuits, similar in texture to ladyfingers, are filled with chocolate pastry cream. The outside of the pastry is brushed with apricot glaze then completely coated with chocolate fondant.

Overflodigshorn   A Scandinavian specialty cake that is traditionally served as a wedding cake in Denmark. The cake is also called a cornucopia cake or horn of plenty because of its shape. It is made of several marzipan rings of descending sizes held together and filled with a rich chocolate cream to create a horn shape that has symbolized abundance since the days of ancient Greece.

P

pain au chocolat   A French pastry made from croissant dough cut into a rectangle, rolled around a bar of dark chocolate, and baked until golden brown and flaky. The chocolate melts into the pastry and when bitten into, a burst of liquid chocolate comes through. Pains au chocolat are a breakfast delicacy and a favorite after-school snack of French children.

palets d'or   Translated from French as golden chocolate coins or disks, this delectable confection is a two-bite–size disk of rich chocolate truffle cream dipped in chocolate couverture and decorated with flecks of edible gold leaf. Versions of palets d'or are made with ground toasted hazelnuts mixed into the center truffle cream. Although dark chocolate is the most common type, there are also milk chocolate and white chocolate versions.

pampepato   *See* **panforte.**

panforte   A classic Italian confection that has been made since the early Middle Ages. Panforte is a thin, dense, rich cake chock-full of dried fruits, nuts, and spices held together with a honey syrup mixture. Cocoa is used to create a dark-colored and chocolate-tasting version of panforte. Often panforte is given the name panforte di Siena, indicating the origins of the famous version made in Siena. In the city of Ferrara a version of panforte, called pan pepato or pampepato, is made that is completely covered with chocolate, and in Umbria chocolate is folded into the mixture before it is baked. Panforte is usually baked in a low round pan between sheets of edible rice paper, edible wheat starch paper, called ostia, or parchment paper. Because it is so dense and rich, panforte is cut into thin slices or squares for serving. Often it is accompanied by a glass of Asti Spumante. Panforte is a traditional Italian Christmas confection.

Pará   A variety of forastero cacao bean cultivated in the Brazilian state of the same name. *See also* **forastero**.

Patisfrance   A brand of premium-quality chocolate and couverture used by professionals.

pavé au chocolat   A square or rectangular chocolate pastry with several alternating layers of chocolate cake and chocolate buttercream, ganache, or mousse filling.

peanut butter cups   This is an all-time favorite American candy of molded chocolate cups that completely enclose a creamy center of peanut butter. Peanut butter cups come in both milk chocolate and dark chocolate versions and in various sizes from miniature to $2^1/_2$-inches in diameter. Reese's is a popular brand name of these candies.

pear and chocolate tart   A specialty of Milan, Italy, this tart has three parts: an unbaked chocolate pastry shell filled with a mixture of sliced pears combined with butter, sugar, and pear eau-de-vie, and sprinkled with chocolate crumb topping before baking. Pear and chocolate tartlets are a variation found in Normandy, France. Line tartlet pans with a sweet pastry crust, fill the bottom of the shells with finely shaved dark chocolate, top with a kirsch-flavored custard and thinly sliced, peeled, and cored fresh pears. Serve warm with a fresh raspberry sauce.

Pernigotti An Italian chocolate and confectionery company founded by the family of the same name in 1868 in Novi Ligure, Italy. Pernigotti is well known for their Dutch-processed, unsweetened cocoa powder with a slight vanilla flavor and for high-quality chocolates including the Luna Stelle (Moon and Stars) collection.

Perugina A world famous Italian confectionery company based in Perugia in central Italy. Perugina was originally founded in 1907 by Francesco Buitoni of the well-known pasta-making family. In 1913, Francesco's son Giovanni took over the company. Giovanni and confectioner Luisa Spagnoli together created Baci, those familiar silver-wrapped, kiss-shaped, hazelnut-filled chocolate candies that are beloved around the world. Introduced in the United States at the 1939 New York World's Fair, Perugina is the largest importer in the United States of fine boxed chocolates. Perugina makes a wide range of boxed assortments of premium-quality chocolates. The company is well known for innovative and seasonal packaging. *See also* **Baci.**

Peter Daniel Peter, one of the Swiss chocolate pioneers, created milk chocolate in 1875 using Henri Nestlé's condensed milk. In 1904 Peter Chocolate merged with Kohler to become the Swiss General Chocolate Company, which licensed the rights to market their milk chocolate to Nestlé for ninety-nine years. In 1929 the company merged with Nestlé and Peter's Chocolate became a division of the larger company, making a wide variety of chocolate products, including couvertures, compound coatings, and cocoa powder. *See also* **Nestlé**.

pot de crème A very rich, creamy, silky smooth, baked chocolate custard. Pot de crème is a classic French dessert. The custard is traditionally baked in specially designed pot de crème cups that have tight-fitting lids, or it can be made in any single-serving container and covered tightly with foil before baking. Pot de crème is always baked in a bain marie so it is cushioned by the hot water and retains its delicate texture.

CHOCOLATE-ESPRESSO POTS DE CRÈME

This sophisticated version of chocolate pudding is rich, creamy, and seductive. It's also deceptively easy to prepare. If you don't have covered pot de crème cups, use ¹/₂-cup soufflé or custard cups and cover them with foil before baking.

Six ¹/₂-cup servings

- 2 cups heavy cream
- 1 tablespoon plus 1 teaspoon instant espresso powder
- 5 ounces bittersweet or semisweet chocolate, finely chopped
- 6 large egg yolks, at room temperature
- 2 tablespoons sugar
  Pinch of salt
- 1 teaspoon pure vanilla extract

GARNISH
- ¹/₄ cup heavy cream
- 6 candy mocha or coffee beans

1 Center a rack in the oven and preheat to 325°F.

2 Place the cream in a 1-quart saucepan over medium heat and scald. Add the espresso powder and stir to dissolve it completely. Cover the pan and set aside briefly.

3 Melt the chocolate in the top of a double boiler over hot, not simmering, water, stirring frequently with a rubber spatula. Remove the top pan of the double boiler and wipe very dry. Pour the cream into the chocolate and stir to blend until very smooth.

4 In a separate mixing bowl whisk together the egg yolks, sugar, salt, and vanilla until smooth and well blended. Add this mixture to the chocolate mixture and blend well.

5 Place six ¹/₂-cup soufflé or custard cups or 8 pot de crème cups in a 3-quart baking pan. Strain the custard into a 4-cup measuring cup or a pitcher. Divide the custard evenly among the cups, leaving a bit of room at the top. Cover the cups with their tops or tightly with foil. Place the pan in the oven and pour boiling water into the pan until it reaches halfway up the sides of the custard cups.

6 Bake the custard for 25 minutes. The custard will still look soft, but will firm up as it cools and chills. Remove the pan from the oven, remove the custard cups from the pan, remove the tops of the cups, and cool on a rack. Chill the custard for at least 2 hours before serving. The custard will keep for up to 3 days, well covered, in the refrigerator.

7 For the garnish, whip the cream until it holds soft peaks. Fit a pastry bag with a large, open star tip and pipe a large rosette in the center of each tart. Place a candy mocha or coffee bean in the center of each rosette.

pot de crème cup   Similar to a custard cup, a *pot de crème* cup is a rounded cylinder, about 2 inches deep and 3 inches wide at the top. It has small loop handles on each side and a snug-fitting lid. The cups are smooth inside and sometimes ribbed on the outside or have an outer decoration. *Pot de crème* cups are made of porcelain. They are available in cookware and restaurant supply shops and are usually sold in sets of six.

Poulain   The French chocolate company started in 1847 by Auguste Poulain when he opened his first chocolate shop in Blois. He developed the slogan "Taste and compare," which became famous in France. His son, Albert, revolutionized the company when he created an instant chocolate breakfast drink in 1884. In 1904 another version of the instant chocolate drink mix, Poulain Orange, was launched, which continues to be sold in France today as Grand Arôme. Today the Poulain company is a part of the conglomerate Cadbury-Schweppes.

pralinés   The French term that refers to the category of elegant, high-quality chocolate candies with fillings of praline (ground caramelized almonds or hazelnuts) or praline paste (similar in texture to almond paste, made from praline). The name derives from the Count of Plessis-Praslin, whose chef created it, quite by accident, in the seventeenth century.

PRALINE PASTE

Praline paste is used as an ingredient in a variety of desserts, pastries, and confections. It is a versatile kitchen staple. Hazelnuts are usually used to make praline paste, but almonds or a combination of both hazelnuts and almonds can be used. If you are adventurous you can try using other nuts as well.

Makes 1 cup

1 cup toasted hazelnuts, almonds, or other nuts
3 to 4 tablespoons unflavored vegetable oil

Place the nuts in the work bowl of a food processor fitted with the steel blade and pulse until they are very finely ground. Add the vegetable oil and process until the mixture forms a thick paste, similar to peanut butter. Store praline paste in a tightly sealed container in the refrigerator for up to 3 months. Bring to room temperature before using.

PRALINE, PRALINÉ, PRALINES

Praline [PRAY-leen] is the French term for the finely ground mixture of caramelized almonds or hazelnuts. The name derives from the Count of Plessis-Praslin, whose chef created praline in the seventeenth century by accidentally combining caramelized sugar and almonds. Praliné is the French term for the category of elegant, high-quality chocolate candies with fillings of praline or praline paste, similar in texture to peanut butter, made from praline. Pralines [PRAH-leens] are a specialty fudgelike candy of New Orleans, Louisiana, made with pecans and brown sugar and shaped into a round, flat patty.

---

presscake *See* cocoa cake.

Prince Regent torte A classic German cake composed of five thin, round cake layers that are filled with a rich, whipped-creamy, chocolate mixture. The torte is completely covered with a smooth, shiny chocolate glaze. As an option the torte can be decorated with blanched almonds.

profiteroles   These are tiny cream puffs filled with either chocolate pastry cream, sweetened whipped cream, or chocolate or coffee ice cream. Five of these filled puffs are stacked in a serving dish in a low pyramid and drizzled with hot chocolate sauce to form the classic dessert, profiteroles au chocolat.

pyramid cake   A stunning and delightful chocolate cake composed of seven rectangular layers of almond sponge cake spread with rich dark chocolate buttercream that are stacked upon each other. After chilling, the stack is cut all the way through on a diagonal, forming two triangles that are then joined together into a pyramid with a layer of the chocolate buttercream. The entire cake is completely iced with chocolate buttercream.

Q

Queen of Sheba cake   *See* **Reine de Saba gâteau.**

Quetzalcoatl   The mythical plumed serpent god worshiped by the Aztecs. Quetzalcoatl provided his people with cacao, which they considered to be divine. He was supposed to return to earth in the year "one-reed" and bring the treasures of paradise. When Hernán Cortés landed in the sixteenth century, in the year "one-reed," he was mistakenly thought to be Quetzalcoatl and warmly welcomed by Montezuma, the Aztec ruler. This ultimately led to the enslavement and destruction of the Aztec people by the Spanish. *See also* **Cortés, Hernán.**

quick tempering   A method of stabilizing the cocoa butter in chocolate so the chocolate has a shiny, even appearance and smooth texture. Finely chop the chocolate to be tempered and melt two thirds of it in the top of a double boiler over low heat. Stir often with a rubber spatula so it melts evenly. Remove the top pan from the water and wipe very dry. Stir in the remaining third finely chopped chocolate in two or three stages until smooth. To check for the right temperature, place a dab under your lower lip. It should feel comfortable.

R

Rademaker   This Dutch company, based in Amsterdam, is a manufacturer of high-quality chocolate couverture, bars, filled candies, and sugar-free chocolates.

Reese   The brand name of a manufacturer of peanut butter cups, a popular American candy. *See also* **peanut butter cups**.

Rehrücken   This Austrian delicate chocolate and almond cake is baked in a specially designed long, curved mold that resembles the shape of a saddle of venison, hence the cake's alternate name, "mock saddle of venison." A shiny chocolate glaze completely coats the cake. It is decorated with rows of blanched whole or slivered almonds that pierce the top. These mimic the fat used to lard a real venison roast.

Rehrücken mold   The specially designed tinned-steel or aluminum baking pan created to shape the classic Austrian "mock saddle of venison" cake. It looks like a long loaf pan that is curved in a half-moon shape and has deep, evenly spaced grooves across the width. Some versions of the pan also have a groove down the center to represent the bone of the saddle of venison. The cake is recognized by its classic curved, ridged shape, which it takes from the pan. A typical Rehrücken mold measures between 10 and 14 inches long, $4^1/_2$ inches wide, and $2^1/_2$ inches deep.

Reine de Saba gâteau   A dense, rich single-layer French chocolate and almond cake whose name translates as Queen of Sheba. The cake has a characteristic creamy center. On the outside it is coated with a layer of whipped ganache, covered with a shiny chocolate glaze, and decorated with sliced almonds.

religieuse   A French pastry whose name means "nun" because it looks like a nun wearing her habit. The pastry is made of two choux pastry puffs filled with chocolate, coffee, or vanilla pastry cream. The puffs are stacked on top of each other and frosted with chocolate fondant or glaze. Although typically these are made as individual pastries, religieuse can also be made as a large cake.

Rigó Jancsi This Hungarian chocolate pastry takes its name from a legendary nineteenth-century violinist who was reputed to break many women's hearts. Two layers of chocolate cake enclose a whipped chocolate filling flavored with rum or orange liqueur. A shiny chocolate glaze coats the pastry, which is cut into individual-size squares.

rochers An elegant candy that take its name from the French word for rock. Rochers are made with toasted slivered almonds coated with tempered milk or dark chocolate, formed into irregularly shaped clusters. Variations of this classic bonbon include toasted coconut. Another version of rochers are also made by the Italian company Ferrero. Their candy is shaped like a dome. It has a center of roasted hazelnut paste covered with dark chocolate. *See also* **Ferrero.**

Rowntree One of the pioneering entrepreneurial families in the English chocolate business. The Rowntrees, like the Cadburys, Frys, and Terrys, were Quakers and had a social conscience. Joseph Rowntree, the founder of the family business, built a factory town near York to house his workers. They also received free education and medical care. Rowntree chocolates are famous for their After Eights, peppermint chocolates traditionally served as after dinner mints. *See also* **Cadbury; J. S. Fry & Sons; Terry.**

S

Sacher, Franz In 1832 Sacher was the pastry chef to Prince Metternich for whom he created a dense, rich chocolate cake covered with apricot preserves and chocolate glaze. The cake, named Sachertorte in honor of its creator, has become world famous. *See also* **Sachertorte.**

Sachertorte A world-famous Austrian chocolate cake created in 1832 by Franz Sacher, pastry chef to Prince Metternich. The rich, dense cake is available in two versions. One version is cut into two horizontal layers and filled with apricot preserves. The other is left intact and coated on the outside with a layer of apricot glaze. Both versions are completely covered with a glassy, smooth chocolate glaze and the word *Sacher* is written on top with piping chocolate. Sachertorte is traditionally served with schlag, whipped cream in German. There is a great rivalry between the Hotel Sacher and Demel's pastry shop in Vienna, Austria, that developed in the 1950s. Both locations claim original versions of the torte that were passed down from the descendants of Franz Sacher. A court decision gave the Hotel Sacher the right to place a chocolate plaque on top of each of their tortes that states it is the "genuine" Sachertorte. *See also* **chocolate glaze; schlag.**

Sarah Bernhardt An individual pastry created in Denmark and named after the legendary nineteenth-century actress. The pastry is composed of an almond macaroon topped with a pointed mound of chocolate ganache, completely encased in dark chocolate. Occasionally, flecks of edible gold leaf decorate this chocolate delicacy.

Scharffen Berger chocolate An American manufacturer of premium-quality couverture chocolate. 1997 was the first year of operation for this rapidly growing company, which follows traditional European methods to produce excellent chocolate with 70 percent cocoa components.

schlag The German word for whipped cream, which is the traditional accompaniment to many chocolate pastries and desserts.

semisweet chocolate Chocolate liquor with the addition of cocoa butter, a small amount of sugar, lecithin, and vanilla. Semisweet chocolate has a deep, rich flavor that is mildly sweet. It is used for making all types of desserts, pastries, and confections and is excellent for eating out of hand. Semisweet chocolate can also be couverture chocolate, which has more cocoa butter than regular chocolate, and is used by professionals. Semisweet chocolate can be easily interchanged with bittersweet chocolate without having to alter the other ingredients in a recipe. It will keep for a few years if stored under optimal conditions. *See also* **baking chocolate; bittersweet chocolate; couverture; extra-bittersweet chocolate; "Chocolate Tips"; "From the Bean to the Bar."**

snap   A technical term that describes one of the characteristics of well-tempered chocolate. It should break cleanly and crisply, with a sharp snap and should not be crumbly or soft.

Snickers   A popular classic American candy bar introduced in 1930 and manufactured by Mars, Inc., whose motto is, "Packed with Peanuts, Really Satisfies." Each rectangular bar is 4 inches long, $^5/_8$ inch deep, and $1^1/_4$ inches wide. The inside of the bar is composed of three layers, a light tan-colored nougat filling topped with roasted peanuts that are covered with creamy caramel. The entire bar is surrounded by milk chocolate. Each bar is considered to be one serving with a caloric content of 280.

Snickers ice cream cone   Manufactured by Mars, Inc., this is an ice cream version of the popular candy bar. The single-serving sugar cone is a total of 4 ounces. It is lined with chocolate, enclosing a peanut-caramel filling and chocolate-peanut ice cream. The cone is topped with chocolate and chopped peanuts.

Spanish rolls   Chocolate in solid tablet form as it was available in the early seventeenth century in Europe. The Spanish had brought chocolate to Europe from Mexico. They mixed it with sugar to make it more palatable and formed it into solid tablets, which they carried with them. These tablets could easily be dissolved in water and made into drinking chocolate.

Sprüngli   One of the founding pioneer families of the Swiss chocolate industry. David Sprüngli started the family business in the early part of the nineteenth century when he apprenticed himself to a confectioner in Zurich. His sons joined him in the business and expanded it to include chocolate factories and a world-famous pastry and confectionery shop in the heart of Zurich. In 1899 Sprüngli merged with Lindt to become Lindt & Sprüngli, one of the world's finest chocolate manufacturers.

sugar bloom   A white crust of sugar crystals that forms when moisture accumulates on the surface of chocolate and chocolate candies. The moisture draws the sugar to the surface where it dissolves. This is visible as white streaks and dots and causes a grainy texture. Sugar bloom is caused by storing loosely wrapped chocolate and candies in the refrigerator where they are exposed to too much moisture. It is not the same as chocolate bloom, which occurs when the cocoa butter in the chocolate rises to the surface. *See also* **chocolate bloom; crystallization**.

T

tartufo   The Italian word for truffle. *See also* **chocolate truffle**.

tempering   A process that sets cocoa butter at its most stable point. Cocoa butter has four different types of crystals and each has a different melting point. Tempering chocolate captures the beta crystal, the most stable of the four. Because chocolate has these different melting points it is unstable and causes the cocoa butter to easily rise to the surface of chocolate. This creates a condition called chocolate bloom, which results in unsightly white and gray streaks and dots, a grainy texture, and makes unmolding difficult. When chocolate is tempered it has a shiny, even appearance and smooth texture. It breaks with a sharp snap, sets up rapidly, and releases easily from molds. All chocolate comes from the manufacturer tempered but when it is melted it loses the temper and must be tempered again for dipping and molding. To temper chocolate, it is heated so it melts completely, stirred to cool to approximately 78°F (below the melting point of cocoa butter), then heated again to an exact temperature, depending on the type of chocolate it is, that is, dark, milk, or white. Tempering is accomplished through different methods and by machine. *See also* **chocolate bloom; chocolate thermometer; classic tempering; quick tempering; tempering machine**.

TEMPER, TEMPER

There are several hand methods for tempering chocolate, including the classic (table) method and the quick (pot) method. Chocolate is also very easily tempered with a chocolate tempering machine.

Classic tempering, also called the table method, involves melting the chocolate until it is completely smooth and fluid. Chop the chocolate very finely and melt in the top of a double boiler over warm water. Stir often with a rubber spatula so it melts evenly. Pour two thirds of it onto a marble slab and spread from one side to the other with an offset spatula. Then gather the chocolate into the center with a plastic scraper. Repeat this several times until the chocolate noticeably thickens. Use a specially designed chocolate thermometer that reads in one-degree gradations in the range of 40°F to 130°F to take its temperature, which should be at 78°F to 80°F. Return this chocolate to the remaining third liquid chocolate and stir together for a couple of minutes until thoroughly blended. The final temperature should be 89°F to 91°F for dark chocolate and 85°F to 88°F for milk and white chocolate. If the temperature is below this, reheat carefully until it reaches the correct point. If the chocolate is too warm it is necessary to repeat the tempering process.

Quick tempering, also called the pot method, is a technique of stabilizing the cocoa butter so the chocolate has a shiny, even appearance and smooth texture. To temper chocolate using this method, very finely chop the chocolate and melt two thirds of it in the top of a double boiler over low heat. Stir often with a rubber spatula so it melts evenly. Remove the top pan from the water and wipe very dry. Stir in the remaining third finely chopped chocolate in two or three stages until smooth. To check for the right temperature, place a dab under your lower lip. It should feel comfortable, not hot or cool. Properly tempered chocolate is a few degrees less than body temperature.

A variation of this method involves adding a large chunk of chocolate to the melted chocolate and stirring continuously until the chocolate is cool. The chunk is then removed from the liquid chocolate and can be used again.

Although accuracy is very important when tempering chocolate, this method does not rely on an exact temperature. To test if the chocolate is tempered, place a teaspoonful on a piece of aluminum foil or waxed paper, then place this in the refrigerator to set up for a few minutes. If it is well tempered the chocolate will set quickly, be shiny, and have an overall even color without streaks or dots. If it is not tempered the chocolate will be dull and cloudy, which means you will need to start the tempering process again.

To hold tempered chocolate at the same temperature, place the bowl over a bowl of water that is two degrees warmer than the chocolate. Be sure the bowl fits snugly so there is no danger of water mixing with the chocolate. It may be necessary to change the water in the lower pan so it stays at a constant temperature. Another method of keeping the chocolate warm is to place the bowl on a heating pad set at its lowest setting. But do make sure this setting is not too hot. Stir the chocolate often while you work with it so it doesn't begin to set up.

To temper chocolate using a tempering machine closely follow the manufacturer's directions to achieve the desired results. Once tempered, the machine will hold the chocolate at the correct temperature by heating and cooling it, for a long time.

tempering machine   A machine designed specifically for melting and tempering chocolate. Tempering machines come in many different sizes and capacities with small machines available for home use. The machine melts the chocolate, tempers it, and holds it at the correct temperature for dipping and molding truffles and candies. The small tempering machines have a plastic or metal casing that holds the electrical components, with a control panel on the front with knobs and switches that turn the machine on and off, control the temperature, control the mode of either melting or tempering, and a switch that controls the bowl motor. A stainless steel bowl sits on top of the casing and is divided in half horizontally by a large plastic scraper, which holds a probe and on some machines, a chocolate thermometer. Finely chopped chocolate is placed behind the scraper, the machine is set to a specific setting or temperature, and the bowl is set to revolve. As the bowl rotates, the melted chocolate moves to the front of the scraper. Tempering machines are easy to use. Simply turn on the machine, put in the finely chopped chocolate, and set the mode temperature according to the type of chocolate, following the manufacturer's instructions. It takes approximately 30 minutes to 1 hour to temper chocolate in the machine and perfect results are guaranteed. A unique feature of some of these machines is that chocolate can be held at a constant temperature to keep it liquid for several hours or overnight. This means that chocolate can be tempered faster than by starting with chopped chocolate. The bowls of the tempering machines lift out for cleaning and extra bowls and scrapers are available. *See also* **tempering;** "Sources for Chocolate Equipment, Tools, and Utensils."

Terry   One of the founding families of the English chocolate business. The Terrys, like the Cadburys, Frys, and Rowntrees, were Quakers and had a social conscience. In 1886 the Terrys built a factory and a nearby town to house their workers, where they also received free education and medical care. *See also* **Cadbury; J. S. Fry & Sons; Rowntree.**

Theobroma bicolor   Called *Theobroma pataxte,* or pataste by the Maya, this is a species of the genus *Theobroma,* grown primarily in Mexico.

Theobroma cacao   The Latin name given to cacao by Linnaeus, the Swedish naturalist who codified the plant world in 1753. Linnaeus bestowed the name with a bow to the drink savored by the Maya and Aztecs and to the myth of Quetzalcoatl. *Theobroma* translates as "food of the gods." *See also* **Quetzalcoatl.**

Theobroma grandiflorum   A species of the genus *Theobroma,* grown in the Amazon rain forest in Brazil, also called cupuaçu. The product of this fruit is a light-colored chocolate that has a delicate, mild bittersweet flavor with fruity undertones. *See also* **cupuaçu.**

3 Musketeers   This popular American candy manufactured by Mars, Inc., and introduced in 1932, originally had three distinct parts—chocolate, vanilla, and strawberry. In the 1940s it was changed to its current all-chocolate formula of milk chocolate nougat completely covered with milk chocolate. Each 2.13-ounce bar measures 5 inches long, $1^{1}/_{4}$ inches wide, and $^{3}/_{4}$ inch thick. Each bar is considered to be one serving with a caloric content of 260.

Tobler   The Swiss chocolate company that invented and produces the famous Toblerone candy bar. Jean Tobler, the company founder, was one of the pioneers of the Swiss chocolate industry. In 1899 he began to manufacture sumptuous chocolate bars and boxed assortments of chocolates in Bern.

Toblerone   A classic Swiss candy bar created in 1908 by Jean Tobler. The name is a combination of the name of its creator and torrone, Italian nougat, that is combined with chocolate to make the confection.

Toblerone bars are known for their triangular shape, reminiscent of the Swiss Alps. Toblerone bars are available in dark, milk, and white chocolate versions, and white chocolate–filled coated with dark chocolate. The bars come in a wide variety of sizes. *See also* **Tobler.**

Tootsie Rolls   A popular American candy, these chewy chocolate logs, introduced in 1896, are named after the daughter of their creator, Leo Hirschfield. Her name was Clara, but her dad always called her "tootsie."

torrone   An Italian confection made with honey, egg whites, toasted almonds, pistachios, and other nuts, such as hazelnuts. Chocolate torrone is also made and chocolate-dipped torrone is often available.

torta barozzi   A dense, moist, fudgy, flourless chocolate cake that is a specialty of the town of Vignola near Modena, Italy. The cake has an intriguing legend surrounding it regarding the ingredients and their proportions. It was invented by pastry chef Eugenio Gollini in 1897 to celebrate the birthday of the architect Jacopo Barozzi, native of Vignola, who created the spiral staircase during the Renaissance. Gollini's descendants still make the cake today in their bakery, but have taken the family vow to never disclose the recipe, even though the ingredients are printed on the box. The cake contains peanuts, a very unusual ingredient for Italy, but the family offers no explanation for how they became part of the cake.

torta gianduia   An Italian chocolate-hazelnut layer cake renowned throughout the Piedmont region, where hazelnuts are grown. Three layers of rich gianduia cake are filled and frosted with a creamy gianduia ganache cream and the cake is decorated with ground toasted hazelnuts.

trembleuse   A cup for chocolate devised in the early eighteenth century to prevent the beverage from spilling. The cup is placed in a holder, in the center of a saucer, that keeps it erect and steady.

trichocolate terrine   A cold molded dessert of a creamy, velvety mousse, ice cream, or custard fashioned of three layers, each flavored separately with dark chocolate, milk chocolate, and white chocolate. Terrine refers to the narrow, long earthenware dish in which a meat or fish dish is molded and from which the dessert takes its name. The dessert is generally molded in a glass or metal loaf pan. It is unmolded and sliced across the width before serving, exposing the three distinct chocolate layers. Trichocolate terrine is usually served with a fruit or custard sauce.

trinitario   One of the three main types of cacao beans used to make chocolate, trinitario beans are a cross between criollo and forastero beans. They are cultivated primarily in Central and South America and Indonesia. Trinitario beans produce flavorful, high-fat cocoa. Some are sweet, some strongly flavored, while others have an acid edge. The particular flavor characteristics are determined by the soil where the beans are grown. As with the other two main types of cacao beans, trinitario beans have several hybrids and varieties, many of which are named by their places of origin. *See also* **amenolado; Bahia; balao malacha; chuao; criollo; forastero; Guayaquil.**

truffle   *See* **chocolate truffle.**

truffle cups   Chocolate truffle cream is piped into bite-size firm, pleated foil candy cups, then chilled. When the foil cups are peeled away they leave a fluted design in the chocolate.

tuiles au chocolat   *See* **chocolate tuiles.**

turtles   A delectable cluster candy made from pecan halves topped with a layer of creamy caramel followed by a layer of chocolate. Turtles are also completely dipped in chocolate.

Twix   A popular American chocolate cookie bar manufactured by Mars, Inc., since 1977. Twix are made with butter cookies topped with a thick layer of caramel, completely coated with milk chocolate. Each cookie bar measures $4^1/_4$ inches long, $^3/_4$ inch wide, and $^1/_2$ inch high. Each 2-ounce wrapped serving contains two cookie bars with a caloric content of 280.

V

Valrhona   A French manufacturer of premium-quality chocolate couvertures. Valrhona produces what many consider to be the world's finest chocolate. The company is known for their Grand Cru chocolates, made from single-origin cacao beans. Valrhona is some of the world's most expensive chocolate.

Van Houten, Coenraad   In 1828 Van Houten developed the hydraulic press that extracts cocoa butter from cocoa liquor, leaving cocoa cake, which is further refined into cocoa powder. This revolutionized the manufacturing of cocoa powder. He also discovered that by adding alkali to cocoa powder, which is naturally acid, the powder becomes mellower in flavor and is more soluble in liquid. This process is called dutching. Today Van Houten is one of the leading manufacturers of high-quality cocoa powder. *See also* **Dutch-processed cocoa.**

vanilla bean   The fruit of a climbing orchid vine native to southern Mexico, vanilla beans have been used as a flavoring for hundreds of years. The Aztecs used the beans to flavor chocolate. The plants are widely grown in tropical climates such as Tahiti and Madagascar, which produce the most moist and flavorful beans. The pods are picked green, then cured. The curing process begins with a boiling water bath, then the beans are wrapped and left to sweat in the sun. This sweating process is alternated with drying, which produces the characteristic shriveled, dark brown appearance of the long, thin beans and causes the outside of the pods to become encrusted with frosty white crystals, called vanillin. Vanillin gives the beans their fragrant flavor and aroma. Vanilla beans are used extensively to flavor deserts, pastries, and confections. Vanilla particularly intensifies the flavor of chocolate. To use the bean for flavoring, it is split open and steeped in liquid. The tiny black grains that fill the inside of the bean contain the potent vanilla flavor, which is released during the steeping. Vanilla beans will dry out if exposed to air. To keep them plump and flexible they should be stored wrapped in plastic in a tightly covered container in a cool, dry place, where they will last for several months. *See also* **vanilla extract; vanillin.**

vanilla extract   Produced by steeping vanilla beans in an alcohol and water solution, pure vanilla is concentrated and therefore, only a small amount is needed for flavoring. Vanilla is an expensive flavoring to produce, which has led to the proliferation of synthetically produced vanilla. According to United States law, if the product is labeled as pure vanilla extract, it must be made from vanilla beans. If synthetically produced vanillin is used as a flavoring, the label must state that the product is artificially flavored. If a combination of pure and artificial vanillas are used to produce the flavor, the label will state that the product is vanilla flavored. Mexican vanilla, which is much cheaper than vanilla in the United States, often contains coumarin, a potentially toxic substance. It is banned by the U.S. Food and Drug Administration. Vanilla extract will last indefinitely if stored in a tightly covered glass or plastic bottle in a cool, dark, dry place. *See also* **vanilla bean; vanillin**.

vanillin   A substitute for natural vanilla produced synthetically as a by-product of the paper industry and treated with chemicals. Vanillin is used to flavor some chocolate and candies. Synthetic vanillin is easily detected because it tastes artificial. *See also* **vanilla bean**.

viscosity   A measure of the coating thickness of melted chocolate, which determines its ability to coat or enrobe confections. Melted chocolate has varying degrees of viscosity depending on its type (dark, milk, or white) and whether or not it is couverture, which contains a higher percentage of cocoa butter than regular chocolate. *See also* **couverture; enrobe**.

W

water bath   *See bain marie;* **double boiler**.

white chocolate   Made from cocoa butter pressed from chocolate liquor during the processing of the cacao bean. Sugar, milk solids, vanilla, and lecithin are added to the cocoa butter to complete the formula. Technically the U.S. Food and Drug Administration does not consider white chocolate to be chocolate because it contains no chocolate liquor.

They require it to be labeled "confectionery" or "confectioners' coating," which makes it easy to confuse with "summer coating," a product that contains no cocoa butter and is made with other vegetable fats. Cocoa butter is what gives white chocolate a true chocolate taste. It also means that white chocolate needs to be tempered to stabilize the cocoa butter for dipping and molding. White chocolate cannot be substituted for milk or dark chocolate in recipes because it has less body than either. White chocolate is also available as couverture. *See also* **dark chocolate; milk chocolate;** "From the Bean to the Bar."

White's　One of the famous early chocolate houses in London, established in the late seventeenth century. These establishments were gathering places, similar to coffeehouses. Many supporters and members of the Whig party, writers, and gamblers frequented White's. In 1787 White's ceased to exist because it had become a gambling club and been forced to move many times. Finally it had no location. *See also* **Cocoa Tree.**

Wilbur Chocolate Company　An American manufacturer of chocolate and compound coatings and cocoa powders for the candy manufacturing, bakery, and dairy industries, based in Pennsylvania. Wilbur was founded in 1865 and has been through several mergers with other companies and company name changes throughout the years.

winnowing　The process of removing the outer husk of the cacao bean to release the inner nibs during the manufacturing of chocolate. *See also* "From the Bean to the Bar."

X, Y, Z

xocoatl　The Aztec word for bitter water, a drink made from cacao beans, from which the word *chocolate* derives.

York　A popular American candy manufactured by Hershey Chocolate U.S.A. The candy is a $2^1/_2$-inch round, $^3/_8$-inch thick peppermint patty completely covered with dark chocolate. Each patty is considered to be one serving with a caloric content of 170.

CHRONOLOGY OF CHOCOLATE HISTORY

Seventh Century

600   The Maya migrate from their home in Guatemala to the Yucatán peninsula in Mexico, where they establish cacao plantations. Archaeological findings strongly suggest that the Maya have been cultivating and using cacao for hundreds of years. Cacao brought the Maya, who were significant traders, great wealth.

Lord Cacao was the name of one of the last three rulers at Tikal in Guatemala. This gives a little insight into how highly cacao was valued by the Maya.

Eleventh Century

1000 Evidence exists of the use of cacao beans by the people of Central America as a form of currency. Ten beans would buy a rabbit, twelve bought the use of a prostitute, and a hundred beans bought a slave. In Mexican picture writings, a basket of eight thousand cacao beans is used to depict the number eight thousand.

Thirteenth Century

1200 The Aztec's supremacy in Mexico is strengthened by their subjugation of other native peoples, including the Maya. Records indicate the Aztecs imposed tributes on the conquered people in the form of payment in cacao beans, which were a precious commodity.

Sixteenth Century

1502 Christopher Columbus tastes the native drink, *xocoatl* (the native word for chocolate), made from cacao beans, on board his ship in the Gulf of Honduras. He is not impressed with the drink and is not interested in cacao. He brings some of the beans back from his voyage merely as a novelty.

1519 Hernán Cortés lands in Mexico and has encounters with the Aztec people who greet him warmly. They think he is the legendary god Quetzalcoatl, who has come back to earth from "the Land of Gold." This is because Cortés's appearance takes place during the year "one reed" of the Aztec calendar, which coincides with the predicted return of Quetzalcoatl. Cortés uses this opportunity to bring about the destruction of the Aztec civilization and to enslave the people. Cortés quickly recognizes the value the Aztecs place on cacao beans and notes that they use the beans as a form of currency. This motivates him to establish a cacao plantation in the name of Spain.

1528 Hernán Cortés returns to Spain from Mexico and brings along some cacao beans and the utensils for preparing them in the Aztec manner.

1560   Criollo cacao is transported from Caracas, Venezuela, to the island of Celebes (Sulawesi) in Indonesia, where plantations are established.

1585   The first commercially grown shipment of cacao beans from South and Central America is unloaded in Spain. This signals the beginning of regular shipments of cacao beans from the colonies to Spain.

Seventeenth Century

1606   Antonio Carletti, a Florentine merchant, visits Guatemala and observes the importance of cacao there. He writes a manuscript describing the procedures for growing and processing cacao into a drink, which he presents to the Grand Duke of Tuscany, Ferdinand I de' Medici.

1609   The first book completely devoted to the subject of chocolate is published in Mexico. It is titled *Libro en el cual se trata del Chocolate* (*The Book Which Treats About Chocolate*).

1615   Anne of Austria, the Spanish Infanta, marries Louis XIII of France and introduces the Spanish custom of chocolate drinking to the French court.

1648   Thomas Gage, an English Dominican friar who has spent much time in the New World with Cortés and his troops, publishes his book, *A New Survey of the West Indies*, in London, which reports on the discovery of cacao and chocolate in the New World.

1657   The first chocolate house is opened in England by a Frenchman. This propels chocolate's popularity with the general population.

Chocolate has had its share of intrigue. During the seventeenth century, the British government enforced high duty on the import of raw cacao beans to increase revenue. If someone was caught smuggling, the penalty was a year in jail.

The June 6, 1657, issue of the London publication, *Public Advertiser*, contained the first notice of chocolate for sale in England, 130 years after it was first brought to Spain: "In Bishopsgate Street, in Queen's Head Alley, at a Frenchman's house, is an excellent West India drink, called Chocolat, to be sold, where you may have it ready at any time; and also unmade, at reasonable prices."

1659 David Chaillou, the first chocolate maker in France, obtains a permit from Louis XIV for the exclusive right to produce and sell chocolate.

1660 The British Parliament imposes a duty on each gallon of chocolate made and sold to raise income for Charles II.

Maria Theresa of Austria marries Louis XIV of France. Her love of chocolate knows no bounds and her enthusiasm for it spreads outside of the nobility to the public.

It is said of Maria Theresa, wife of Louis XIV, that "Chocolate and the King were her only passions." It's interesting that chocolate comes before the king.

Maria Theresa's maid was named "La Molina" by the queen's courtiers. The name derived from the stick used to beat the chocolate the queen loved to drink.

"*Well-made chocolate is such a noble invention that it, rather than nectar and ambrosia, should be known as the food of the gods.*"
—Dr. Bachot, physician to Maria Theresa

The French establish cacao plantations on Martinique.

1663   Pralines are created by a cook in Regensburg, Germany, by mixing together almonds and marzipan, then covering them with chocolate. He does this to please the refined palate of the duke of Choiseul, descended from the counts of Plessis-Praslin, after whom the new delectable confection is named.

> "*T*o a coffee-house, to drink jocolatte, very good."
> —Samuel Pepys, from his diary, November 24, 1664

1674   The first solid eating chocolate appears in stick form, called "in the Spanish form," in London at a famous coffeehouse, At the Coffee Mill and Tobacco Roll.

1677   A royal decree allows Brazil to establish its first cacao plantations in the state of Pará. Brazil later becomes one of the world's largest producers of cacao.

1685   Philippe Dufour, a French author, publishes his cookbook in London titled *The Manner of Making Coffee, Tea, and Chocolate.*

1690   The British Parliament passes a law that forbids selling drinking chocolate without a license, thereby creating income for the ruling monarchs, William and Mary.

Eighteenth Century

1704   Interested by the expanding import of chocolate, Frederick I of Prussia imposes a tax of two talers on every purchase of chocolate.

Giovanni Maria Lancisi, the physician to Pope Clement XI in the early eighteenth century, decreed that chocolate had no ill effect on habitual users. In a treatise published in London in 1706, Daniel Duncan, a French Huguenot doctor, declared that chocolate was healthful if taken moderately.

1705   Parisian café owner Pierre Masson publishes a book that includes a recipe for his method for preparing chocolate as a drink.

1711   Charles VI moves his court from Madrid to Vienna, bringing chocolate to Austria.

1720   Coffeehouses in Florence and Venice serve chocolate, whose reputation spreads far beyond the borders of Italy.

1728   Walter Churchman, a British manufacturer, installs the first hydraulic chocolate press in Bristol.

1732   A French inventor named Monsieur Dubuisson creates a table for grinding chocolate that allows the workers to stand up while grinding the beans, thereby making the operation more productive. The table is heated from underneath by charcoal. This is a technological breakthrough in the processing of cacao beans.

1746   The first plantings of cacao in the Brazilian state of Bahia are made using seeds brought from the state of Pará by a French planter.

1753   Carl von Linné, the celebrated Swedish naturalist known as Linneaus, gives the cacao tree the scientific name *Theobroma cacao*, meaning "food of the gods," when he codifies the plant world.

1764   Baker Chocolate Company is established in a mill in Dorchester, Massachusetts, by James Baker, a physician, and John Hannon, an Irish-American chocolate maker.

Even after John Hannon and Dr. James Baker set up their chocolate manufacturing facilities in Dorchester, Massachusetts, chocolate wasn't really accepted by the colonists until a group of fishermen from Gloucester, Massachusetts, accepted cacao beans in payment for cargo.

1767   Bayldon and Berry confectioners is established in York, England. Joseph Terry will marry into the Bayldon family, take charge of the company, and rapidly expand it.

1770 The Compagnie Francaise des Chocolats et Thés Pelletier & Cie, a chocolate and tea company, is founded in Paris.

1773 In Madrid, Spain, a guild of chocolate grinders is formed with over 150 members. In order to join the guild one must have six years of apprenticeship.

1776 English chocolate maker Joseph Fry petitions the Lord Commissioners of the Treasury to lower the tax on chocolate so it will be less expensive and available to more people to drink. In time he succeeds.

1779 Dr. James Baker takes over the chocolate business he started with John Hannon in 1764 when Hannon is lost at sea in the West Indies on a mission to buy cacao beans.

1780 The first machine-made chocolate is produced in Barcelona, Spain.

Chocolate factories in Bayonne, France, are outfitted with steam-driven machinery.

Dr. James Baker labels his chocolate products "Baker's Chocolate."

1792 Two brothers named Josty, from the Grisons region of Switzerland open a confectioner's shop and chocolate factory in Berlin, Germany. The Josty brothers' chocolate receives high praise.

1795 In England, J. S. Fry & Sons use steam power to grind cacao beans for the first time, a revolutionary breakthrough.

1796 Majani Chocolate Company is founded in Bologna, Italy.

"I have met with few things more remarkable than the Chocolate which is the finest I ever saw."

—**John Adams, American diplomat and future second president of the United States, traveling in Spain in 1799**

Nineteenth Century

1800 The firm of Debauve & Gallais is founded in Paris. This famous company has the distinction of being the oldest firm to make handmade chocolate in France.

1818 Amédée Kohler, a Swiss chocolate maker, establishes the firm of the same name that concentrates on making chocolate confections.

1819 François-Louis Cailler returns from Italy where he has studied the art of chocolate-making and establishes the first Swiss chocolate factory in an old mill in Corsier, near Vevey. Cailler specializes in making eating chocolate in the form of fondant, which is used by others in the manufacture of candy. He produces chocolate in small individual blocks, a new form, and introduces specialty chocolate products with the addition of the distinctive flavors of vanilla and cinnamon.

1822 John Cadbury opens a tea and coffee shop in Birmingham, England, which quickly expands to include chocolate manufactured on the premises.

Cacao cultivation is introduced to Príncipe, a small island close to the West African coast.

1825 Philippe Suchard opens his first confectionery shop in Neuchâtel, Switzerland.

1826 Giuseppe Maestrani, who learned the art of chocolate making in the Lombard region of Italy, begins production of handmade chocolates in Lugano, Switzerland.

Pierre-Paul Caffarel begins production of chocolate in Turin, Italy.

1828 Coenraad Van Houten, a Dutch chocolate maker, invents a method for removing most of the fat from chocolate. The remaining mass is processed into cocoa powder. He also discovers that by adding some of the extracted cocoa butter and sugar to the mass, the resulting mixture becomes firm and can be molded.

1830 Charles-Amédée Kohler sets up facilities to manufacture chocolate in Lausanne, Switzerland.

Cacao cultivation spreads from Príncipe to São Tomé, an island close to the West African coast.

1832   Franz Sacher, a sixteen-year-old Austrian apprentice chef, develops the renowned chocolate torte named after him, the Sachertorte. The Sachertorte is still made today and versions are served at the Sacher hotel and Demel's pastry shop in Vienna.

François-Louis Cailler opens a new, larger chocolate manufacturing plant in the town of Corsier, Switzerland.

1840   Cailler opens a second chocolate factory in Vevey, Switzerland, which he sells twenty years later to brothers Julien and Daniel Peter, who invent milk chocolate.

English confectioner Joseph Terry dies. His three sons take over and change the company name to Joseph Terry & Sons. They continue to expand the business.

1842   Englishman Charles Barry begins production of Cacao Barry chocolate and cocoa in France, which become very well known.

1845   Swiss confectioner David Sprüngli begins production of chocolate in Zurich. He is the first to make chocolate in German-speaking Switzerland.

Italian chocolate maker Pierre-Paul Caffarel dies. He is succeeded by his son, Isidore Caffarel.

1846   Aquilino Maestrani succeeds his father, Giuseppe, as head of their family chocolate company.

1847   The first manufacturer of chocolate in England sets up shop with the name J. S. Fry & Sons. They create the first chocolate bars for eating.

1848   Auguste Poulain, the French chocolatier, opens his first chocolate shop in Blois, France, where all his chocolates are made completely by hand.

1852   Aquilino Maestrani moves his chocolate company to Lucerne, Switzerland, and opens his own shop in Krongasse.

1852 Louis Fouquet opens his shop in Paris on Rue Lafitte to produce artisinal chocolates and jams, which remain some of the world's best into the late twentieth century.

Caffarel chocolate company introduces gianduia, a completely new type of chocolate made with hazelnuts grown locally in the Piedmont region of Italy. With the new invention they produce gianduiotti, a candy that instantly becomes popular and remains so well into the late twentieth century.

Swiss chocolate pioneer François-Louis Cailler dies at the age of sixty-five. His widow takes over the direction of the company until their two young sons are old enough.

1854 Cacao cultivation spreads to Fernando Póo (now known as Bioko) a small island close to the West African coast.

1856 Jacques Klaus, a Zurich native, establishes a chocolate factory in Le Locle after an extensive tour of Switzerland and France. His chocolate goes on to attain a significant reputation.

1857 Neuhaus, the oldest Belgian producer of chocolate bonbons, establishes a shop in Brussels.

1859 Swiss confectioner David Sprüngli et Fils opens a second confectionery shop at the Neumarkt (later to become Paradeplatz), which becomes their flagship location. This is the first elegant establishment in Zurich to offer confections.

Aquilino Maestrani transfers his chocolate company to St. Gallen and establishes himself in the Multergasse.

1861 Richard Cadbury, the son of the founder of Cadbury Ltd., creates the heart-shaped candy box for Valentine's Day and starts a trend of enclosing delicious chocolates in a heart-shaped box that lasts to this day.

1862 Domingo Ghirardelli establishes himself in the confectionery trade in San Francisco, California. He ultimately specializes in the production of chocolate bars.

Baker's Chocolate Company acquires the rights to use the painting *La Belle Chocolatiere*, by Swiss artist Jean-étienne Liotard, that hangs in a Dresden, Germany, art gallery. The painting depicts the wife of Prince Dietrichstein as a maid serving chocolate, which is how she was dressed when they first met. Baker's Chocolate Company will use this painting as their company trademark. It proves to be one of the oldest product trademarks in the United States.

Swiss chocolate maker David Sprüngli dies at the age of eighty-six. He is succeeded by his son, Rudolf.

1864 Jean Tobler begins production of handmade confections in Bern, Switzerland.

Henry Rowntree buys a foundry in York, England, and transforms it into a production facility for chocolate and cocoa.

1865 Samuel Croft and H. O. Wilbur establish their confectionery business on Third Street in Philadelphia. The partners later separate and Wilbur focuses on producing cocoa and chocolate products for the industry.

1867 French chocolatier Auguste Poulain devises his company's slogan, "Taste and Compare," which shows their commitment to produce good-quality chocolate sold at reasonable prices.

Daniel Peter establishes a chocolate firm under the name Peter Cailler & Compagnie in Vevey, Switzerland. His experiments with combining condensed milk and chocolate will prove successful in 1875 when he invents milk chocolate.

1868 Etienne Guittard, who had learned the chocolate trade in France, opens his chocolate business in San Francisco, California.

Ulysses B. Brewster of Newark, New Jersey, founds the Brewster Chocolate Company, which will merge with Ideal Cocoa and Chocolate Company and ultimately with Wilbur-Suchard Chocolate Company.

The Pernigotti family founds the chocolate company of the same name in Novi Ligure, Italy, first producing torrone, then expanding to include chocolate torrone and gianduiotti, and a full line of chocolates and confections.

1869   Henry Rowntree and his brother Joseph establish their business under the name of H. I. Rowntree & Co. They produce and market two main products, Superior Rock Cocoa and Homeopathic Cocoa.

On April 8, Italian chocolate maker Caffarel, based in Turin, receives a grant of patent from Victor Emmanuel II of Italy.

1870   Belgian chocolate maker Charles Neuhaus opens the Côte d'Or chocolate firm, which specializes in making dark chocolate bars.

Rudolf Sprügli, who succeeded his father David in 1862, sets up his chocolate factory at Werdmühle outside Zurich, Switzerland.

Runkel Brothers, Inc., begins operations and soon becomes a major manufacturer of cocoa and chocolate in the United States. They supply bulk chocolate to many Chicago, Illinois, confectioners such as Fannie May, DeMets, and Curtiss.

1872   Baker's Chocolate Company begins to use the Chocolate Girl painting, acquired in 1862, as the company trademark.

Chocolates Arumi is founded in Barcelona, Spain, which will become Chocovic. They produce artisanal chocolates for the important families of the region.

1874   Charles-Amédée Kohler, Swiss pioneer chocolate manufacturer, dies in Lausanne, Switzerland. He is succeeded by his son Charles-Amédée, Jr.

Cacao cultivation is introduced into Nigeria from the West African island of Fernando Póo.

1875   Madame Charbonnel, invited by the future king Edward VII to leave her French chocolate shop, opens a chocolate shop with a Mrs. Walker in Bond Street, London, where to this day, high-quality chocolates are sold in lavish surroundings.

Daniel Peter, a Swiss inventor, successfully combines milk with chocolate after eight years of experimentation and sells the first milk chocolate.

> "*S*ince the Spaniards brought it [chocolate] to Europe at the beginning of the seventeenth century, it has come into more and more widespread use. Like coffee, it is now a regular part of people's diet, but its nutritional value is higher."
> —**Daniel Peter, Swiss inventor of milk chocolate, in 1875**

1876 The Ganong brothers of Saint Stephen, New Brunswick, Canada, formally enter the candy-making business.

1878 Daniel Peter's milk chocolate wins a silver medal at the International Exhibition in Paris.

Italian chocolate maker Caffarel merges with Michele Prochet & Co. The company name becomes Messrs. Caffarel, Prochet & Co.

1879 Rodolphe Lindt invents the conch, a machine that stirs liquid chocolate to break down any remaining particles left after processing. This revolutionary process makes the first smooth, melt-in-the-mouth eating chocolate. Lindt calls this chocolate fondant and labels his bars Lindt Surfin.

1880 Swiss chocolate maker Philippe Suchard opens a branch of his chocolate factory in Lörrach, Germany. This is the first Swiss foreign branch.

Daniel Peter's milk chocolate wins a gold medal at the International Exhibition in Zurich, Switzerland.

1883 Henry I. Rowntree of the English chocolate company dies. His brother and business partner, Joseph, retains sole control of the company.

1884 Albert Poulain, son of French chocolatier Auguste Poulain, develops a new chocolate breakfast drink that is easily mixed. This is the forerunner of Poulain Orange instant cocoa drink mix.

H. O. Wilbur separates from his partner, Samuel Croft, and establishes H. O. Wilbur & Sons to manufacture cocoa and chocolate.

1884 Charles-Amédée Kohler Jr., Swiss chocolate manufacturer, dies in Lausanne, Switzerland. He is succeeded by his sons Amédée-Louis and Jean-Jacques who change the company's name to Les fils de Charles-Amédée Kohler. They continue to produce excellent quality chocolate for which the company is famous.

1887 H. I. Rowntree & Co. of England produce Elect Cocoa, a powdered dark chocolate, which they manufacture and market very successfully.

Christopher's Candy Company is founded in Los Angeles, California, specializing in the manufacture of chocolate products.

1888 Ganong Brothers, Ltd., of Saint Stephen, New Brunswick, Canada, are the first to imprint chocolates on the bottom by using embossed celluloid pads, which are patented by Gilbert Ganong.

Alexandre Cailler Jr., grandson of Swiss pioneer chocolate-maker François-Louis Cailler, completes his training at Turin, Italy, and becomes director of the company his grandfather founded.

1890 In July Henri Nestlé, founder of the company of the same name, dies at Montreux, Switzerland. His name and company will survive and thrive well into the next century and beyond, and become a household word throughout the world.

1892 Rudolf Sprüngli settles the question of succession of his family chocolate empire. Son Rudolf receives the chocolate factory complex located at Werdmühle. The other son, David, takes over the original property in Marktgasse and the confectionery shop on Paradeplatz in Zurich.

1893 Milton Hershey attends a demonstration of German-made chocolate manufacturing equipment at the World's Columbian Exposition in Chicago. He is so impressed that on the spot he declares "caramels are only a fad, chocolate is a permanent thing," although he has been successfully producing and selling caramels for several years. He makes the decision to change his focus completely to chocolate. He buys the demonstration equipment and has it shipped to his caramel factory in Lancaster, Pennsylvania.

C. J. Van Houten Company of Holland erects a full-scale chocolate reproduction of a sixteenth-century Dutch town hall, called a chocolate house, at the World's Columbian Exposition in Chicago.

Italian chocolate maker Caffarel, Prochet & Co. receives a Certificate of Merit for Purity and Excellence of Preparation, at the World's Columbian Exposition in Chicago.

The Stollwerck Chocolate Company of Cologne, Germany, uses thirty thousand pounds of chocolate to erect a ten-foot-tall statue of Germania within a thirty-eight-foot-tall Renaissance temple at the World's Columbian Exposition in Chicago.

H. O. Wilbur & Sons produce their soon-to-be-famous candies, Wilbur Buds.

1894 Milton Hershey creates his first candy bar. His chocolate company begins production of baking chocolate, cocoa, and chocolate coatings for caramels.

Otto J. Scholenleber founds Ambrosia Chocolate Company in Milwaukee, Wisconsin, and begins production of candy for the consumer, but switches in the mid-twentieth century to the production of bulk chocolate for use by large food production corporations such as Hostess, Pillsbury, and Nabisco.

Arms and the Man is a play by George Bernard Shaw, first produced in 1894. A box of chocolates takes center stage when a fugitive Swiss soldier of fortune from the Bulgarian-Serbian conflict of 1885 shows up at the home of Raina Petkoff, a young Bulgarian gentlewoman. She is enchanted with him and he asks for chocolates, which she gives him from a half-eaten box. He becomes known as the chocolate cream soldier and by the end of the play they are in love with each other and have become engaged to be married.

1896 Inventor Leo Hirschfield introduces the Tootsie Roll candy, which he names after his daughter.

1896 Richard Cadbury, writing under the pseudonym Historicus, publishes *Cocoa—All About It* in London. In the book he has photographs of and describes the Cadbury chocolate factory in Bournville.

Swiss chocolate pioneer Daniel Peter founds the corporation, Société des Chocolate au Lait Peter, with the financial backing of Albert Cuénod and L. Rapin and capitalization of 450,000 Swiss francs. Gabriel Montet, a banker from Vevey, is instrumental in constructing the deal.

Antoine Jacques founds his chocolate company in Verviers, Belgium.

The Stollwerck Chocolate Company of Cologne, Germany, begins production of chocolate in a newly renovated factory in Bratislava, Czechoslovakia.

On January 14 Le Cordon Bleu Ecole de Cuisine hold its first cooking class in the Palais Royal in Paris. The school goes on to become one of the best-known cooking schools in the world, teaching thousands how to create classic desserts, pastries, and confections and how to work with chocolate.

1897 The English chocolate company Rowntree incorporates and changes its name to Rowntree & Company Ltd. Joseph Rowntree, one of the original founders, is the company's first chairman.

The Italian chocolate firm of Caffarel, Prochet & Co. is taken over by other partners who change the company name to The Successors to Messrs. Caffarel, Prochet and Co.

Chocolate consumption in England is recorded at 36 million pounds, in Europe as 100 million pounds, and in the United States as 26 million pounds.

1898 Alexandre Cailler Jr., director of the company founded by his grandfather, Swiss pioneer chocolate maker François-Louis Cailler, sets up a new chocolate factory in Broc, Switzerland, and begins manufacture of milk chocolate for which the Gruyère region is famous.

Fabrique de Chocolat Amédée Kohler & Fils is incorporated in Morges, in the canton of Vaud, Switzerland, by the great-grandsons of Swiss pioneer chocolate manufacturer Charles-Amédée Kohler. They are capitalized with 3 million Swiss francs.

1899 Rodolphe Lindt sells his secret formula for making fondant chocolate to David Sprüngli for the sum of 1.5 million Swiss francs. He becomes a partner in the new company, Lindt & Sprüngli.

Rudolf Sprüngli moves the family's chocolate manufacturing facility to Kilchberg on the outskirts of Zurich, where it remains today.

Jean Tobler starts his chocolate company in Bern that will become world famous. He begins to manufacture sumptuous chocolate bars and boxed assortments of chocolates.

Twentieth Century

1900 The Kendig Chocolate Company receives its charter from the Commonwealth of Pennsylvania on November 2. Shortly thereafter the company builds its factory on Broad Street in Lititz, Pennsylvania. This will eventually become the home of the Wilbur Chocolate Americana Museum.

Milton S. Hershey introduces his new Milk Chocolate Bar. Hershey Chocolate Company also begins production of Sweethearts, a vanilla sweet chocolate candy with a heart imprinted on the base. These will be discontinued in 1931.

The Swiss chocolate company François-Louis Cailler becomes a corporation with a capitalization of 1 million Swiss francs.

1901 The Swiss chocolate company Suchard introduces the Milka chocolate bar.

Daniel Peter opens a new, well-designed chocolate factory at Orbe in the canton of Vaud, Switzerland, a region well known for its milk production.

Swiss chocolate manufacturers form an association whose goal is to protect their joint interests.

> "*I*t may be of interest to you (Walter Baker & Co.) to know that while on the toughest mountain trail one of my partners and myself ate nothing from breakfast til supper but your chocolate. We ate about one ounce only at a time and finished the day in better shape than those who ate the usual hearty lunch. This might not be generally believed, but numbers of Yukon travelers can testify to the sustaining powers of cocoa and chocolate."
>
> **—An early twentieth-century traveler from Alaska
> writing to Walter Baker & Co.**

1902   Kendig Chocolate Company changes its name to Ideal Cocoa and Chocolate Company.

Joseph Rowntree, chairman of the English firm of Rowntree & Co. Ltd., begins publication of *Cocoa Works* magazine, forerunner to *Rowntree Mackintosh News*, the company newspaper that will be published in 1969.

1903   Milton Hershey builds his chocolate factory and a surrounding town to house its workers near Harrisburg, Pennsylvania.

1904   Swiss chocolate companies Kohler and Peter merge to become the Société Générale Suisse de Chocolats. Jean-Jacques Kohler assumes control of the new firm. The words *Peter et Kohler réunis* are retained for use on product packaging. The company licenses the rights to market their milk chocolate products to Nestlé for ninety-nine years, which merges with this company in 1929.

Poulain chocolate company launches their instant cocoa drink mix, Poulain Orange, with a marketing strategy designed to build brand loyalty, that includes a small metal figurine and a color picture card inside each tin.

The Cadbury company develops a dairy milk chocolate, breaking the long-held Swiss monopoly on milk chocolate.

1905   The brand name and logo of Antoine Jacques Chocolatier is registered with the commerce tribunal in Verviers, Belgium. The logo states a guarantee of quality of cocoa and sugar used in the house brand of Le Sameur chocolate.

Cadbury company debuts its Dairy Milk candy bar.

1906   The Ganong Brothers of Saint Stephen, New Brunswick, Canada, begins to manufacture its own chocolate for use in creating the company's candies.

Italian chocolate maker Caffarel, Prochet & Co. receives a gold medal at the International Exposition in Milan, Italy.

The town of Derry Church, Pennsylvania, officially changes its name to Hershey, Pennsylvania, in honor of its famous resident entrepreneur, Milton S. Hershey, and his chocolate company.

Hershey, Pennsylvania, has been dubbed "The Sweetest Place on Earth."

1907   On July 1 the Hershey company begins to manufacture its famous Kisses, which are hand-wrapped in silver foil.

Exactly how Hershey's Kisses got their name is a bit of a mystery. One popular theory is that the candy was named for the sound of the chocolate being deposited by machine during the manufacturing process.

The only time production of Hershey's Kisses has been interrupted since their introduction in 1907 was during the war years of 1942–1949 due to the rationing of silver foil. The mixing machinery used to produce the candy was used instead to temper the mixture for the military ration chocolate bar that Hershey Chocolate produced for the U.S. military. It is estimated that more than 3 billion of these ration bars were produced during this time.

1907 The Buitoni family of Italy, famous for its pasta, begins production of Perugina chocolates in Perugia. They will become famous worldwide for their Baci candies, chocolate kisses wrapped in silver foil with blue stars, that carry a hidden message.

Richard Purdy opens his first chocolate shop on Robson Street in downtown Vancouver, British Columbia, Canada. Using family recipes brought from England, he begins the tradition of creating fine-quality, hand-crafted chocolates.

1908 Theodor Tobler, son of the founder of the Tobler company, develops the unique triangular, nougat-filled chocolate candy bar, Toblerone, that makes the company famous.

Max Felchlin begins manufacture in Schwyz, Switzerland, of high-quality specialized chocolates and other products for pastry shops and bakeries, which are in use today by many top chefs, confectioners, and bakers throughout Europe, the United States, and Japan.

Hershey Chocolate Company introduces its milk chocolate with almonds bar.

1909 Hershey Chocolate Company begins production of Silvertops, a version of its Hershey's Kisses made to be sold individually. These will be discontinued in 1931.

1910 Leonidas chocolate company is founded in Brussels, Belgium, by Leonidas Kesdekidis, a member of the Greek delegation to the International Exposition. He creates a broad range of pralines which become famous.

Henri Wittamer founds the bakery named after himself in Brussels, Belgium, which is the cornerstone of a family empire that will include pastries, confectionery, and ice cream and gain a worldwide reputation for making excellent quality products.

Arthur Ganong, nephew of the chocolate manufacturing Ganong brothers of New Brunswick, Canada, creates their famous five-cent milk chocolate candy bar.

1911   The Dutch chocolate company De Zaan is founded.

The Swiss chocolate company Cailler, established in 1819 by François-Louis Cailler, merges with the Swiss General Chocolate Company to become Peter Cailler & Kohler Chocolats Suisses, S.A.

The Belgian confectionery company Callebaut, begins production of chocolate bars and tablets.

Frank and Ethel Mars found their candy company in Tacoma, Washington, which goes on to become Mars, Inc., one of the world's largest candy manufacturers.

1912   Jean Neuhaus Jr., grandson of the founder of Neuhaus chocolates, invents the first chocolate praline by filling an empty chocolate shell with some of the delectable creations developed by his father, Frederick, who produced pralinés by experimenting with almonds and sugar.

J. C. Haley joins Harry Brown to form the Brown and Haley Candy Company in Tacoma, Washington.

Louise Agostini, Jean Neuhaus's wife, creates the ballotin, a box to hold chocolates so they will not damage each other as they do when packed in a cone. The ballotin is recognized throughout the world as the symbol of Belgian chocolates. It is adopted by all top-quality chocolate makers.

The Whitman Company produces their soon-to-be famous boxed assortment, Whitman's Sampler. It is the first to offer a diagram of where the chocolates are located in the box.

John Mackintosh, Ltd., of Halifax, Nova Scotia, begins marketing its first chocolate product.

1913   Jules Séchaud of Montreux, Switzerland, invents the filled chocolate candy bar using fondant cream.

1914   L. S. Heath & Sons, Inc., manufacturers of the popular Heath Bar candy bar, begins operations in Robinson, Illinois.

1914   The first recipe for brownies appears as Bangor Brownies in a cook-book published by the Bangor, Maine, YWCA. This chocolate confection is destined to become an American classic favorite.

1915   The American Chocolate Mould Company begins to manufacture metal chocolate and ice-cream molds in Oceanside, New York.

Antonio Peyrano, a food chemist, opens his chocolate factory in a house on the Po River, in Turin, Italy. The Peyrano firm becomes one of the most celebrated Italian chocolatiers, known worldwide for their fine-quality chocolates.

1918   The English chocolate companies of Fry and Cadbury merge.

Hershey Chocolate Company begins production of Silverpoints, a product made with a chocolate paste that contains more milk than their popular Hershey's Kisses.

1919   The Fannie Farmer chain of candy shops begins operation in Rochester, New York. Frank O'Connor, the owner, names his business in honor of one of the first American cookbook authors because she and her career fascinated him.

1920   Brown & Haley introduces its Almond Roca buttercrunch candy, which becomes world famous and is the company's most widely distributed candy, sold worldwide.

Antoine Jacques goes into partnership with William Zurstrassen to create Chocolaterie Jacques Ltd. in Verviers, Belgium. Wallonia is the newly registered brand name of the company.

1921   Bendicks chocolate shop, maker of the famous Bendicks Bittermint is established in the Mayfair section of London, the outcome of a successful partnership between Colonel Bendick and Mr. Dickson.

Hershey Food Corporation begins to wrap it Kisses by machine and adds the familiar flag to the wrapping.

Milton Hershey has been called "the Henry Ford of chocolate" for making chocolate affordable and available to the consuming public.

John Mackintosh, Ltd. of Halifax, Nova Scotia, changes its name to Mackintosh & Sons, Ltd.

The Mounds candy bar is invented by Peter Paul Halijian, who markets it under the name Peter Paul Mounds.

See's Candy is founded in Culver City, California, by Charles A. See and his mother, Mary See. They use her home recipes as the basis for the candy and other confections made by hand in See's kitchens. Charles chooses Mary's portrait to adorn the boxes of See's candy and to symbolize the company's motto of "Old Time," and "Homemade."

1922   De Zaan chocolate company of the Netherlands ceases to produce chocolate and concentrates solely on the production of cocoa.

French chocolate couverture manufacturer Valrhona establishes its production facilities in the Rhone Valley in France.

H. B. Reese, a former dairy employee of Milton S. Hershey, founder of Hershey Chocolate Company, is inspired by Mr. Hershey's success and begins production of Reese's peanut butter cups using Hershey's milk chocolate.

Giovanni Buitoni and Luisa Spagnoli of La Perugina, the Italian chocolate company, create Baci, the world-famous chocolate candy kisses made with ground hazelnuts covered with dark chocolate, wrapped in silver foil with blue stars. Each candy kiss carries a hidden love message within its wrapping.

The Belgian company Chocolaterie Jacques Ltd. moves its headquarters and production facility to Eupen, Belgium.

See's Candy becomes a corporation on June 2 with a capital stock value of $100,000.

1923 In Switzerland Alexandre Cailler creates Frigor, the Nestlé candy bar with a praline filling.

Alexander LaCarre takes over control of the Cacao Barry chocolate company.

Frank Mars creates the Milky Way candy bar using high-quality ingredients. The candy bar has a chocolate nougat center enrobed in milk chocolate and remains popular for over seventy years.

Hershey Foods Corporation registers the name Hershey's Kisses as a trademark.

Chocolaterie Jacques Ltd. opens a new factory in Eupen, Belgium.

1924 Hershey Foods Corporation registers the size, shape, and configuration, including the wrapping of Hershey's Kisses as a trademark.

Nestlé acquires an interest in the Italian firm, Industria Riunita Cioccolata at Intra.

1925 The New York Cocoa Exchange is created. It is modeled after the Chicago Board of Trade and allows purchasers to buy cocoa futures.

Belgian chocolate company Callebaut begins the production of high quality couverture, which is sold to other chocolate manufacturers.

Richard Purdy sells his chocolate company to Hugh Forrester who keeps the company afloat during the Depression years by staying open late and offering a weekend special of a pound of peanut brittle and a half pound of another candy for a dollar.

Nestlé builds a chocolate production factory in Auckland, New Zealand, to increase the company's sound financial footing. In France Nestlé sets up a production center in Lisieux. Société Nestlé (Belgique) begins to operate a chocolate factory in Antwerp in cooperation with Peter Cailler & Kohler Chocolats Suisses S.A.

French chocolate maker Joseph Richart establishes his chocolate company, Richart Design et Chocolat, in Lyons using the world's finest cacao beans to produce some of the most exquisite and unusual chocolates.

August Fauchon opens his food emporium in Paris, which becomes renowned for the quality and quantity of items, including exquisite chocolates and pastries made in-house.

On November 20 Hershey Chocolate Company introduces its chocolate bar, Mr. Goodbar.

1926   Ganong's of Canada introduces its five-cent molded Chocolate Peppermint Rolls, Pepts, which become the company's most popular candy.

Joseph Terry & Sons introduce their Chocolate Apple, twenty sections of chocolate flavored with apple, in the shape of an apple. It proves to be very popular.

1927   Baker's Chocolate Company is acquired by General Foods Corporation and is relocated to Delaware.

H. O. Wilbur & Sons merges with Suchard Société Anonyme of Switzerland and the name changes to Wilbur-Suchard Chocolate Company, Inc.

Ideal Cocoa and Chocolate Company merges with Brewster Chocolate Company on December 2.

The board of directors of Brewster-Ideal Chocolate Company authorize its sale to Wilbur-Suchard Chocolate Company of Philadelphia, Pennsylvania.

On October 24 Hershey Chocolate Company is renamed Hershey Chocolate Corporation.

Nestlé and the Swiss Company of Peter Cailler & Kohler Chocolats Suisses S.A. open a chocolate factory in Turkey and set up a production center in La Penilla, Spain, run by the small company of Sociedad Espanola de Chocolates S.A. Nestlé also sets up a chocolate factory in Saavedra, Argentina. In addition, Nestlé begins to market its products in Peru and Portugal.

1928   Artisan chocolatier Fouquet opens a second location in Paris on rue François 1er to sell their high-quality chocolates, sweets, and jams.

1928   Italian chocolate maker Caffarel, Prochet & Co. is awarded a gold medal at the Commercial Exposition in Turin, Italy.

L. S. Heath & Sons, Inc., develop their English toffee candy bar, Heath Bar, and market it in a unique way, providing a box to check to order it on their home-delivered dairy order forms. The candy bar becomes one of the world's most popular.

Nestlé acquires an interest in the large German chocolate company Sarotti AG, based near Berlin.

Cadbury chocolate introduces its Fruit & Nut candy bar.

Bosco chocolate syrup is invented by a Camden, Massachusetts, doctor and marketed by William S. Scull Company. The syrup sells briskly.

> "*I* love Bosco
> it's rich and chocolaty,
> chocolate-flavored Bosco
> is mighty good for me.
> Mama puts it in my cup
> for extra energy.
> Bosco gives me iron
> and sunshine Vitamin D."
>
> —Promotional jingle for Bosco chocolate syrup

1929   On January 1 the Swiss chocolate company Peter Cailler & Kohler Chocolats Suisses S.A. merges with Nestlé to become the world's largest chocolate manufacturer.

Camille Bloch founds Chocolates Camille Bloch S.A. in Bern, Switzerland, a manufacturer of fine-quality couverture and pralines.

Candy manufacturer Frank Mars opens his Chicago candy plant that quickly becomes a success by producing quality candy bars utilizing a fluffy nougat center. Snickers, 3 Musketeers, and the

Mars Bar are on their way to becoming all-time favorite American candy bars.

Jose Rafael Zozaya and his father-in-law, Carmelo Tuozzo, found Tuozzo Zozaya & Cia. in Caracas, Venezuela, to produce premium-quality chocolate couvertures from cacao grown only in Venezuela. In time the company will change its name to Chocolates El Rey.

The Belgian Drap family establishes Godiva chocolates. The fourteen-year old son, Joseph, creates chocolate truffles, which become an instant success.

1930   Frank Mars, creator of the Mars candy empire, introduces the Snickers candy bar.

1931   Joseph Terry & Sons introduce their Chocolate Orange, twenty sections of milk chocolate flavored with orange oil, shaped like an orange. It proves to be more popular than their Chocolate Apple, introduced in 1926.

Carl Maentler begins production of Carma chocolates and glazes in Dübendorf, Switzerland.

Mr. and Mrs. Prodromos Daskalidès-Kestekidès establish Daskalidès chocolate company and shop in Ghent, Belgium, specializing in pralines made by Mr. Daskalidès. The company quickly gains a reputation for producing high-quality pralines and expands rapidly.

1932   Frank Mars, creator and driving force behind the Mars candy empire gives his son Forrest $50,000 and the foreign rights to Milky Way and other Mars candy bars so he will leave the country and start his own business because they do not get along well together. Forrest opens a factory near London and christens his business Mars, Ltd. He quickly becomes a pacesetter in the British confectionery business.

The Wilbur-Suchard Chocolate Company sells its Newark, New Jersey, plant back to Albert E. Brewster, founder of Brewster Chocolate Company, which had merged with Ideal Cocoa and Chocolate Company, and ultimately with Wilbur-Suchard in 1927.

1932 John Mackintosh & Sons, Ltd., acquires the Caley Chocolate Company, founded at Norwich in 1860. This enables Mackintosh to develop products that combine chocolate and toffee, for which Mackintosh is famous. Rolo and Quality Street candies quickly become Mackintosh's most important brands.

1933 Elite Industries Ltd. is established in Israel by a group of immi-grants from Latvia and begins to manufacture chocolate and con-fectionery products.

Rosemary Hume, a former student at Le Cordon Bleu école de Cuisine in Paris opens a campus of the school in London.

Cadbury chocolate introduces its Whole Nut candy bar.

1935 Basile Kesdekidis, nephew of Leonidas's founder, takes over as head of the company and begins use of the logo that shows the effigy of the Greek warrior Leonidas, king of Sparta. He opens a store front on Boulevard Anspach in Brussels where he can display his freshly made pralines in the windows and customers can easily purchase them.

Camille Bloch moves his company, Chocolates Camille Bloch S.A., to a former paper pulp factory at Courtelary, in the watch-making region of the Jura in Switzerland.

1937 Caffarel begins using specially designed extrusion pourers to shape their famous confection, Gianduia 1865, in their factory in Turin, Italy. This new machinery enables the company to develop auto-matic wrapping machines.

Ben Meyerson forms his namesake candy company in Los Angeles, California.

1938 On September 14 Hershey Chocolate Corporation introduces its chocolate bar, Krackel.

1939 Bloomer Chocolate Company, which will become the United States' largest commercial chocolate manufacturer, begins manu-facturing operations in Chicago, Illinois.

Joseph Terry & Sons have to cease production of their Chocolate Apple and Chocolate Orange confections. Due to World War II the factory is unable to receive shipments of ingredients from Europe.

Chocolate Ibarra is founded in Guadalajara, Mexico, by the husband-and-wife team of Maria Ruiz and Camilo Gomez Ibarra.

Hershey Chocolate Corporation introduces Hershey's Miniatures chocolate bars.

Joseph L. Hooper and his wife open their small chocolate company in a garage in Oakland, California.

1940 Edmond Opler Sr. founds World's Finest Chocolate Company, Inc., in Chicago.

1941 Forrest Mars returns to the United States from England and goes into business partnership with Bruce Murrie, the son of the president of the Hershey Chocolate Company. They name their company M & M Ltd. Their first product is called M & M's, pellets of chocolate coated with hard candy in a variety of pastel colors, which become wildly popular.

Caffarel begins use of automatic wrapping machines to wrap their famous confection, Gianduia 1865, in their factory in Turin, Italy. This increases their production and ensures uniformity.

1942 The Hershey Chocolate Company develops a candy bar without cocoa butter, which gives it a long shelf life, to be carried as rations by soldiers of the United States Army. This bar is dubbed "Ration D."

Walter Baker and Company, Ltd., produce a candy bar called the Flying Fortress, which is a civilian version of the army ration bar they produce. The Flying Fortress airplane, the mainstay bomber of the U.S. Army during World War II, is featured on the candy bar wrapper.

Chocolates Camille Bloch S.A. introduces Ragusa a chocolate bar filled with roasted hazelnuts, which becomes a market leader of international renown.

1944 On January 10 the first Helen Grace Chocolates shop opens in San Pedro, California, producing candies using old-fashioned recipes that is an instant hit with their customers.

1945 Herb Knechtel develops the popular chocolate Frango Mint candy for the Marshall Field department stores of Chicago, Illinois. The candy name is borrowed from a candy made by the Seattle department store, Frederick and Nelson, owned by the Field company.

Chocosuisse, the Association of Swiss Chocolate Manufacturers, is formed. The goals are to promote the Swiss chocolate industry and protect its members interests in issues of international trade, and agreements with local trade unions and to support its members with a variety of services and advice. Chocosuisse maintains a worldwide publicity and public relations network.

1947 The Almond Joy candy bar is introduced by Peter Paul.

1948 Chocolates Camille Bloch S.A. introduces Torino, chocolate sticks with a praliné filling, which become a market leader.

Marc Cluziel establishes his chocolate company in Damville, Normandy, France and names it Michel Cluziel in honor of his son, who at the age of fourteen is his first employee.

Bloomer Chocolate Company expands to Los Angeles, California, with the addition of a new chocolate factory.

Joseph Terry & Sons start production again of their popular confections, Chocolate Apple and Chocolate Orange.

1950 Ganong's is forced to stop manufacturing their most popular chocolate candy bar, Pepts, due to a heavy excise tax on confectionery imposed by the Canadian government.

Sam Altshuler founds the Annabelle Candy Company, Inc., named after his daughter, which produces the Rocky Road candy bar.

1951 The Annabelle Candy Company begins production in San Francisco of the Rocky Road candy bar.

Wilbur Chocolate Company pioneers the delivery of liquid chocolate in tank trucks to their clients who include candy manufacturers, bakeries, and dairies.

Ferrero company, which will manufacture filled chocolates Mon Cherí, Rocher, and Pocket Coffee, is founded in Italy.

1952   Henri-Alexandre LaCarre takes over management of the Cacao Barry chocolate company from his father. He changes the company's direction to produce semifinished chocolate products, such as cocoa liquor, cocoa butter, and cocoa powder for other large manufacturers and artisanal bakers and confectioners.

Hoopers Chocolates moves to its current location at 4632 Telegraph Avenue in Oakland, California. The building is painted pink, Barbara Hooper's favorite color.

1954   Finding their Chocolate Orange more popular than their Chocolate Apple, Joseph Terry & Sons, discontinue production of the Chocolate Apple.

1955   The Bernachons establish their artisan chocolate company and shop in Lyons, France.

Ben Meyerson Candy Company of Los Angeles, California, acquires Christophers Candy Company.

1957   In August H. B. Reese Candy Company, Inc., manufacturer of the popular candy, Reese's Peanut Butter Cups, opens its new hundred-thousand-square-foot production facility on Chocolate Avenue in Hershey, Pennsylvania.

Chocolat Alprose S.A. is founded at Caslano (near Lugano), Switzerland, under the name Titlis S.A.

1958   On December 31 the Wilbur-Suchard Chocolate Company dissolves and the name changes to Wilbur Chocolate Company.

1962   Ghirardelli Chocolate Company becomes a division of Golden Grain Macaroni Company.

1962 For the first time Hershey's Kisses are wrapped in colors other than silver. During the Christmas season they are wrapped in red, green, and silver.

1963 Purdy's Chocolates is sold to Charles Flavelle who takes the company from a small chain of four shops to forty-two throughout British Columbia and Alberta, Canada.

Hershey Chocolate Company buys its neighbor, the H. B. Reese Candy Company, Inc., for $23.5 million.

1964 The American conglomerate W. R. Grace buys the Dutch cocoa company De Zaan and Ambrosia Chocolate Company of Milwaukee, Wisconsin.

1965 The Belgian chocolate manufacturer Callebaut begins to export its products beyond the boundaries of the European Economic Community.

1966 The Campbell Soup Company acquires Godiva Chocolatier, Inc., of Belgium.

1967 Dilettante Chocolates opens in the Capitol Hill District in Seattle, Washington. To create his chocolates Dana Davenport uses his father's notebook and his grandfather's recipes, whose brother was chocolatier by appointment to Tsar Nicholas II.

1968 On October 18 Wilbur Chocolate Company becomes a wholly owned subsidiary of MacAndrews & Forbes Company.

Caffarel, Prochet & Co. builds a new factory and moves its headquarters from Turin to Luserna San Giovanni in the Piedmont region of Italy, where the company founder was born.

Antonio Escriba opens his confectionery and pastry shop in Barcelona, Spain. He quickly becomes recognized throughout the world as a chocolate magician, able to produce art through his chocolate.

1969 The Rowntree Company, Ltd., of York, England merges with John Mackintosh & Sons, Ltd., of Halifax, Nova Scotia, and changes its name to Rowntree Mackintosh, Ltd. Shortly thereafter they begin publication of a company newspaper titled *Rowntree Mackintosh News*.

Bloomer Chocolate Company builds a new manufacturing facility in Union City, California, which becomes the company's West Coast headquarters.

Alajos Jámbor, a new immigrant to the United States from Hungary, buys a thriving chocolate shop in Los Angeles, known as Bit of Sweetland, where he makes candies and pastries in the Hungarian tradition using recipes that dated back to the turn of the century, inherited from the original shop owners.

1970 The chocolate companies Tobler and Suchard merge to form one of the world's largest chocolate companies.

Due to the popularity and success of Reese's Peanut Butter Cups, ground is broken to double the size of the manufacturing plant.

Camille Bloch, founder of Chocolates Camille Bloch S.A., dies at the age of eighty. Rolf Bloch, Camille's son, continues to manage the company.

Christian Constant establishes his chocolate shop in Paris and produces exotically flavored ganache-filled chocolates that are renowned worldwide for their exquisite flavor and texture.

1971 Rowntree Mackintosh, Ltd., acquires the French company Chocolat-Menier S.A.

The See family sells their company to Berkshire Hathaway, Inc. Charles Huggins, a twenty-year See's executive is appointed president and CEO, a position he retains to this day.

1973 The Cadbury Company opens Chocolate World, its Disney-like theme park, in Bournville, England.

Neuhaus Chocolates is sold to the General Biscuits Group, then to Jean-Jacques and Claude Poncelet, who extend its product line while maintaining its tradition of quality.

1973 Tuozzo Zozaya & Cia. in Caracas, Venezuela, sets up a stock company named Chocolates El Rey C.A. and begins to orient the company toward production of premium-quality Venezuelan chocolate couvertures and derivatives such as cocoa butter and cocoa powder for export.

Rowntree Mackintosh Ltd. acquires the French company Ibled S.A.

On June 30 Hershey Foods Corporation opens the visitor center to its theme park, Hershey's Chocolate World.

On December 12 Hershey Foods is the first to add nutritional labeling to its candy bars.

1975 Joseph Terry & Sons introduces a dark chocolate version of their popular Chocolate Orange. It garners a loyal following, but the milk chocolate version remains most popular.

The German chocolate company Stollwerck AG acquires Titlis S.A., parent company of Alprose S.A. based in Caslano (near Lugano), Switzerland.

1976 The Hershey Chocolate Company introduces Reese's Crunchy, the first variation to its popular candy, Reese's Peanut Butter Cups, with the flavor and texture of chopped peanuts.

On December 5 Alice Medrich opens her European-style chocolate pastry shop, Cocolat, in Berkeley, California. She popularizes French-style chocolate truffles and creates the oversize American chocolate truffle.

1977 The Nederland Group buys Chocovic of Barcelona, Spain, and changes the company's focus to target small confectioners and patissiers.

Rowntree Mackintosh, Ltd., acquires the French company Chocolaterie Lanvin S.A. based in Dijon.

Robert Linxe establishes his chocolate shops in Paris and produces some of the world's finest chocolate bonbons and pralines.

On September 2 Hershey Foods introduces its Golden Almond chocolate bar.

1979   The New York Cocoa Exchange merges with the Coffee and Sugar Exchange to form the Coffee, Sugar, and Cocoa Exchange Inc. The Exchange operates to trade in futures and options contracts on its commodities.

Rowntree Mackintosh, Ltd., acquires the Dutch company Nuts Chocoladefabriek BV.

Joseph Terry & Sons introduces Chocolate Lemon in both milk and dark versions, variations of their popular Chocolate Orange.

1980   Cocoa consumption throughout the world is three times as much as thirty years ago. The biggest consumers are the European countries, led by Switzerland.

Forrest Mars opens a candy factory in Henderson, Nevada, to produce a line of liquor-filled chocolates using top-quality ingredients. He names the company Ethel M in honor of his mother.

Due to growth, Bloomer Chocolate Company builds its third manufacturing plant in East Greenville, Pennsylvania, making the company one of the largest chocolate manufacturers in the United States.

In a real life espionage story an employee of the Swiss company Suchard-Tobler unsuccessfully attempts to sell secret chocolate recipes to Saudi Arabia, China, and Russia.

1981   Belgian chocolate manufacturer Callebaut is sold to the Swiss company Interfood.

Joseph Terry & Sons discontinues production of their Chocolate Lemon to concentrate on their much more popular Chocolate Orange.

1982   Cacao Barry chocolate company is acquired by Sucres et Denerees, an International Trading Group.

Jacobs coffee company and the Suchard-Tobler chocolate company merge to form Jacobs Suchard.

Rowntree Mackintosh, Ltd., changes its name to Rowntree Mackintosh PLC.

1982 Terry's of York is acquired in England by United Biscuits.

The Belgian chocolate company, Chocolaterie Jacques Ltd. is acquired by the German Stollwerck group.

Bernard Callebaut emigrates to Canada from Belgium and begins production of his own line of high-quality hand-crafted European-style pralines and chocolates in Calgary.

1983 Joseph Schmidt Confections opens a small shop in San Francisco.

Chantal Coady opens her tiny chocolate shop, Rococo, in London, specializing in private label grand cru chocolate bars, exotically flavored and unusual artisanal chocolates and bonbons.

Klaus J. Jacobs buys the Interfood Group, which owns Belgian chocolate manufacturer Callebaut and Dutch cocoa producer Van Houten.

Katalin Coburn starts Jerbeau chocolates, the wholesale side of her family's Bit of Sweetland chocolate shop, which her parents bought in Los Angeles, California, in 1969.

1985 Bosco Products, Inc., takes over production of Bosco chocolate syrup from Corn Products Company, which had acquired the product from its inventor in the mid-1950s.

Daskalidès pralines from Ghent, Belgium, are introduced to the foreign market and are very well received, resulting in brisk sales.

Katalin Coburn of Jerbeau Chocolates sells the family retail chocolate shop, Bit of Sweetland, in Los Angeles, California, to concentrate on the thriving wholesale business.

1986 Belgian chocolate company Côte d'Or is acquired by the Swiss chocolate company Jacobs Suchard.

Joseph Schmidt Confections moves its production facilities to a large facility to keep up with the demand for its products.

Rena Pocrass founds Chocolates a la Carte, a company specializing in high-quality chocolate designs that can be imprinted with company logos and other custom artwork, in Los Angeles, California.

1987 Tiense Raffinaderijen, the most important Belgian sugar refinery, takes over Neuhaus Chocolates. Within a short time the company becomes N.V. Neuhaus-Mondose S.A. and is sold to Belgian Holding Artal, a leading company in top food sectors in Europe and Asia.

Rowntree Mackintosh PLC changes its name to become Rowntree PLC.

Elite Industries Ltd., Israel's largest exporter of food products and manufacturer of 69 percent of Israel's chocolate and confectionery, is acquired by the E. D. & F. Man Group.

In July the Belgian company Chocolaterie Jacques Ltd. begins production in its newly built factory.

Daskalidès pralines from Ghent, Belgium, are awarded the prestigious French gold medal, Laurier d'Or de la Qualite.

1988 Perugina chocolate company becomes part of the multinational food company Nestlé, yet maintains its distinctive image and product line.

Nestlé acquires the British chocolate and candy manufacturer Rowntree, the world's fourth-largest manufacturer of chocolates and confectionery items, after Mars, Hershey, and Cadbury. This makes Nestlé the world's largest chocolate and confectionery manufacturer.

United Biscuits, which owns Terry's of York acquires Callard & Bowser Toffees and Butterscotch.

Cadbury Schweppes PLC of Britain acquires Poulain of France.

Hershey Chocolate Company is renamed Hershey Chocolate U.S.A. The company acquires Peter Paul, manufacturer of Almond Joy and Mounds candy bars. On August 25 the company acquires the U.S. confectionery operations of the British company, Cadbury Schweppes.

In Italy, Andrea Slitti begins to pursue his passion and creates his own line of chocolates. He soon becomes world famous for the quality and uniqueness of his products.

1988 Richard Donnelly establishes his chocolate shop in Santa Cruz, California, specializing in top-quality European-style truffles and pralines using California ingredients such as pistachio nuts and macadamia nuts.

1989 In September Hershey Chocolate U.S.A. introduces Symphony milk chocolate bar and Symphony milk chocolate bar with almonds and toffee chips.

1990 Alice Medrich sells Cocolat, her European-style pastry shop that popularized French-style chocolate truffles and oversize American chocolate truffles.

In July Hershey Foods Corporation opens Hershey's Visitor Center in Oakdale, California, as the gateway to their West Coast plant. In September the company introduces nationally the new variation to their perpetually popular candy, Hershey's Kisses with Almonds. In December Hershey provides U.S. Army troops in the Gulf War, Desert Storm, with 144,000 of their heat-resistant candy bars, Hershey's Desert Bar.

To announce the introduction of Hershey's Kisses with Almonds in September 1990, a five-hundred-pound, six-foot-tall milk chocolate replica was lowered from a sixty-foot flagpole in New York City's Times Square.

1991 In February Steven C. Wallace founds the Omanhene Cocoa Bean Company in Ghana as a joint venture with the Ghanaian government. The company produces fine-quality chocolate with locally grown cacao beans.

In March Reese's Peanut Butter Cups are reformulated to contain three times the amount of peanuts of the original recipe introduced in 1976.

Josephine Fairley and Craig Sims found Green & Black's in London to produce high-quality chocolate with organically grown cacao from Togo and Belize. The company establishes a Fair Trade policy, which pays a fair price to the farmers and offers a long-term contract so they can continue to grow the cacao organically and are ensured of income to provide a decent life for their families. The chocolate is very well received by the public.

Chocolat Alprose S.A. opens its chocolate museum, SCHOKOLANDALPROSE—The World of Chocolate, in Caslano (near Lugano), Switzerland. It is the first and only chocolate museum in Switzerland, attracting over 700,000 visitors in its first year of operation.

1992 Kraft General Foods International purchases a majority stake in Figaro, the foremost confectionery company in the Slovak Republic and expands their equity in Pavlides, a Greek chocolate confectionery company.

Janele Smith opens Fenton & Lee Chocolatiers in Eugene, Oregon, and wins the National Association for the Specialty Food Trade (NASFT) award for Best Confection at the Fancy Food and Confection show for her Chocolate Espresso Wafers. The company name comes from the middle names of her two sons.

Callebaut Asia Pacific, a division of Callebaut chocolate, is established in Hong Kong and Singapore.

1993 Kraft Jacobs Suchard is formed to manage the European interests of Kraft General Foods International. The company acquires majority stakes in Republika, the principal chocolate producer in Bulgaria. The company also acquires Terry's Group, based in Cheltenham, England, from United Biscuits. This creates the United Kingdom's fourth-largest confectionery manufacturer named Terry's Suchard.

Larry Burdick locates his artisan chocolate company, L. A. Burdick Chocolates in Walpole, New Hampshire.

In August Hershey Foods Corporation introduces nationally two new versions of their popular Hershey's Kisses candies, Hershey's Hugs, mini Hershey's Kisses wrapped in white chocolate, and another version with almonds.

1993 Newman's Own Organics, the organic food division of Newman's Own is formed. Based in Santa Cruz, California, the company produces a variety of chocolate bars using completely organic ingredients. The company motto, like its parent company, is "All Profits, After Taxes, Go to Charity."

In October Italian chocolatier Andrea Slitti is convinced by his colleagues to participate in the International Chocolate Show held in Larange, France. He takes the gold medal, the first Italian to do so in a French show. This gives him the right to participate in the final competition of the International Grand Prix of Chocolate, held every two years in Paris, where he also wins the gold medal, beating competitors from the United States, Japan, France, Spain, and England.

1994 Kraft Jacobs Suchard obtains majority interest in Rumania's largest chocolate manufacturer, Poiana.

1995 In January the Averna company acquires the Italian chocolate and confectionery company Pernigotti.

In Boulder, Colorado, Timothy Love starts Chocolove to produce premium-quality Belgian chocolate bars with high cocoa content. The bars are packaged to resemble love letters with classic love poems printed inside each label.

1996 Kraft Jacobs Suchard launches Toblerone Blue, a new filled rendition of their famous Toblerone candy bar. This bar has an outer milk chocolate shell that encloses a white Toblerone filling in the familiar triangular shape.

Chocolates El Rey introduces its Carnero Superior line of Venezuelan chocolates to the United States and Venezuelan mass consumption markets.

Consumer Reports rates L. A. Burdick Chocolates of Walpole, New Hampshire, number one in the United States for quality and taste.

Bernard Callebaut travels to the International Festival of Chocolate in Montelimar, France where he is the festival's only invited North American guest. He wins three prestigious awards at the festival: one for superior chocolate to accompany wines, one for superior children's chocolate product, and the overall Prize of Excellence. Additionally, he is inducted into the Nougat Guild and the International Order of the French Gastronomy, bestowed by the French government.

In September Chocolove introduces two new premium Belgium chocolate bars, Rich Dark Chocolate with 65 percent cocoa content and Strong Dark Chocolate with 70 percent cocoa content. Both are very well received by the chocolate-eating public.

Robert Steinberg and John Scharffenberger begin production of Scharffen Berger Chocolate in South San Francisco using old world techniques. They travel the world to buy vintage equipment and the best-quality cacao beans, then blend several varieties to produce chocolate of extremely high quality, rivaling some of the world's finest.

1997 In February Archer Daniels Midland Co. (ADM) of Decatur, Illinois, buys Grace Cocoa from W. R. Grace & Co., a deal that includes Grace's major Dutch processor, Cacao De Zaan, renamed ADM Zaan.

In June ADM buys E. D.& F. Man Group Plc's cocoa processing unit, making ADM the world's largest cocoa processor.

Chocovic chocolate, made in Barcelona, Spain, from high-quality single-origin cacao beans is introduced into the United States.

In July San Francisco Venture Group acquires the beloved fifty-eight-year-old Hooper's Chocolates of Oakland, California, known for its exclusive use of Belgian chocolate and its assorted creams. The group plans to revitalize the company and continue to produce its well-known line of premium chocolates. On September 16 Hooper's officially reopens for business in its pink building on Telegraph Avenue in Oakland.

1998 In January Ghirardelli Chocolate Company is acquired by Switzerland's Chocoladefabriken Lindt & Sprüngli AG. Ghirardelli continues to operate under its own name and produce its line of products as a wholly owned subsidiary of Lindt & Sprüngli.

$\mathscr{F}$ROM THE BEAN TO THE BAR

"No other factory in the world mixes its chocolate by waterfall."
—Willy Wonka in the movie, *Willy Wonka and the Chocolate Factory*, 1972

In 1753 the celebrated Swedish naturalist Linnaeus named the cacao tree *Theobroma cacao*, "food of the gods." It's likely that his idea for the name came from the Maya, Toltecs, and Aztecs who believed the gods had given them cacao as a gift. Today the "food of the gods" is still thought to be divine by devoted chocolate eaters.

The origins of the cacao tree (technically it is cacao until the beans are made into cocoa) are cloudy, but it is thought that the first trees grew wild in the Orinoco and the Amazon basins in northern Brazil. Today cacao is cultivated in tropical climates within 10 to 20 degrees north and south of the Equator; it is also being grown on the semitropical Big Island of Hawaii, with measured success. In order to thrive, the evergreen cacao trees require warm, very humid conditions with loose, nutrient-rich soil, shaded sunlight, little or no wind, lots of rain, and a short dry season. The main cacao-producing countries are Brazil, Ghana, the Ivory Coast, and Nigeria. Cacao is also grown in Bolivia, Cameroon, Colombia, Costa Rica, Cuba, the Dominican Republic, Ecuador, Fiji, Grenada, Haiti,

Indonesia, Malaysia, Madagascar, Mexico, Peru, the Philippines, Papua New Guinea, São Tomé, the Seychelles, Sierra Leone, Sri Lanka, Togo, Trinidad, Venezuela, and Zaire.

There are three main varieties of cacao beans: criollo, forastero, and trinitario. The criollo bean is native to Central America and was the first cacao grown. It is known as the flavor bean because it produces the best-tasting, highest quality cocoa. Criollo accounts for only about 10 to 15 percent of the world's cacao output because the trees are small and difficult to cultivate. Forastero cacao is heartier and makes up the majority of the cacao grown worldwide, about 70 percent. It is not nearly as tasty as the criollo variety, producing beans that are harsher and more bitter. Generally the two varieties are blended together, although in some cases criollo beans are used exclusively to produce "grand cru" chocolates, considered by many to be the world's finest. Within these two main varieties of cacao there are many hybrids and different flavor notes are highlighted depending on soils and growing conditions.

Trinitario cacao is a hybrid of criollo and forastero that has been cultivated in Trinidad and the Caribbean for many years. It has developed into a major category of beans that accounts for approximately 20 percent of the world's cacao harvest. Trinitario has many of the flavor characteristics of the criollo beans with much of the heartiness of the forastero beans.

Cacao trees can grow as tall as sixty feet in the wild, but on plantations they are kept to a height of about twenty feet, to make it easier to harvest the pods. Cultivated trees grow in the shade of tall, large-leaved "mother" trees, usually banana trees, rubber trees, or coconut palms, depending on where they are grown. Large groves or orchards of the trees are called "cacao walks." Young trees begin to bear fruit between four and five years and continue to produce crops for up to thirty years.

At any time the tree supports simultaneously as many as five thousand tiny white flowers, which will develop into pods, and twenty to thirty pods in various stages of ripeness. These all grow in unique fashion not only on the branches, but on the trunk as well. The oval-shaped pods are large, hard, and deeply ridged, approximately the size of a football. They come in a rainbow of colors—green, yellow, orange, and red. Generally the unripe pods are green and yellow, the ripe ones orange and red, but unripe pods can also be red or orange, making it hard to tell when they are ripe. Pods that are not completely ripe will ferment adequately, and even if the pods are ripe it doesn't hurt them to remain on the trees for a few weeks. Generally the pods take five to six months to develop, so they are harvested twice a year. Within each pod a milky-white, pulpy membrane holds from twenty to forty ivory to purple-colored, almond-shaped beans. The beans taste bitter at this point, but the pulp is tasty and sweet and is often eaten by the plantation workers.

When ready for harvest, the pods are cut off the trees using a machete or other type of sharp knife, split open, and the beans and pulp are removed. The beans are placed on banana leaves, in large wooden boxes, or in baskets, covered with leaves, and left to ferment for several days. Criollo beans usually ferment for two to three days, forastero and trinitario beans for three to seven days. The beans are turned a few times during the process to ensure even fermentation. During this time the sugar-loaded membrane evaporates, raising the heat that stops the germination process. The beans become darker and wrinkled. This is when the beans lose their bitterness and first begin to develop a faint chocolate taste. If the fermentation stage is skipped, the beans will never fulfill their true flavor potential and will taste inferior. After fermentation the beans are sun-dried for several days on special drying racks if the weather permits, or in large mechanical drying machines. Drying enhances the aroma of the cacao beans and evaporates much of their water content, which helps keep mold and mildew from developing. Next, they are packed into burlap sacks and shipped to factories where they become cocoa and chocolate.

During the process of making cacao beans into chocolate there are four key factors that determine the final flavor of the finished product: roasting time and temperature, blending of types of cacao beans, proportions of ingredients, and conching, the final stirring stage that produces a velvety smooth texture. This is where the skill and knowledge of the chocolate maker comes into play to create exactly the product the company wants. Many chocolate manufacturers closely guard the specific formulas that they use.

When the beans arrive at the chocolate factory they are first sorted and cleaned of any extraneous matter. Blending of the beans takes place at various stages during the processing (before or after roasting, before or after grinding), depending on the manufacturer. The next step is to roast the beans at a temperature of 250 to 350°F for thirty minutes to two hours, depending on their type and the desired end result. They are roasted in large, revolving drums. The main purpose of roasting is to bring out the flavor of the beans. This is when the aroma of chocolate develops. It's what you smell upon arrival at a chocolate factory. If the beans are roasted too long they will develop a bitter edge, which is not desirable. In most cases the beans that are roasted for cocoa powder will be roasted longer than those for chocolate because chocolate goes through other processes after roasting that also develop its flavor.

One of the differences between European and American chocolates is how they are roasted. Generally the European manufacturers roast the beans at a lower temperature for a longer period of time. This develops deep flavor. Many American chocolate manufacturers roast their beans at higher temperatures for shorter periods of time, which makes the flavor rougher, requiring more sugar to mellow it.

After roasting the beans are winnowed, a process that cracks and removes the outer shell, leaving the inner nib. The shells are generally sold for animal feed. The nibs are crushed, then heated to melt the cocoa butter, and ground to a thick paste similar to peanut butter, called chocolate liquor (cocoa mass in the United Kingdom), which contains absolutely no alcohol, despite its name. At this point depending on whether the chocolate liquor is to become chocolate or cocoa powder, it goes through different processes. If the nibs are to become Dutch-processed cocoa, they will have been treated with an alkali either after roasting or after grinding. The alkali darkens the color of the mixture, softens the flavor, and makes the final product easier to disperse in liquid. (It was a Dutchman, Coenraad Van Houten, who developed the press that extracts cocoa butter from chocolate liquor to produce cocoa powder. He also discovered that by treating the mixture with an alkaline substance, it became easier to mix with water or milk. This occurred in the mid-nineteenth century and revolutionized the manufacture of cocoa and chocolate.) If left untreated with alkali the chocolate liquor is processed into natural cocoa powder.

Cocoa is the world's third-largest agricultural export crop, following closely on the heels of coffee and sugar.

To make cocoa powder, large presses extract the cocoa butter from the chocolate liquor. The result is a dry cake called presscake or cocoa cake,

Amsterdam is the world's largest transshipment port for unprocessed cacao, where approximately 20 percent of the world's cacao harvest is unloaded.

which is ground and then sifted through fine nylon, silk, or wire mesh. There is some cocoa butter left in the cocoa cake after pressing, between 10 and 25 percent, producing low-fat and high-fat cocoas. Low-fat cocoa contains between 10 and 13 percent fat, whereas high-fat cocoa contains between 15 and 25 percent. Low-fat cocoa is generally used for cocoa drinks, high-fat to flavor desserts and for products that contain vegetable fats other than cocoa butter.

To make unsweetened or "baking" chocolate, pure chocolate liquor is molded and solidified. Dark chocolate is made by combining chocolate liquor with varying amounts of sugar, depending on whether it is to be extra-bittersweet, bittersweet, or semisweet, cocoa butter that was extracted during the processing of cocoa cake, and vanilla. To make milk chocolate the same ingredients are combined in different proportions with milk solids or powder. White chocolate is made from pure cocoa butter, sugar, and milk solids or powder.

The proportion of ingredients is another of the key factors that distinguishes one brand of chocolate from another. Because white chocolate contains no chocolate liquor, the U.S. Food and Drug Administration will not allow it to be labeled chocolate. It is called confectionery coating. This can be confusing because there are also products labeled compound coating and summer coating that are made with fats other than cocoa butter which are passed off as white chocolate. Cocoa butter is what gives the chocolate flavor to white chocolate, so make sure you read the label before you buy and know what you are getting.

Couverture, the French word for coating or covering, is chocolate that has more cocoa butter than regular eating chocolate. It makes a thin coating on dipped truffles and candies. Professional chocolatiers and confectioners use couverture chocolate not only for dipping but for fillings and centers. It is also delicious for eating and works very well for baking. Most of the high-quality chocolate brands are also available as couvertures. Dark, milk, and white chocolates are all made as couvertures.

Another ingredient that is added to chocolate is lecithin, primarily extracted from soybeans. Lecithin is an emulsifier. Its purpose is to help disperse any remaining solids left in the chocolate mixture and to make it smoother and more fluid. Although lecithin accounts for only .3 to .5 percent of the finished product, it is important because it keeps the chocolate from becoming too hard and brittle.

There is another type of chocolate called gianduia. This is a blended mixture of chocolate and roasted hazelnuts with a velvety smooth texture. Often roasted almonds are used in place of the hazelnuts or in combination with them. Although milk chocolate is most commonly used, occasionally gianduia is made with dark chocolate and even with white chocolate. Gianduia is one of the true wonders of the world. Once tasted, it is impossible to forget. Its flavor is so subtle that it is practically impossible to pick out the separate ingredients. Gianduia is used in the same way as chocolate, to flavor a wide variety of desserts, pastries, and confections.

Once all the ingredients are combined, the chocolate mixture goes through a refining process where it is kneaded between several large steel rollers. This reduces the particle size to make a smooth paste mixture. Next it is conched, a process that develops the flavor by aerating the chocolate and driving off any volatile acids to reduce acidity, making a homogenous mixture. During conching the liquid mixture is heated and continuously mixed, ground, and stirred, which stabilizes the emulsion, making a velvety smooth, melt-in-the-mouth chocolate. The conch, Spanish for shell, which was its original shape, was developed by Rodolphe Lindt in 1879 and was a revolutionary step in producing high-quality, smooth eating chocolate. How long chocolate is conched is another key factor in determining the quality of the finished product. High-quality chocolates are conched for several days, whereas lower-quality chocolates may be conched for hours. Because there is some flavor loss during conching, chocolate makers must strike a balance between texture and flavor.

After conching the chocolate is tempered, a process that gradually raises, lowers, and raises the temperature to set degrees. This stabilizes the cocoa butter crystals, which have six different melting points, and prevents chocolate bloom, a condition that occurs when cocoa butter rises to the surface. It also gives chocolate its snap, gloss, and smooth texture, and makes it easy to unmold.

If the finished chocolate is to be sold to other product manufacturers, it is kept in its liquid state and flows through large pipes to tanks. If it is to be molded into chocolate bars and other products it goes through that process now. Any additions, such as nuts and fruit, are made at this point. Once the chocolates are molded, they are solidified, then wrapped and stored.

Unsweetened or bitter chocolate contains no sugar. Extra-bittersweet, bittersweet, and semisweet chocolates range between 35 to 50 percent sugar. Milk chocolate contains about 50 percent sugar. One indication of quality of chocolate is the amount of cocoa mass it contains. Some of the world's finest quality chocolates state that they contain between 60 to 70 percent cocoa mass. Be sure to read labels so you know what to expect from your chocolate of choice.

Organic chocolate is grown and processed in much the same way as described above. What makes organic chocolate different is whether or not and which types of fertilizers and pest controls are used in the growing of the cacao. Also, organic chocolate is processed without the use of artificial stabilizers or emulsifiers. In addition, other normal ingredients, such as sugar and nuts or dried fruits, come from organic sources. Because there are no set standards for organic chocolate, it's really pretty difficult to say that chocolate is truly organic. My best advice is to read the label before you make your choice.

MAKING CHOCOLATE AND COCOA

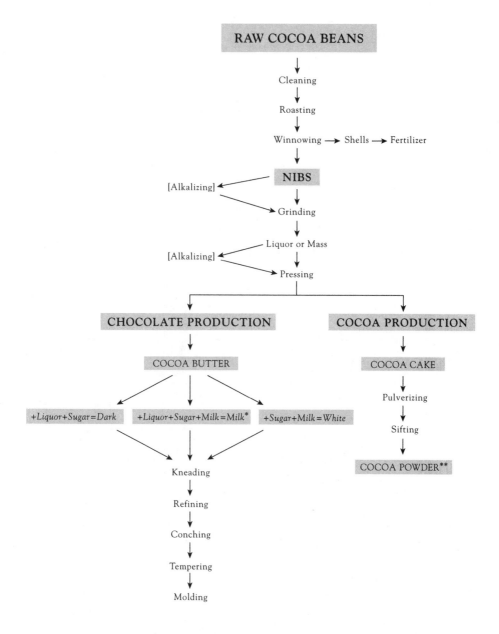

RAW COCOA BEANS

↓ Cleaning

↓ Roasting

↓ Winnowing → Shells → Fertilizer

NIBS

[Alkalizing] ← Grinding

↓ Liquor or Mass

[Alkalizing] ← Pressing

CHOCOLATE PRODUCTION   **COCOA PRODUCTION**

COCOA BUTTER   COCOA CAKE

+Liquor+Sugar=Dark   +Liquor+Sugar+Milk=Milk*   +Sugar+Milk=White   Pulverizing

Kneading   Sifting

Refining   COCOA POWDER**

Conching

Tempering

Molding

*Liquor+Sugar+Milk+Hazelnuts = Gianduia
**Cocoa Powder+Sugar+Milk = Cocoa/Chocolate Drink

TASTING CHOCOLATE

Chocolate contains more than 500 flavors, which makes it more complex than any other food. No wonder it's capable of satisfying practically everyone's sensory taste.

—**Debra Waterhouse, Why Women Need Chocolate, 1995**

We all have flavor preferences based on our unique chemical makeup. Which chocolate we like best is personal. How and where we had our first encounters with chocolate are factors to be considered because they do affect our preferences, oftentimes subliminally. However, there are several universally recognized key factors to be aware of when tasting chocolate. These enhance the appreciation of chocolate and indicate quality.

Appearance: Chocolate should be lustrous and evenly colored, with no gray streaks or dots, known as bloom. Dullness and signs of bloom indicate the chocolate has not been handled properly. One type of bloom is a result of the chocolate going through rapid temperature changes. This does not affect the taste, but it is unsightly. Another type of bloom is the result of moisture drawing the sugar up to the surface. This will affect the texture and flavor. Some of the most common words used to describe the appearance of chocolate are gloss, sheen, dull, cracks, dots, and streaks.

Aroma: Chocolate should smell rich and flavorful, not burned or smoky. The aroma should be primarily chocolate. There should be no musty or chemical scent. Even if the chocolate is filled, the other aromas should not overpower the chocolate, but should enhance it. Often-used words to describe the aroma of chocolate are fresh, subtle, mellow, spicy, floral or flowery, fruity, berry, citrusy, winy, pungent, sour, grassy, woody, mildew, or straw.

Snap: Chocolate should break firmly and cleanly, not crumble or splinter. The only exception to this is if the chocolate comes directly from the refrigerator and has not had time to warm up to room temperature. Then it may splinter, which is a better sign than crumbling. To describe the snap of chocolate words used often are crisp, brittle, clean, dry, coarse, crumbly, hard snap.

Texture/Mouthfeel: Chocolate should be smooth and creamy, not greasy, waxy, or gritty. It should melt in your mouth because chocolate melts at close to body temperature and it should melt evenly. Some of the most common words used to describe the texture and mouthfeel of chocolate are smooth, velvety, creamy, soft, greasy, chalky, sticky, gummy, waxy, sandy, gritty, grainy, coarse, and dry.

Flavor: The flavor should be pleasing, harmonious, and well-balanced, not bitter or too sweet. The other flavors, such as vanilla, spices, and nuts, should blend well and enhance the chocolate, not overpower it. Terms used to describe the flavor of chocolate are rich, round, caramel, fudgy, roasted grain, toasted nuts, malt, mellow, spicy, floral, fruity, citrusy, earthy, salty, bitter, burned, smoky, artificial, harsh, tart, and flat.

Aftertaste: The flavor should linger in your mouth pleasantly, without an overpowering burned quality. Some words to describe the aftertaste of chocolate are long, short, soft, even, and flat.

High-quality premium chocolate is easy to distinguish from the inferior, low-grade variety. Read the label and look for the percent of cocoa content. In general, the higher the percentage, the better the quality of chocolate, although more than 72 percent cocoa can be unpalatable. Another factor is the use of real cocoa butter rather than substitutes, such as other vegetable fats, which leave a detectable residual greasiness in the mouth. Artificial vanilla leaves an artificial aftertaste. The better-quality chocolates use real vanilla. The quality of the cacao beans used and how they are roasted also affect the quality and flavor of chocolate. Finally, be aware of the sugar content. Sugar is used to mask the flavor of inferior chocolate. It should be used sparingly.

One way to explore the many qualities of chocolate is to set up a tasting. A good way to do this is to gather two to three brands of pure chocolate of various types, such as extra-bittersweet, bittersweet, semisweet, milk, and white. The best way to taste chocolate is straight off the bar because that flavor is how the chocolate will taste when it is used in baking, to make candies and confections, or any chocolate dessert. It's best to use plain chocolates, not filled or flavored bars. Chop each type of chocolate into small chunks and place them on separate plates.

Provide each participant with a Chocolate Tasting Score Card (following). To hold a blind tasting, write the brand name and type of each chocolate on a card and tape it to the bottom of each plate. Also, attach a card to each plate with a number and the type of chocolate (e.g., #1 bittersweet). Participants will need to write these numbers and types of chocolate at the top of the columns on their score cards to keep track of what they are tasting.

If you wish to reveal the identity of each chocolate before the tasting, attach a card with the name and type of chocolate to each plate (e.g., Valrhona bittersweet). Have the participants copy these onto their score cards. Briefly describe to everyone how to use the score card, including explaining what factors to be aware of when tasting.

It's a good idea to have water and plain bread on hand for palate cleansing. After the tasting it's fun and informative to share your results.

When selecting chocolates for a tasting, I have found that generally the European brands of chocolate are the highest quality and best tasting, although there are very good American-made brands. Some of the most popular European brands, and I think best tasting, are Callebaut (Belgian), Cacao Barry (French), and Valrhona (French). The most popular, and my preference for the best-tasting American brands, are Scharffen Berger and Guittard.

To make your tasting exciting, mix diverse types of chocolates from a variety of sources, but limit the number so it's not an overwhelming experience. You may choose to restrict your tasting to a single type—bittersweet or semisweet, for example. You might prefer to taste chocolates from one country—Switzerland, France, or Belgium, or from a single manufacturer.

For filled chocolates, bonbons, and truffles, cut one open and examine it. If it is a top-quality piece, the outer shell will be thin rather than thick and the bottom will not have a large "foot" but will look as trim as the top. Look at the center and see if you can discern its composition. Perhaps it is made of ganache. If so, it will be smooth and creamy.

The main point is to learn more about chocolate and increase its overall enjoyment, so it's really not important exactly how you set up your tasting. Chocolate should make you smile!

CHOCOLATE TASTING SCORE CARD

Chocolate Name				
Chocolate Type				
Appearance				
Aroma				
Snap				
Texture/Mouthfeel				
Flavor				
Aftertaste				
TOTAL				

Rating system: Excellent = 5, Very good = 4, Good = 3, Fair = 2, Bad = 1, Very bad = 0

CHOCOLATE TIPS

Choosing Chocolate
- Taste chocolate straight off the bar. Be sure you like the chocolate "plain" before using it, because the flavor of chocolate doesn't change when it is used in baking, pastry making, and candy making. For more tips on what to look for in tasting chocolate see the section titled "Tasting Chocolate."

Chocolate Substitution
- In most recipes semisweet and bittersweet chocolate can be substituted for each other without having to make any adjustments in the ingredients. However, milk chocolate and white chocolate cannot be substituted directly for dark chocolate as they all have different amounts of body. In most cases more milk chocolate and white chocolate are needed than dark chocolate if it is to be used in the same recipe. There is no set formula for the amount to substitute.

Also, it may be necessary to adjust the proportions of other ingredients in the recipe. In many cases it is not advisable to replace one chocolate with another because it will greatly change the taste and texture of the finished product, which may not be as enjoyable as expected. In some instances milk chocolate and white chocolate can be substituted for each other, but usually more white chocolate is needed if it replaces milk chocolate. It's a good idea to make a trial recipe to see what adjustments need to be made.

Handling Chocolate

- To melt chocolate, chop it into tiny pieces using a chef's knife with a large blade on a cutting board. It can be chopped in a food processor, but the machine beats up the chocolate and the heat of the motor may melt it before you are ready.
- Chocolate should not be heated over 120°F or it will begin to disintegrate.
- Don't let chocolate come in direct contact with heat. It burns very easily.
- Melt chocolate in the top of a double boiler over hot, not simmering, water. Stir it frequently with a rubber or plastic spatula to ensure even melting. Don't use a wooden spoon to stir chocolate because it is porous and holds other flavors that will taint your chocolate.
- You can create your own double boiler with a saucepan and a stainless steel bowl.
- Be sure the top pan or bowl of the double boiler fits snugly over the bottom pan, so no water or steam can leak out and mix with the chocolate. Make sure the top pan or bowl is large enough to hold the amount of chocolate you need and there is room to stir.
- Keep the water level in the bottom pan low, about 1 inch deep, or it may spill out and mix with the chocolate.
- Melt chocolate slowly over low heat. Don't allow the water in the bottom pan to boil. Dark chocolate should not be heated over 120°F. Milk chocolate and white chocolate should not exceed 115°F.
- White chocolate is the most delicate to melt. The milk solids easily coagulate (forming lumps) if exposed to too much heat. Most people think the lumps are from unmelted chocolate and turn up the heat,

when it is too much heat that has caused the chocolate to become lumpy.

- Water or other liquids are chocolate's main nemesis. A few drops of liquid will cause chocolate to thicken up and become like mud. This is called seizing. Once this happens there is nothing that can be done to restore chocolate to its original smooth, velvety condition. It is possible to mix a small amount of vegetable oil with the seized chocolate, but then it is no longer pure chocolate. You can also add a larger quantity of liquid and the mixture will become smoother, but it still is not pure chocolate. If chocolate seizes, toss it out and start over. The best thing to do is make sure no liquid comes in contact with chocolate, unless a recipe calls for a specific ingredient. Be sure all utensils that come in contact with chocolate are completely dry.

- To combine chocolate with other ingredients, such as butter or liquid, it is best to melt them together to prevent seizing. To do this there must be more than a tiny amount of liquid. Eminent food scientist Shirley O. Corriher has determined that the best proportion is to use 1 tablespoon liquid for every 2 ounces chocolate.

- When the top pan or bowl is removed from the double boiler wipe the bottom and sides very dry so no water can mix with the chocolate when it is poured out.

- Chocolate chips don't completely lose their shape as they melt until they are stirred. Be sure to use a rubber spatula to stir them or you will think they are not thoroughly melted and may apply too much heat.

- Humidity can also affect how chocolate acts. Try to avoid working with chocolate on rainy, foggy, or hot summer days.

- Chocolate can be melted in a microwave oven, although I don't recommend this because it is much too easy to burn it. Use low power for 10- to 15-second intervals and stir the chocolate after each interval. Since microwave melts chocolate from the inside out, stirring it is the only way to tell if it is melting.

- Burned or overheated chocolate is grainy and has a burned taste.

- Leftover chocolate that has been used for dipping can be saved as long as nothing has mixed with it. Transfer the chocolate to a clean container, cover it tightly, and store at room temperature. It can be chopped and used again. The chocolate will have to be tempered again if it is to be used for dipping or molding, because once it cools, it will go out of temper.

- When adding other ingredients to chocolate have them all at a similar temperature. If a cold liquid is blended with warm chocolate, lumps will form.

Storing Chocolate

- Store plain or bar chocolate at room temperature (ideally 65 to 75°F) in a dark, dry place tightly wrapped in foil or brown paper. If stored in the refrigerator or the freezer, chocolate will pick up moisture that will condense on it, causing it to thicken and/or seize when melted.
- Chocolate that comes in contact with moisture or becomes too cold during storage develops tiny white or gray sugar crystals on its surface. This is known as sugar bloom. It is the result of moisture that condenses on the surface of the chocolate, which draws out sugar that dissolves and leaves crystals after the liquid evaporates. Sugar bloom will affect the texture of the chocolate, making it grainy.
- If chocolate becomes too warm during storage, some of the cocoa butter may rise to the surface causing a white bloom, which is visible as streaks or dots. This does not affect the taste of the chocolate and when the chocolate is melted, the cocoa butter will go back into its emulsion.
- Properly stored dark chocolate will last indefinitely. Properly stored milk chocolate and white chocolate will last approximately 10 months to a year.
- If you are unsure whether chocolate is still good, check its aroma. If it has an "off" smell, don't use it. Also, taste a small piece. If the taste is good, the chocolate is still good to use.
- Store finished chocolate desserts, pastries, and confections in the refrigerator, tightly covered, to guard against moisture condensation. If the chocolate is shiny, refrigerating it will cause its sheen to dull. There are some chocolate desserts and pastries that can be stored at room temperature. Be sure they are tightly covered. Be careful what you place next to the chocolate because it is like a sponge and will easily absorb other flavors. Some chocolate candies and confections

can be frozen. To do so, place them in airtight containers and wrap with several layers of foil and plastic wrap. Defrost them in the refrigerator for at least 24 hours before letting them stand at room temperature. The main factor to guard against is moisture condensation. By wrapping the candies very well and defrosting them slowly, this can be minimized.

- Quick temperature changes cause the outer chocolate coating to crack and discolor.

Packaging and Shipping Chocolate

- To ensure that your chocolate candies and confections arrive in good condition, pack them carefully in a tin or box no more than three layers deep. Place layers of waxed paper or food-safe coated quilted sheets between the layers of candies to protect them from bumping into each other.
- Wrap the container in bubble wrap or Styrofoam and place in a snug-fitting box or a padded envelope.
- Ship via first-class mail or an overnight carrier service.
- If the weather if very warm when shipping the chocolate, include a cold pack with it to help stabilize the surrounding temperature.
- Include a note for the recipient with tips about how to store and serve the chocolate, for example: "Store in the refrigerator wrapped in aluminum foil away from strong-flavored foods for up to 3 weeks. Let stand at room temperature at least 20 minutes before serving for the full flavor to develop. Alternately, store at cool room temperature in a dark cabinet in an airtight container for up to 1 week. Enjoy!"

How to Present and Serve Chocolate

- All chocolate tastes best at room temperature. Remove chocolate desserts, pastries, and confections (except ice cream and other easily melted items) from the refrigerator 20 to 30 minutes before serving so they can warm up. If chocolate is eaten too cold it's wonderful full flavor will not be apparent and it won't be as well appreciated as it is when eaten at the proper temperature.

CHOCOLATE AND HEALTH

"People who habitually drink chocolate enjoy unvarying health, and are least attacked by a host of little illnesses which can destroy the true joy of living."
—**Anthelme Brillat-Savarin, *The Physiology of Taste*, 1825**

". . . good, well made chocolate can be assimilated by any stomach which can still digest even feebly."
—**Anthelme Brillat-Savarin, *The Physiology of Taste*, 1825**

Chocolate and health may seem like an oxymoron. However, chocolate may be a lot better for your health than you ever thought. This may not be news to those of us who have been happily consuming chocolate all of our lives. Actually, for hundreds of years chocolate has been thought to be a healthful food.

There are some scientific reasons why chocolate makes us feel good and is good for us. To begin with, the main factors of sugar, fat, and carbohydrate provide a boost of energy. Then there is chocolate's seductive mouthfeel, the result of cocoa butter, which melts at close to body temperature. Also, chocolate contains theobromine, caffeine, phenylethylamine (PEA), and anandamide that add to its appeal. These chemical substances have a profound effect on the brain and demonstrate that chocolate has a definite physiological effect on the body.

Theobromine and caffeine are both stimulants. Phenylethylamine is a chemical that our brain releases when we fall in love. It also acts as an antidepressant by combining with dopamine that is naturally present in the brain. Anandamide helps to stimulate and open synapses in the brain that allow "feel good" waves to transmit more easily. These are the same brain receptors that respond to the psychoactive ingredients in marijuana and hashish. But one would have to ingest more than twenty-five pounds of chocolate at one sitting to get "high" in the same way. Anandamide was discovered by a scientist in 1992. He named it after the Sanskrit word *ananda*, which means bliss.

> *"The divine drink of chocolate builds up resistance and fights fatigue. A cup of this precious drink permits a man to walk all day without food."*
> —Hernán Cortés, Spanish conqueror of the Aztecs,
> in a letter to Charles V, king of Spain

> *"The superiority of chocolate both for health and nourishment will soon give it the same preference over tea and coffee in America which it has in Spain."*
> —Thomas Jefferson

Two other factors that also fit into the picture are serotonin and endorphins. These have been talked about often in the context of exercise, but they are important here. Serotonin is a chemical in the brain that is released after eating carbohydrates. It is a neurotransmitter that communicates a feeling of calm to the brain and helps to stabilize moods. Endorphins are another chemical that act to send high levels of energy and feelings of euphoria to the brain. In addition, endorphins have been shown to be effective painkillers, much like morphine. Both serotonin and endorphins are released when chocolate is eaten and, in turn, bring on a sense of well-being. If all of this is not enough, chocolate also contains magnesium, which helps the body manufacture serotonin, that all-important calming brain chemical. Chocolate also contains vitamins A1, B1, B2, C, D, and E, as well as calcium, potassium, sodium, and iron.

These chemical components present in chocolate may explain why some people crave chocolate more than others and certainly why we reach for chocolate when we're depressed. Interestingly, it's dark chocolate and milk

> "Whoever has drunk a cup of chocolate can endure a whole day's travel."
> —Johann Wolfgang von Goethe

chocolate that contain these compounds. They are absent from white chocolate, which contains cocoa butter, but no cocoa liquor (see "From the Bean to the Bar").

There's even more good news about chocolate. Although cocoa butter is a fat, it is derived from plant matter, so it contains no cholesterol. The fat in cocoa butter is stearic acid, which is a unique fatty acid that reacts differently than most fats and does not raise blood cholesterol levels. Also the phenols present in chocolate act as antioxidants, which inhibit oxygen from combining with other substances, most noticeably fat. So eating chocolate can block the bad effect that fats have on the body.

Some people are worried about the amount of caffeine in chocolate. As it turns out, there are only between five and ten milligrams of caffeine in one ounce of dark chocolate and only five milligrams in milk chocolate, the same as a cup of decaffeinated coffee. One cup of regular coffee contains between 100 and 150 milligrams of caffeine. Quite a difference.

Chocolate gets blamed for some health problems, but in reality the truth is otherwise. Chocolate does not cause acne. In fact, dermatologists have determined that diet has little to do with acne. Chocolate does not cause tooth decay, either. Cocoa contains substances that may inhibit the growth of bacteria that converts sugar into polysaccharides, which cause tooth decay. As long as the chocolate consumed is not too sugary and sticky, it will not harm the teeth. Studies have shown that chocolate causes less harm to teeth than other foods with the same amount of sugar.

Chocolate is not physically addictive, even though some people crave it. It tastes divine, which is reason enough to want to eat chocolate regularly. Even though you may think of yourself as a chocoholic, your body will not experience withdrawal if you stop eating chocolate.

On the other hand, headaches may be caused by the phenylethylamine (PEA) in chocolate because it dilates blood vessels in the brain, which can trigger migraines. But some cheeses and red wine contain the same substance. Chocolate can also promote heartburn by causing a backup of acids from the stomach into the esophagus.

If you are a chocoholic in need of resisting your favorite food, there is help available in the form of a stick-on patch. Liz Paul has developed Diet Scent Plasters, which are impregnated with the scent of a tropical orchid. Smelling the particular scent acts to make certain foods, in this case chocolate, easy to resist.

It appears from all the scientific studies and information available that chocolate is not "bad" for us. If eaten in moderation, it is actually good. Think about how good it makes you feel and you be the judge. Bon appétit!

". . . *In* the Indies, I comming in a heat to vitife a sick person, and asking water to refresh me, they persuaded me to take a draught of chocolate; which quencht my thirst: & in the morning (I took it fasting) it did warme and comfort my stomack."

—Antonio Colmenero de Ledesma, *Chocolate: or an Indian Drinke*, 1652

"*To* every 100 cacaos, you must put two cods of the long red Pepper, of which I have spoken before, and are called in the Indian tongue, chilparlangua, and instead of those of the Indies, you may take those of Spaine, which are broader, & less hot. One handful of annisseed orejnelas, which are otherwise called vinacaxlidos: add two of the flowers called mechasuchil, if the Belly be bound. But instead of this, in Spaine, we put in six roses of Alexandria beat to powder: One cod of Campeche, or Logwood: Two drams of cinnamon; Almons and Hasle-Nuts; of each one dozen: of white sugar, half-a-pound; of Achiote enough to give it the colour. And if you cannot have these things, which come from the Indies, you make it with the rest."

—Antonio Colmenero de Ledesma, *Chocolate: or an Indian Drinke*, 1652

"I recommend good chocolate to nervous, excitable persons. Also to the weak, debilitated, and infirm; to children and women. I have obtained excellent results from it in many cases of chronic diseases of the digestive organs."
—Christoph Wilhelm Hufeland, distinguished nineteenth-century physician

"Chocolate of good quality, well made, properly cooked, is one of the best aliments that I have yet found for my patients and for myself. This delicious food calms the fever, nourishes adequately the patient, and tends to restore him to health. I would even add that I attribute many cures of chronic dyspepsia to the regular use of Chocolate."
—François-Joseph-Victor Broussais, celebrated nineteenth-century physician and member of the French Institute

"Chocolate is not only proper to prolong the life of aged people, but also those whose constitution is lean and dry, or weak and cacochymical, or who use violent exercises, or whose employments oblige them to an intense application of mind, which makes them very faintish. To all these it agrees perfectly well, and becomes to them an altering diet."
—A French officer, author of a Natural History of Chocolate

CHOCOLATE LORE

In the ancient Quiché Maya *Popul Vuh* or "Book of Counsel," the story of the creation of the world is told. In this story the maize god meets his untimely demise in the underworld, and his head is hung in a cacao tree. The book also recounts the story of the Hero Twins, magically conceived by the severed head of the maize god and the daughter of the ruler of the underworld. She is exiled to the surface of the earth and gives birth to the Hero Twins. They have a series of heroic exploits, which include creating humans and the foods to sustain them. One of the achievements they are credited with is the invention of the methods for processing cacao beans so they can be consumed.

• • •

In Quiché Maya culture, during the marriage ceremony, cacao beans were exchanged by the bride and groom to signify their acceptance of each other.

• • •

In Aztec culture, chocolate was thought to be divine, having come to earth as a gift of the god Quetzalcoatl. Chocolate is still considered by many to be divine.

• • •

The Aztecs believed that wisdom and power came from eating cacao beans.

• • •

Chocolate has long been thought to be an aphrodisiac. It is said that the Aztec ruler Montezuma drank fifty cups of chocolate a day from golden goblets, usually before visiting his harem.

• • •

Chocolate was revered by the Aztecs who preferred it to their other native drink, octli, because it was nonalcoholic.

• • •

In Aztec song and poetry, chocolate was symbolic of luxury and sensuality.

• • •

Chocolate is valued as a quick source of energy. Even Napoleon I thought so because he is reputed to have carried it with him on military campaigns to eat when he needed an energy boost.

• • •

Chocolate is associated with love. Eating chocolate can make you feel a similar euphoria because it contains phenylethylamine (PEA), a naturally occurring substance that releases the same endorphins in the brain. Feeling blue and lonesome are great excuses for indulging in chocolate.

The Italian lover Giovanni Casanova favored chocolate as an aid in his seduction of women. In his memoirs he mentioned often that he liked to drink a cup of chocolate for breakfast.

"It's not that chocolates are a substitute for love. Love is a substitute for chocolate. Chocolate is, let's face it, far more reliable than a man."
—Miranda Ingram

The Ganong Brothers of Saint Stephen, New Brunswick, Canada, are reputed to have created the first candy bar in 1910. However, Milton Hershey is reputed to have had a candy bar on the market in 1894. And to further muddy the waters, Squirrel Brand of Cambridge, Massachusetts, created a peanut candy bar in 1906. Which of these is the true creator of the candy bar is hard to tell.

• • •

For over two centuries, there was a raging ecclesiastical debate about whether the taking of chocolate was a drink or a food. If it was considered a food, then indulging was breaking the Lenten fast. Several popes were consulted, including Gregory XIII, Paul V, Pius V, and Benedict XIV. They all said it was a drink. Finally the argument was put to rest when in 1662 the Bishop of Rome, Cardinal Francesco Maria Brancaccio, pronounced that even though chocolate was nourishing, it was considered a drink and as such did not break the fast.

Death by Chocolate

In seventeenth-century Chiapas, Mexico, upper-class women found themselves so hungry during mass that they were unable to continue without a cup of hot chocolate to sustain them. Their maids brought the hot chocolate during the service, which was disruptive. The bishop of Chiapas warned the ladies several times to stop, but they ignored him. Out of desperation he declared that he would excommunicate anyone who continued this practice. Oddly, it was not long before the bishop died from drinking a cup of hot chocolate that had been poisoned.

A tale recounted in 1625 by Thomas Gage, an English friar living in New Spain

• • •

In Baroque Spain chocolate was used to disguise the taste of poison. A popular story that circulated in seventeenth-century France told of a Spanish noblewoman who was deceived by her lover and retaliated by feeding him a poisoned cup of chocolate. The story goes that he drank it, and upon collapsing complained that the poison gave the chocolate a bitter taste and it would have been better if she had added more sugar.

COCOA
FUTURES

Are you the betting type? If so, do you want to bet that chocolate will be more popular in the near future? It's easy enough—all you need to do is buy some cocoa futures and hope they go up in price within a fixed period of time, then sell them at the higher price. You pocket the difference, which is your profit, and you can use it to buy more cocoa futures or simply buy more ready-to-eat chocolates.

Here's how it works. You must first open an account with a broker who can do business with the Coffee, Sugar & Cocoa Exchange in New York City or the London International Financial Futures and Options Exchange. You then place your buy order through the broker who has someone at the exchange actually place the order. For example, you may ask your broker to buy a cocoa contract for ten metric tons of cocoa at a particular price per ton to be sold at a certain time in the future, usually no more than eighteen months from the purchase date. Then sit tight until the time comes for your contract to be sold. If the price of cocoa has gone up, as you hoped it would, you earn the difference from what you initially paid. And if the price goes down you lose the difference from what you initially paid. Because you have actually bought the cocoa, when your contract is up you must make sure that it is sold or you personally must take delivery. Beware that your garage may not be large enough to store a couple hundred two-hundred-pound sacks of cacao beans.

As with the stock market, there are many variations on buying and selling futures (including something called cocoa options). However most individual speculators follow the above formula. Please note that playing the futures markets is very risky. Do your research and get all the advice you can before placing your bets. Futures markets move in strange ways that sometimes seem to defy normal economic principles. The best bet for a sure thing is to stop by your local chocolate shop and buy directly over-the-counter.

For information about cocoa futures contact:

Coffee, Sugar & Cocoa Exchange, Inc.
4 World Trade Center
New York, NY 10048
Phone: (212) 742-6106
FAX: (212) 748-4321
E-mail: csce@ix.netcom.com
World Wide Web Address: www.csce.com

London International Financial Futures and Options Exchange
Cannon Bridge
London, EC4R 3XX
United Kingdom
Phone: 011 44 171 623 0444
FAX: 011 44 171 588 3624
E-mail: cocoa@liffe.com
World Wide Web Address: www.liffe.com

PART II

All About Where to Find Chocolate

CHOCOLATE FESTIVALS, EVENTS, AND TRADE SHOWS

How to spot a chocoholic: Someone who is grumpy because they haven't had their "chocolate fix" for the day. You know you are one if you can't go more than a few hours without thinking about and desiring chocolate.

Events

January

THE BLACKHAWK CHOCOLATE TRAIL

Northwestern Illinois

A four-county region offers a self-guided tour of fifteen sweet and treat shops that meanders through the Blackhawk waterway. Included are cafes, candy stores, general stores, restaurants, tearooms, bakeries, gift stores, and old-fashioned soda fountains. Many offer free samples. Also on the chocolate trail are award-winning bed and breakfasts (Sharon Burdick of Pinehill Bed & Breakfast listed below is the originator of the Blackhawk Chocolate Trail) and country inns. Every January 15 the Blackhawk Chocolate Trail Treasure prizes are awarded, drawn from those who have visited ten or more of the shops and have received the shops' stamps on their cards. These are submitted to the Convention and Visitors Bureau to be entered in the prize drawing. First prize is $100, second $50, and third $25 in Blackhawk Chocolate gift certificates.

Contact: **Blackhawk Waterways Convention and Visitors Bureau**
            Tel: (800) 678-2108

CHOCOLATE FEST

Knoxville, TN

This annual event is a benefit for the National Kidney Foundation of East Tennessee. The fest is sponsored by Aubrey's Cafe and takes place from 10 A.M. to 4 P.M. on the third or fourth Saturday in January at the East Towne Mall. For a $10 donation, each participant receives a flyer with a map of the vendors' locations and a page with boxes for each vendor to check off as they dispense their samples. Live entertainment and contests punctuate the day, along with cookie decorating and face painting.

Contact: **Helen Harb, Assistant Executive Director**
            National Kidney Foundation of East Tennessee, Inc.
            4450 Walker Blvd., Suite 2
            Knoxville, TN 37917
            Tel: (615) 688-5481
            FAX: (615) 688-0196
            E-mail: hharb1@korrnet.org

February

CELEBRATION OF CHOCOLATE TEAS AND ACCOMMODATIONS

Pinehill Bed & Breakfast
400 Mix Street
Oregon, IL 61061

During the month of February, Sharon Burdick, winner of the 1995 Illinois Governor's Award for Bed & Breakfast, Best Special Promotion, offers afternoon teas with a menu of top-quality European and American boxed chocolates and her own handmade historic Prairie confections, including the Pinehill Fudge collection, a large variety of exotically flavored, shaped, and decorated handmade fudge. A selection of chocolate-flavored beverages accompany the treats. There are also seasonal celebrations for Hanukkah, Kwanzaa, and Christmas. Fund-raising events such as Brownies at Brunch to benefit the Illinois prairie are scheduled at various times throughout the year. These delightful and delicious experiences take place in an 1874 Italianate country villa listed on the National Register of Historic Places.

Pinehill Bed & Breakfast offers five different themed rooms with private baths. Turndown service includes chocolate kisses on the pillows and chocolates are always available for nibbling. Innkeeper Sharon Burdick also maintains a large chocolate library.

Contact: **Sharon Burdick**
             Tel: (815) 732-2061

CHOCOLATE LOVERS WEEKEND

Hotel Hershey
Hershey, PA

This annual gathering of chocolate enthusiasts takes place during the weekend closest to Valentine's Day. Cupid's buffet dinner featuring chocolate in most courses, starts the weekend on Friday night. Daily breakfast features chocolate pancakes, croissants, bread pudding, and chocolate milk. A "choctail" reception includes outrageous chocolate confections and make-your-own chocolate sundaes. The Chocolate Gallery is a featured event where pastry chefs compete for prizes with their specialty chocolate desserts. Decadent samples of chocolate are offered in the Taste of the Valley event, which spotlights local merchants and their chocolate treats. Throughout the weekend there are a variety of workshops, demonstrations, and lectures all focused on chocolate with tastings available. Package price is $124 per person, per night (double occupancy), which includes daily breakfast and dinner, workshops, receptions, and accommodations.

Contact: **Hotel Hershey**
                  Tel: (800) 437-7439 (information)
                  (800) 533-3131 (reservations)
                  (717) 533-2171

CHOCOLATES OF THE WORLD

English Oak Room at The Avenue at Tower City
Cleveland, OH

This annual event is sponsored by the Cleveland Council on World Affairs. The main mission is to educate the public on the topic of chocolate. Many aspects of this delectable topic are explored during the day-long presentations, such as chocolate history, uses of chocolate, and chocolate's role in the global economy. Several chocolate companies participate and provide samples such as Cacao Barry, Godiva, Harry London, Lindt & Sprüngli, M & M Mars, and Prairie Confections. For an admission fee of $5 per adult or $10 per family (two adults, two children) you can attend all of the day's lectures and tasting events.

Contact: Cleveland Council on World Affairs
             Tel: (216) 781-3730
             Internet: www.ccwa.org/cowII.html
             E-mail: info@ccwa.org

CHOCOLATE FESTIVAL

Browning Mansion, Kellogg and North Streets
Galesburg, IL

This annual event benefits the Galesburg Historical Society. It is held at the Browning Mansion, home of the Historical Society, on the weekend closest to Valentine's Day. The two-day event is open from 11 A.M. to 4 P.M. and a donation of $6 per person, per visit is suggested. The chocolate cakes, cookies, candies, and confections are made primarily by local Historical Society members. Some commercially made chocolates are also available, such as Fannie Mae and Godiva chocolates. Once inside, attendees are free to eat as much as they can on the premises.

Contact: **Raleigh Barnstead**
             Tel: (309) 343-2925

CHOCOLATE FANTASY FAIR

Columbus Convention Center
Columbus, OH

In its fourteenth year (1998) this one-day annual event takes place every February on the Sunday before Valentine's Day. It is a fund-raiser for the Central Ohio Breathing Association. For $5 per adult, eight tickets are issued that can be exchanged for tastes from the vendors who offer a wide variety of chocolate candy, cookies, cakes, and ice cream. There are also chocolates for sale by the vendors, most of whom are major chocolate manufacturers. Between six thousand and ten thousand people attend this popular chocolate event. For patrons of the Breathing Association, the event includes an opening brunch featuring a large chocolate bar for dessert.

Contact: **Central Ohio Breathing Association**
Tel: (414) 457-4570

FETZER VINEYARDS RED WINE & CHOCOLATE SPECTACULAR

Fetzer Vineyards
Hopland, CA

The weekend before Valentine's Day has been set aside for the past thirteen years for this red wine and chocolate event at the Fetzer Vineyards tasting room in Hopland, in Mendocino county, north of San Francisco. Admission is free, but there is an $8 per person charge for wine and chocolate tasting, which includes a souvenir glass. The winemakers are present to lead the tastings of vintage Fetzer red wines. Truffles, chocolate-dipped strawberries, and fine-quality chocolate accompany the tasting. Live music is part of the weekend festivities and discounts are offered on select Fetzer and Bonterra wines.

Contact: **Fetzer Vineyards Tasting Room & Visitor Center**
Tel: (800) 846-8637

FIREHOUSE ART CENTER CHOCOLATE FESTIVAL

Firehouse Art Center
University of Oklahoma Campus
Norman, OK

In its seventeenth year (1998), this annual festival takes place in February the Saturday before Valentine's Day. There is a gala dinner event with entertainment and chocolate desserts for an admission fee of $35 per person. A Chocolate Art Competition is part of the festivities. For an admission fee of $12 per person a book of ten tickets is issued, which can be exchanged for tastes of the chocolate desserts provided by area restaurants.

Contact: **Firehouse Art Center**
Tel: (405) 329-4523

CHOCOLATE LOVER'S FANTASY

Lincoln, NE

This annual event, now in its twelfth year (1998), takes place in February on the Sunday before Valentine's Day at the Ramada Plaza Hotel. It is a fund-raiser for the Historic Haymarket District, an area in downtown Lincoln that has been completely restored and listed on the National Register of Historic Places, and for its joint partner, the Special Olympics. Doors open for the evening event at 5 P.M. and close at 9 P.M. Admission for all-you-can-eat is $10 per person. About forty local chefs and celebrities either prepare chocolate treats or represent companies who donate chocolate for tasting. Water, milk, and other drinks are available, as well as salty treats such as pretzels and potato chips to assist in cleaning palates in between chocolate tastes. A silent auction with a wide variety of items helps raise money for the beneficiaries of the event.

Contact: **Downtown Lincoln Association**
Tel: (402) 434-6900
FAX: (402) 434-6907

TASTE OF CHOCOLATE

Radisson South Hotel
Bloomington, MN

This annual gathering of several hundred chocolate lovers is a fund-raising benefit for the Bloomington Fine Arts Council. Now in its fourth year (1998), the event takes place on the Sunday before Valentine's Day from 2 to 5 P.M. Eight to ten of the upscale local restaurants participate and provide tastes of their specialty chocolate desserts. The desserts are entered in a competition and judged by local food critics and food specialists, such as cooking school owners and food media people. Prize plaques are awarded for the categories of Best Dessert, Best Presentation, and People's Choice. For the entry fee of $10, attendees receive a taste of each dessert and enjoy the performances of dancers, musicians, and choral groups who are members of the Fine Arts Council. The Radisson Hotel, cosponsor of the event, provides a nonchocolate dessert as well as coffee, tea, and water. Tickets are available in advance and at the door the day of the event.

Contact: **Kate Pettit**
Bloomington Fine Arts Council
Tel: (612) 835-5227

RED WINE AND CHOCOLATE CELEBRATION

Yakima Valley, WA

More than twenty wineries throughout the Yakima Valley participate in this annual celebration. The event takes place from 10 A.M. to 5 P.M. on the weekend closest to Valentine's Day. Each winery serves a different chocolate delight along with its selection of red wines. This free event is open to the public who are invited to visit as many wineries as they like.

Contact: **Yakima Valley Vintners Association**
Tel: (800) 258-7270

American Chocolate Week is always the third full week in March every year.

May

CHOCOLATE CITY FESTIVAL

Festival Grounds
Burlington, WI

This annual event takes place at the home of Nestlé chocolate and is organized by the Chocolate City Festival, a nonprofit organization. Now in its twelfth year (1998), the festival is held in May on the weekend following Mother's Day. Friday evening and all day Saturday and Sunday vendors display their chocolates and offer samples. The vendors are primarily commercial chocolate companies. There is a wide variety of entertainment throughout the weekend, including live bands, big-name entertainers, rides, and games. On Sunday a Chocolate City parade takes place in downtown. The admission fee for each day of the festival is $5. Children age twelve and under attend free.

Contact: **Chocoholic Hotline (Burlington Chamber of Commerce)**
            Tel: (414) 763-6044

FANTASIES IN CHOCOLATE

Reno, NV

An annual chocolate black-tie extravaganza sponsored by the Reno *Gazette-Journal*. The event takes place in early May at the Reno Hilton. Included in the admission fee of $25 are chocolate sampling, champagne tasting, music, and a silent auction. Several local chocolatiers, pastry shops, and restaurants provide samples of their specialty chocolate desserts, pastries, and confections. Proceeds benefit the Lend-A-Hand foundation of northern Nevada.

Contact: **Janis Laycox, Coordinator**
Reno Gazette-Journal
P.O. Box 22000
Reno, NV 89520
Tel: (702) 788-6434

A CHOCOLATE LOVER'S TOUR OF BELGIUM

In May 1997 FPT tours led a week-long tour visiting Brussels, Bruges, and Antwerp, home of some of the world's finest chocolate manufacturers. Included were cooking demonstrations and visits to chocolate kitchens usually closed to tourists, visits to markets, and an optional excursion to Eupen and Cologne to visit the Chocolate Museum. Other tours are planned for 1999 for Belgium, France, and Switzerland.

Contact: **Diana Altman**
FPT Special Interest Tours
Tel: (800) 645-0001
(617) 476-1142 in MA
FAX: (617) 661-3354
E-mail: dma@fpt.com

June

THE SINGLE GOURMET CHOCOLATE FANTASY
TOUR OF EUROPE

In 1997 the group sponsored a ten-day tour of The Netherlands, Belgium, and Switzerland visiting world-famous chocolate and cocoa factories, and artisanal chocolate shops and confiseries for single people. Lodging was in four-star hotels.

Contact: The Single Gourmet
            133 East 58th Street
            New York, NY 10022
            Tel: (212) 980-8788
            FAX: (212) 980-3138

August

CHOCOLATE FEST

St. Stephen, New Brunswick, Canada

This annual Chocolate Festival in the home of the Ganong chocolate factory (Canada's Candy Town), has been taking place during the first week of August since 1985. The Great Chocolate Mousse is their mascot and symbol. A week of chocolate activities include tours of the Ganong chocolate factory, hand-dipping demonstrations, concerts, The Great Chocolate Mousse Chocolate Chip Cookie Decorating Contest, lumberjack competitions, an ice cream social, chocolate bingo, a candy and treasure hunt, chocolate mania games, craft and food sale, and a variety of breakfasts, luncheons, and cocktail parties. Prices vary according to the events, but are very reasonable.

Contact: Chocolate Fest
P.O. Box 5002
St. Stephen, New Brunswick E3L 2X5
Canada
Tel: (506) 465-5616
Internet: www.pcsolutions.nb.ca/ganong

September

MICHIGAN RENAISSANCE FESTIVAL CHOCOLATE FESTIVAL

Holly, MI

An annual one-day event that takes place during the Sweet Endings weekend at the end of the Renaissance Festival. Several local chocolatiers provide free samples and also sell their wares to the festival attendees. The $13.95 per person admission fee to the Renaissance Festival include entrance to the Chocolate Festival. The Tournament of Temptations, a professional competition also takes place during this weekend, and is open to the public for viewing and tasting.

Contact: **Michigan Renaissance Festival**
120 South Saginaw
Holly, MI 48442
Tel: (248) 634-5552
FAX: (248) 634-7590

October

EUROCHOCOLATE

Late October in Perugia, Italy; Amsterdam, The Netherlands; and Copenhagen, Denmark

An annual chocolate extravaganza organized by a group of dedicated chocolate enthusiasts and professionals. The main events take place in Perugia, Italy. The festival features workshops and seminars about chocolate, chocolate techniques, and the psychological, social, and historical importance of chocolate. Chocolate tastings, exhibits, Eurochocolate awards, chocolate competitions, a chocolate photography contest, an international chocolate gallery and bazaar, and many special events are all part of the nine-day event. Events, exhibits, and tastings are ongoing from early in the day until late in the evening. There are several events planned for children. Maps printed on special cocoa-flavored paper provide all the information and a schedule of the events at over two hundred locations throughout Perugia.

Contact: **Eugenio Guarducci, Director**
Eurochocolate
Tel: (011 39 75) 573-2625
FAX: (011 39 75) 573-1100
Internet: www.chocolate.perugia.it
E-mail: cpc@chocolate.perugia.it

HUDSON VALLEY SWEETEST SEASON CHOCOLATE FESTIVAL

Poughkeepsie, NY

1997 was the first of this annual event that takes place in mid-October when the leaves are at their peak of color. The one-day event is a fund-raiser for the Junior League of Poughkeepsie. For a fee of $15 per person you can participate in chocolate tastings offered by many chocolate companies and several local restaurants, chocolate classes by Certified Master Pastry Chef Joe McKenna, Certified Master Chef Fritz Sonnenschmidt, and celebrity chefs, entertainment, and exhibitions. For a fee of $50 you can attend the premiere event, which features a lecture by a renowned wine expert on pairing wine and chocolate, meet the lecturer, other teaching chefs, and celebrity chefs, taste wine with chocolate, participate in a silent auction, and possibly win a door prize, as well as attend all other events. The Chocolate Festival takes place at the Culinary Institute of America. Future plans include a Chocolate Festival Weekend, a Chocolate Ball, and a professional pastry chef competition.

Contact: **Junior League of Poughkeepsie**
Tel/FAX: (914) 471-5330

CHOCOLATE TEMPTATION

Red Rooster Inn
Hillsboro, IL

This annual event is always held on Sweetest Day, a new holiday to celebrate those who have been nice to us, on the third Saturday in October, from 9 A.M. to 3 P.M. 1998 marks the twelfth year. Often there is a tie-in with another local event. Past festivals have included a chocolate banquet and a chocolate cocktail party. Local vendors, highlighting small artisan chocolate companies, showcase their wares and provide samples to those who attend. There is no admission charge. A bake-off is one of the highlights, judged by a media person and a local home economist. All the prizes are chocolate-related and relevant to each year's particular theme.

Contact: **Mary Francis**
Red Rooster Inn
123 East Seward Street
Hillsboro, IL 62049
Tel: (217) 532-6332

November

CHOCOLATE LOVER'S WEEKEND

Ritz-Carlton Hotel
Marina del Rey, CA

Chocolate connoisseurs and enthusiasts gather for a weekend of chocolate demonstrations, cooking classes, tastings, and indulgences in mid-November. Valrhona Chocolate sponsors the weekend of delicious festivities, which is a weekend for the World Pastry Cup to practice and hone their skills. You can attend the entire weekend or choose particular events. There is a separate fee for each event. On Friday evening start off with a champagne and chocolate reception to honor the World Pastry Cup team. Saturday morning offers cooking demonstrations and a hands-on class. In the afternoon attend tastings of tea and chocolate, cognac and chocolate, or pink champagne and chocolate. In the evening a Discovery Dinner features a six-course meal highlighting chocolate in every course. Sunday brings a Chocolate Decadence Brunch with a chocolate sculpture and ice sculpture centerpiece created by the World Pastry Cup team, as well as a sumptuous spread.

Contact: **The Ritz-Carlton, Marina del Rey**
4375 Admiralty Way
Marina del Rey, CA 90292
Tel: (310) 823-1700, ext. 5121
FAX: (310) 823-8241

IN CELEBRATION OF CHOCOLATE

Kohler, WI

In its fourteenth year (1998) this annual event for chocolate lovers takes place in late November or early December at the American Club, a top-class resort, from 7 to 9 P.M. Each year the one-night indulgence has a different theme that directs the menu, devised and executed by Executive Pastry Chef Richard Palm and his staff. The party is not formal, but cocktail dress is expected. An entrance fee of $35 per person gives unlimited access to buffet tables replete with a large variety of chocolate desserts, pastries, and confections. There are also Perugina and Godiva chocolates available for tasting. The event is limited to 450 participants and sells out quickly each year.

Contact: **The American Club**
            Tel: (800) 344-2838
            (414) 457-8000

December

BRACH'S KIDS' HOLIDAY PARADE

Chicago, IL

For over thirteen years, this popular parade has been taking place on the Saturday after Thanksgiving from noon to 2 P.M. Over one hundred floats and exhibits, fifteen marching bands, and ten helium-filled floats, all with themes that appeal to children, wind through the streets of downtown Chicago. Loads of Brach's candy is distributed to spectators. Several large companies sponsor this holiday event and there is no admission charge. Many celebrities participate in the parade.

Contact: **Production Contractors**
            Tel: (773) 935-8747

Professional Trade Shows

THE PHILADELPHIA NATIONAL CANDY, GIFT & GOURMET SHOW

September 13, 14, 15, 1998; January 10, 11, 12, 1999;
August 29, 30, 31, 1999

Twice-yearly trade show sponsored by Retail Confectioners Association of Philadelphia, Inc. Held at Valley Forge Convention and Exhibit Center, Valley Forge, PA. Included are booths, exhibits, roundtable discussions, and seminars.

Contact: **Retail Confectioners Association of Philadelphia**
Tel: (610) 265-4888
FAX: (610) 265-4689

ALL CANDY EXPO

Navy Pier
Chicago, IL

Sponsored by the National Confectioners Association. Every June for four days this trade show combines the Candy Buyers Expo and the Equipment, Ingredient, and Supply Expo. Factory tours, workshops, and continuing education classes are offered in addition to networking opportunities.

Contact: **National Confectioners Association**
7900 Westpark Drive, Suite A-320
McLean, VA 22102
Tel: (800) 433-1200
(703) 790-5750
FAX: (703) 790-5750
E-mail: info@candyusa.org

FANCY FOOD SHOW

Jacob Javits Convention Center, New York, NY
Moscone Convention Center, San Francisco, CA

This trade show is held every summer in late June or early July (July 11–14, 1999) in New York and in San Francisco every winter in late January or February (January 17–19, 1999). The first spring show is planned for Chicago in 1999 (March 21–23). The Fancy Food Show is the premiere event that showcases specialty foods from both large and small manufacturers primarily from throughout the United States, but exhibitors are also present from Canada, Italy, the United Kingdom, and other countries. Food celebrities and cookbook authors also make appearances.

Contact: **The National Association for the Specialty Food Trade (NASFT)**
120 Wall Street
New York, NY 10005-4001
Tel: (212) 482-6440
FAX: (212) 482-6459

THE WEST COAST CANDY AND CONFECTIONS EXPO

Held every August at the Disneyland Hotel in Anaheim, CA (August 15–17, 1999), this three-day event showcases purveyors of chocolate, candy, cake-decorating, and gift-basket products, as well as chocolate equipment and supplies to support producers and retailers. Admission is free to attendees. Exhibitors need to contact the show management for fees.

Contact: **Comprehensive Show Management, Inc.**
P.O. Box 297
Springfield, PA 19064
Tel: (610) 544-5775
FAX: (610) 544-9808

THE INTERNATIONAL PASTRY & SPECIALTY BAKING FAIR

Various locations regionally around the United States

January and late August or early September

Held in conjunction with the Chef des Chef Trade Show & Conference, this is a two-day conference that includes demonstrations and educational seminars taught by industry leaders. A trade show with exhibitors showing their equipment and ingredients, as well as other products also takes place. One of the days of the show is always on Monday so working chefs can attend. Attendees can earn continuing education credits toward ACF certification by attending the seminars and are issued a certificate upon completion of the conference. Fees, which include admission to all events, demonstrations, and seminars plus a reception the first evening of the conference, are: $295 per person; $120 for students and instructors upon submission of verification of status.

Contact: **Von Rabenau Productions**
20 North Wacker Drive, Suite 1865
Chicago, IL 60606
Tel: (800) 299-1967, ext. 69
(312) 849-2220, ext. 27
FAX: (312) 849-2174

CHOCOLATE MUSEUMS, ATTRACTIONS, THEME PARKS, AND FACTORY TOURS

Cadbury World
Linden Road
Bournville, England
Tel: (011 44 121) 451-4159

Hours: Daily throughout the year: 10 A.M. to 5:30 P.M.

Admission: Adult £5
                Senior citizens £4.35
                Children under 5 free
                Children 5 to 15 years £3.45
                Family ticket (2 adults, 2 children) £14.50
                Family ticket (2 adults, 3 children) £17.50

People call a visit to Cadbury World "Chocolate Paradise." You can watch, smell, and taste chocolate as it is produced by hand and see their Luxury Assortment created, decorated, and packaged. Also included is a visit to the Cadbury factory packaging plant to view bars of chocolate wrapped and packed. The Cadbury Collection is a separate exhibition that tells more of the Cadbury story and the history of the Bournville villages. There is the Robert Opie Collection of Cadbury Packaging, "Sweet Delights," a replica of a 1930s sweet shop, and a film show of *The Bournville Story*. Another exhibit is titled Aztec Secrets, and re-creates a Central American rain forest where cacao was first grown. You can sample the spicy drink *chocolatl* and learn about the ingredients with Montezuma. The exhibit traces the story of chocolate throughout Europe to Birmingham. It shows how John Cadbury began to use cocoa and how he created the famous Cadbury's Dairy Milk chocolate bar. See how Cadbury makes chocolate and creates their world-famous products today.

Chocolate Cascade
    The Candy Basket
    1924 NE 181st Avenue
    Portland, OR 97230
    Tel: (800) 864-1924, (503) 555-2000

Located in the lobby of the Candy Basket Chocolate Factory, this is the only known chocolate fountain in the world. Two thousand eight hundred pounds of chocolate are heated day and night to maintain proper viscosity so that it can cascade twenty-one feet over sculpted marble and bronze and create the sounds of a surging chocolate fall. Designed by Marc Accuardi and engineered by Dale Fuhr, this dream of owner Dick Fuhr took six months to construct.

Chocolaterie S.A. Jacques N.V.

Industriestrasse 16
B-4700 Eupen, Belgium
Tel: (011 32 0) 87.59.29.11
FAX: (011 32 0) 87.59.29.29

Hours: Monday through Friday: 9 A.M. to 5 P.M.;
       Saturday: 11 A.M. to 5 P.M.;
       closed Sundays and holidays

Admission: 50 Belgian francs per person
       1 Belgian franc each for a group of 20 or more
       Children under 6 admitted free

Tours last one hour. Reservations are required for a guided tour. Tours include visits to the museum, production facility, and tasting of chocolates. For tour information contact Ms. Cecchini: Tel: (011 32 0) 87.59.29.67.

Ethel M Chocolate Factory Tours

Ethel M Chocolate Factory
One Sunset Way
Henderson, NV 89014
Tel: (702) 433-2500
FAX: (702) 451-8379
Internet: www.ethelm.com
E-mail: chocolatier@ethelm.com

Admission: Free

Self-guided tours are ongoing from 8:30 A.M. to 7 P.M. every day, except Christmas. A free sample of Ethel M chocolates is offered during the tour. Over 800,000 people per year tour this factory located in a suburb of Las Vegas, Nevada.

Haigh's Chocolate Factory Tours
Haigh's Chocolates
154 Greenhill Road
Parkside (near Adelaide) South Australia 5063
Tel: (011 61 8) 8271 3770
FAX: (011 61 8) 8373 0528

Admission: Free

Tours are held Monday through Saturday at 2:30 P.M. and last approximately twenty minutes. Tours include excellent viewing of chocolate manufacturing and candy production. Tastings and a visit to heritage displays of original packaging, old machinery, and early photographs follow the tour. The retail store is open for chocolate tastings, browsing, and purchasing freshly made chocolates and confections. Groups are welcome but do need to reserve in advance.

Harry London Chocolate Factory Tours
Harry London Chocolate Factory
5353 Lauby Road
North Canton, OH 44720
Tel: (800) 321-0444, (330) 494-0833
FAX: (330) 499-6902

Hours: Tours Monday through Saturday every hour from 9 A.M. to 4 P.M.;
Sunday every hour from noon to 3:30 P.M.
Reservations are suggested for groups.

Admission: Adults $2.00
Students 6 to 18 years $1.00
Children under 6 years free

Tours last approximately one to one-and-a-half hours and are held daily, year round. Guided tours in the eighty-thousand-square-foot facility include samples of chocolates as they are made, strolling the Chocolate Hall of Fame, and visiting the Chocolate Store, the Midwest's largest, with over five hundred varieties of chocolate and gourmet candies.

Hershey Town, USA, "The Sweetest Place on Earth"
19 East Chocolate Avenue
Hershey, PA 17033
Tel: (800) HERSHEY (437-7439) for information about attractions
    (800) 533-3131 for information about lodging
Internet: www.800hershey.com/park/index.html
E-mail: hersheyparkpublicrelations

Hours: 10 A.M. to 10 P.M. during the summer months

Admission: Ages 3 to 8 and over 55, $15.95
          Ages 9 to 54, $26.45

Hershey's Chocolate World lets you explore the art of chocolate making during a twelve-minute simulated factory tour ride. The Hershey Museum introduces you to chocolate king Milton S. Hershey and tells about his life, businesses, and his unique creation of Hershey town.

Hershey Park is a world-class theme park with over twenty rides and attractions.

The Imhoff-Stollwerck Museum
Rheinauhafen
50678 Cologne, Germany
Tel: (011 49 221) 931888-0
FAX: (011 49 221) 931888-14

Hours: Tuesday through Friday: 10 A.M. to 6 P.M.;
        Saturday, Sunday, and holidays: 11 A.M. to 7 P.M.

Chocolate production: 10:30 A.M. to 5:15 P.M.

Admission: Adults 10,00 DM
        Reduced rate 5,00 DM (children, students, military, handi-
        capped, senior citizens over 60, and Stollwerck employees)
        Group rates (15 people or more): Per adult 9,00 DM

Walk-in guided tours: Saturday: 2:00 and 4:00 P.M.;
        Sunday and holidays: 11:30 A.M., 2:00 P.M., 4:00 P.M.
        Children's tours: 3:00 P.M.

Tour price per person: 3,00 DM plus regular admission price
        Reduced rate: 4,50 DM

Exhibits include a historical and cultural view of chocolate from three thousand years ago to the present. Chocolate and cocoa packaging and products are included, as well as porcelain and silver chocolate services. A photographic exhibit traces the stages of chocolate from its origins to cultivation and harvest. In a two-story chocolate production facility view how chocolate is processed and made into a myriad of products such as bars, truffles, and hollow-molded figures. Taste chocolate at the fountain that flows with warm chocolate.

The museum also has a chocolate shop and a restaurant overlooking the Rhine that serves chocolate desserts and beverages.

La Cabosse d'Or Miniature Golf Theme Park
973, Ozias Leduc
Otterburn Park, Quebec J3G 4S6, Canada
Tel: (800) 784-6937, (514) 464-6937
FAX: (514) 464-9933
Internet: www.cabossedor.qc.ca

Hours: Summer months: 10 A.M. to 9 P.M.;
    spring and fall open weekends only
    Groups can call in advance to arrange times to attend the park.

Admission: Adults $5.00
    Children to 7 years $3.50
    Children under 7 years $1.00

A 115,000-square-foot miniature golf course with a chocolate theme situated next to the famed chocolate house near Quebec City. Each hole has a plaque with information, written in both English and French, on the history, cultivation, and processing of chocolate.

Melba's Chocolates
Heritage Park
Henry Street
Woodside, South Australia 5244
Tel: (011 61 8) 8389 7868
FAX: (011 61 8) 8389 7977

Hours: Monday through Friday: 10:00 A.M. to 4 P.M.;
    Saturday, Sunday, and holidays: noon to 5 P.M.

Admission: Free

Self-guided tours of this facility include viewing old-fashioned chocolate-making equipment and seeing chocolate made in the time-honored fashion. Tastings of the chocolate and a visit to the retail shop follow the tour. Any size group is welcome, but appointments are recommended.

Nestlé Suisse S.A.
1636 Broc (Gruyere), Switzerland
Tel: (011 41 26) 921.51.51
FAX: (011 41 26) 921.55.25

Hours: Monday: 1:30 P.M. to 4 P.M.;
   Tuesday through Friday: 9 A.M. to 4 P.M.
   Saturday in late August through mid-September: 9 A.M. to 4 P.M.

Admission: Free

By appointment only from mid-April through October, visits can be made to the factory that include a forty-minute film presentation of chocolate manufacture, viewing a chocolate workshop, tasting chocolates, and a visit to the chocolate shop. Presentations are scheduled every half hour.

SchokoLand Alprose—The World of Chocolate
Chocolat Alprose S.A.
Via Rompada, P.O. Box 147
CH-6987 Caslano-Lugano, Switzerland
Tel: (011 41 91) 71.66.66, 606.66.66, 606.61.43
FAX: (011 41 91) 71.51.85

Hours: Monday through Friday: 9 A.M. to 6 P.M.;
   Saturday and Sunday: 9 A.M. to 5 P.M.

Admission: Adults 3 Swiss francs
    Children 6 to 16 years 1 Swiss franc
    Groups of 10 or more free
    Advance booking strongly recommended for a
    guided tour

Sponsored by the Alprose Chocolate Company, this museum includes photographs, chocolate utensils, antique chocolate vending machines, and a tasting tour through its factory. A unique feature of the museum is the catwalk through its chocolate factory.

Wilbur Chocolate Candy Americana Museum
48 North Broad Street
Lititz, PA 17543
Tel: (717) 626-3249
FAX: (717) 626-3487

Hours: Monday through Saturday: 10 A.M. to 5 P.M.

Admission: Free

On a self-guided tour through this museum you can enjoy displays of unusual and antique candy packaging items, cocoa tins, advertisements, candy-making equipment and chocolate pots collected from all over the world. Many of the chocolate pots date from the 1700s and come from Dresden and Limoges. In the candy kitchen view candy made by hand, the old-fashioned way. A video presentation takes you through the process of Wilbur chocolate manufacturing. The Candy Americana factory store offers free tastes of Wilbur Buds and has a large selection of chocolate items for sale.

CHOCOLATE COMPETITIONS

SOUTHERN PASTRY CLASSIC

Annually, every February in Atlanta, Georgia
Sponsored by Barry Callebaut Chocolate and RaviFruit; organized by Classic Gourmet, Atlanta

The event also includes a full-day educational seminar on topics such as sorbets, wedding cakes, and rolled fondant.

Each participant prepares:
1. Chocolate sculpture or centerpiece
2. Chocolate cake
3. Plated chocolate dessert
4. Six candies or truffles

All entries must be made entirely of edible ingredients and decorations. Two hours are allowed for set up in the morning.

Participants are judged on these skills:
1. Taste and texture: 50 percent
2. Presentation and creative use of Barry Callebaut products:
   50 percent

Judging is done by a panel of eight judges consisting of pastry chefs and executive chefs. The top three qualify to compete in the national Masters du Chocolat competition held in Philadelphia every September.

Prizes:
- Winner qualifies to participate in the finals of the Masters du Chocolat Competition in Philadelphia in September
- $300 cash
- All-expense paid course at Cacao Barry School in New Jersey
- Trophy

Contact: David Kee at Classic Gourmet, Atlanta, GA
Tel: (404) 767-7655

MICHIGAN STATE UNIVERSITY NEW MUSEUM MASTERPIECE CHOCOLATE COMPETITION

Annually, first Sunday in February at the MSU Kellogg Center, East Lansing, as part of the Museum Chocolate Party Fund Raiser.
Sponsored by Great Lakes Gourmet, U.S. Pastry Alliance, Barry Callebaut Chocolate, and Patisfrance Chocolate

Prospective participants must submit recipes in advance and release them to be included in the MSU Museum Chocolate Party Cookbook, which will be sold to raise funds for the museum. Both amateurs and professionals can compete.

Each is separated into four categories:
1. Cakes and tortes
2. Cheesecakes
3. Other (edible)
4. Display

Judging criteria and scoring for all categories:
Each category is scored from 1 to 5 points. Five points is the top score in each category, with a total of 30 points available. Best of Show is determined by the highest score from combining the scoring sheets of all judges.

1. Visual appearance
2. Taste, flavor, aroma
3. Artistic presentation and technique (for the display category these are two separate categories to replace number 2, taste, flavor, and aroma)
4. Creativity
5. Originality
6. Theme (specified each year)

Judges: Professional and Masterpiece entries are judged by ten to twelve professional chefs and industry professionals. Amateur entries are judged by ten to twelve celebrity judges and industry professionals. There is also a Professional Chef's Choice award given to the amateur entry given the most points by the professional judges. The celebrity judges award the Celebrity Judges Choice to the highest point scorer in the Professional and Masterpiece categories.

Prizes for both amateur and professional levels:
First Place: $1,000 and a trophy
Second Place: $500 plus a tuition of up to $500 for any seminar at the Cacao Barry Chocolate School in New Jersey
Third Place: $250
Special Prize: $500 for best utilization of Patisfrance Couverture Chocolate sponsored by Patisfrance
Best of Show: One round-trip airline ticket on Northwest Airlines in the continental United States

All chocolate for the competition is donated by Patisfrance.
Entry fee is $35 per person for professional and $20 per person for amateurs.
Culinary students can compete in the amateur category.

Contact: **Michigan State University Chocolate Party**
Tom Chaput
Great Lakes Gourmet
12130 Greenfield Road
Detroit, MI 48227
Tel: (313) 270-4433
FAX: (313) 270-4570

MICHIGAN RENAISSANCE FESTIVAL
TOURNAMENT OF TEMPTATIONS

Chocolate Sculpture Competition
Annually, last weekend of September in Holly, MI

Sponsored by Pioneer Sugar and held in cooperation with the American Culinary Federation as a fund-raising event for the ACF's charity, The Chef and the Child Foundation

The cost to enter the competition is $25 per entry, which includes admission to the Renaissance Festival. Entrants must submit their recipes in advance in writing. Judging is done by a team of professional chefs and media celebrities.

All entries are judged on:
1. Visual appearance
2. Taste, flavor, and aroma
3. Creativity
4. Originality
5. Theme (specified each year)

All entries are automatically judged for Best of Show, which has a prize of $1,000. Medals are awarded for first, second, and third place.

Contact: **Michigan Renaissance Festival Tournament of Temptations**
120 South Saginaw
Holly, MI 48442
Tel: (248) 634-5552
FAX: (248) 634-7590

HEARTLAND PASTRY CLASSIC

Annually, first week of October in St. Louis, Missouri
Sponsored by Patisfrance; organized by Classic Gourmet, Atlanta, GA

Prospective participants must submit recipes and photos of the entries in advance to qualify. Ten competitors are chosen.

Each participant prepares:
1. Sugar centerpiece
2. Ornate cake
3. Plated dessert
4. Unique decorative ideas

Judging is done by a panel of five judges consisting of four pastry chefs (one of whom is a celebrity) and one executive chef.

Prizes:
- Winner qualifies to participate in the Patisfrance competition held every February at the New York Restaurant Show
- $1,000 cash
- One week paid course at Lenôtre Pastry School in France
- Gift certificate for MatFer Brand products (French pastry tools)

Contact: **David Kee at Classic Gourmet, Atlanta, GA**
Tel: (404) 767-7655

MASTERS DU CHOCOLAT

Annually, in September in Philadelphia
Sponsored by Barry Callebaut Chocolate

Forty prospective participants must turn in recipes and photos of the recipes in advance to qualify. Fourteen competitors are chosen.

Each participant prepares:
1. Chocolate sculpture or centerpiece
2. Chocolate cake
3. Plated chocolate dessert in 3 fashions
4. Six candies or truffles

Two days are allowed for preparation and set up.

Participants are judged on these skills:
1. Artistic
2. Baking
3. Tempering
4. Plating

Judging is done by a panel of eight judges consisting of pastry chefs, including the corporate chef for Barry Callebaut.

Prizes:
- Top two qualify to participate in InterSuc du Chocolat, a trade show, held in France every February
- Cash prize
- Ten-day all-expenses-paid luxury trip to Paris to participate in the competition. Included are guided tours to Ecole Lenôtre and the Barry Callebaut factory after the competition.

Contact: **David Kee at Classic Gourmet, Atlanta, GA**
Tel: (404) 767-7655

CHOCOLATE CENTERPIECE COMPETITION

American Culinary Federation, Central Florida Chapter
Orange County Convention Center
9800 International Drive
Orlando, FL 32819

Held annually in September, this event takes place during the Florida Restaurant Association International Food Service Expo. The sponsors vary and previous sponsors have included Van Leer Chocolate. Any professional pastry or confectionery chef is eligible to enter by completing the application and paying the entry fee. The competition is a one-day event. Participants bring their completed centerpiece and set it up for the judging. The centerpiece must be at least 70 percent chocolate. The judging is by American Culinary Federation (ACF)–approved judges who are professional pastry chefs.

Participants are judged on:
1. Originality and creativity
2. Composition and artistic impression
3. Degree of difficulty

Points are awarded by the judges for ACF gold (36–40), silver (32–36), and bronze (28–32) medals, and for a diploma (24–28).

Prizes:
First Place: $1,000
Second Place: $500
Third Place: $250

Contact:	American Culinary Federation	or	Steven Jayson
	Tel: (800) 624-9458		Tel: (407) 363-8340,
	FAX: (904) 825-4758		(407) 363-8343
	Internet: www.acfchefs.org		FAX: (407) 363-8349
	E-mail: acf@aug.com		

WORLD PASTRY CUP

Held every other year in the fourth week in January in Lyon, France. The next competition will take place in January 1999. The public is welcome to attend and view the competition. Sponsors include RaviFruit and Valrhona Chocolate. The team from each country also raises money through sponsors. Sixteen countries compete. Each country holds national tryouts for their team members approximately ten months in advance. In the United States, the tryouts usually take place in Chicago and New York. The team positions are open to any professional with a minimum of seven years experience in the field. In the United States, approximately ten people compete for the available positions. They send in an application with photographs and a portfolio of their work in advance. Each team is composed of three members and an alternate. The team members are chosen through a series of regional competitions judged by prominent pastry chefs who have had competition experience and are recognized by their peers. However, the U.S. team for 1999 was appointed by the team captain rather than by holding tryouts. The captain of each team must be born in the country they represent. The other team members can be naturalized citizens. In the United States, the team captain is appointed by the U.S. organizer, currently Roland Mesnier, executive pastry chef at the White House. Mesnier was appointed in 1989 by the International Organizing Committee of the World Pastry Cup. The team captain assists with fund-raising and recruiting sponsors.

Each participant enters 2 of these 3 categories:
1. Ice carving with a frozen dessert
2. Chocolate centerpiece with a plated dessert
3. Sugar work with a chocolate torte

This ensures that each team member is flexible and can work within the three categories. Once the team is chosen they have six practice sessions during eight to ten months. The first four sessions are for ideas and testing. The last two sessions are to perfect timing and teamwork.

The World Pastry Cup competition is a two-day event. Half the teams compete each day. The competition takes nine hours. The same three categories are used as in the national tryouts. Many of the component parts can be prepared in advance such as sponge cakes, cookie dough, ingredients scaled and ready, pastillage that is dried and sanded, but not colored.

Participants are judged on these skills:
1. New techniques
2. Craftsmanship
3. Creativity
4. Degree of difficulty
5. Cleanliness
6. Timeliness

Judging is done by a panel of five to six judges consisting of prominent pastry chefs with a high level of experience who have competed and are recognized as experts by their peers.

Prizes are awarded in ECUs, the European monetary unit.

First Place: 9,000 ECUs
Second Place: 6,000 ECUs
Third Place: 3,000 ECUs

Contact: **U.S. Pastry Alliance**
3349 Somerset Trace
Marietta, GA 30087
Tel: (888) 272-7879
FAX: (770) 980-9573
Internet: www.uspastry.org
E-mail: maison1@compuserve.com

OKLAHOMA STATE SUGAR ART SHOW

Tulsa, OK

Held annually for a week sometime between mid-September and early October, the show takes place at the same time as the Oklahoma State Fair. The purpose is to improve and recognize the areas of sugarcraft and all edible decorative arenas. All profits are donated to the Big Brothers/Big Sisters of Green County, Oklahoma. Each year a different area of cake skills are recognized. In 1998 Here Comes the Groom is the theme, and groom's cakes are the focal point of the cakes displayed at the entrance to the main display area. There are several levels of competition: children, adult beginners, adult advanced, professionals, and masters. There are a variety of categories for entries: special occasion, wedding, novelty, sculptured, foreign techniques, special techniques not on a cake, and gingerbread. Participants can enter more than one category. The entry fee is $20 per person for the front display area and $7 per entry for the main show.

Judging is by a panel of three or four professionals and experts in the field. Some of the judges come from the British Sugarcraft Guild.

Participants are judged on:
1. Neatness of cake covering and decoration
2. Originality and creativity
3. Mastery of the techniques and skill
4. Choice of colors appropriate to the design
5. Number of techniques used
6. Difficulty of techniques used
7. Table draping and decoration
8. Overall appearance

Category winner will be awarded:
1. Gold award
2. Silver award
3. Bronze award

Prizes:

Wedding Cake Spectacular:
- $1,000 cash from C & H Pure Cane Sugar
- Signed Wedgwood fine bone china bride and groom figurine
- Signed copy of *Weddings, A Celebration*
- Silverplated trophy
- $250 scholarship to a pastry course in an Oklahoma school, sponsored by the U.S. Pastry Alliance

Placed Cakes:
- One week tuition for a class at the International School of Confectionery Arts
- $500 cash and a basket of products from Buderim Ginger and Royal Pacific Foods
- KitchenAid Stand Mixer

Contact: **D.L.V. Enterprises**
Kerry Vincent, Show Organizer
Suite 245, 3000 Center
3015 E. Skelly Drive
Tulsa, OK 74105
Tel: (918) 745-0384, (918) 629-9125
FAX: (918) 747-1747, (918) 745-0879
Internet: http://users.aol.com/cakinbake/index.htm
E-mail: cakinbake@aol.com

INTERNATIONAL CAKE EXPLORATION SOCIETE
ANNUAL CONVENTION AND EXHIBITION

Held every August in varying locations

July 29–August 1, 1999, Kansas City, MO

August 2000, Detroit, MI

August 2001, Portland, OR

August 2002, Nashville, TN

August 2003, Hamilton, Ontario, Canada

A slogan is chosen for each year to guide creation of exhibition pieces. In 1999 the slogan is Missouri Loves Company. Approximately one thousand Chocolate and Sugar Art exhibitions are expected. Attendance will be about fifteen hundred to two thousand people from twenty-seven countries. Scholarships will be awarded for the winning exhibits and one need not be a member to qualify. Chocolate and sugar craft demonstrations will take place led by international and national high-profile personalities. Also international and national vendors showcase the latest equipment on the market.

Contact: **Kerry Vincent, Publicity**
10530 South Urbana
Tulsa, OK 74137
Tel: (918) 299-7125
FAX: (918) 745-0879
Internet: www.ices.org
E-mail: dougievin@aol.com

Contact: **Host hotel (1999)**
Marriott Downtown
2000 West 12th Street
Kansas City, MO 64105
Tel: (816) 421-6800
FAX: (816) 471-5631

CLUBS, ASSOCIATIONS, AND PROFESSIONAL ORGANIZATIONS

American Culinary Federation
10 San Bartolo Drive
St. Augustine, FL 32086
Tel: (800) 624-9458, (904) 824-4468
FAX: (904) 825-4758
Internet: www.acfchefs.org
E-mail: acf@aug.com

A professional organization representing working chefs throughout the United States. There are ACF chapters in many cities. The organization sponsors regional and national conferences for networking and continuing education opportunities. Culinary competitions, which offer a chance to compete and win prizes, are held on an ongoing basis throughout the United States.

The Chocolate Society of Great Britain
36 Elizabeth Street
London SW1W 9NZ, England
Tel: (011 44) 171 267-5375
Clay Pit Lane, Roecliffe, Nr. Boroughbridge
North Yorkshire YO5 9LS, England
Tel: (011 44) 1423 322230
FAX: (011 44) 1423 322253
Internet: www.chocolate.co.uk

Founded in 1994. Primarily a mail-order group offering the world's best chocolate with the highest cocoa content to its nine thousand members.

Chocolate Manufacturers Association
7900 Westpark Drive, Suite A-320
McLean, VA 22102
Tel: (703) 790-5011
FAX: (703) 790-5752
Internet: www.candyusa.org

Organized in 1923, the mission of this association is to provide industry leadership to promote, protect, and enhance the chocolate industry's interest through legislative and regulatory programs, and public relations. Membership is open to companies engaged in the manufacture and distribution of cocoa and chocolate products that fall under the definitions of those products by U.S. Food and Drug Administration.

Club des Croqueurs

11 bis, rue de la Planche
75007 Paris, France
Tel: (011 33 1) 42.27.86.27
FAX: (011 33 1) 42.27.04.67

A Paris-based group of chocolate devotees that meets bimonthly to taste and discuss various chocolates. They taste no more than seven different items at a meeting. The club also publishes a guide to chocolatiers in France with descriptions of their specialties, addresses, telephone numbers, opening hours, and ratings of their products.

Compagnia del Cioccolato

Via Ruggero d'Andreotto, 19
06124 Perugia, Italy
Tel: (011 39 75) 573-2625
FAX: (011 39 75) 573-1100

An Italian chocolate lovers association with offices in cities throughout the country. The group has over three hundred members who meet regularly and sponsor events to showcase chocolate.

International Association of Culinary Professionals

304 West Liberty Street, Suite 201
Louisville, KY 40202
Tel: (800) 928-4227, (502) 581-9786
FAX: (502) 589-3602
Internet: www.iacp-online.org
E-mail: iacp@aol.com, iacp@hdqtrs.com

This professional organization represents cooking schools and teachers, cookbook authors and editors, freelance food writers, television cooking celebrities, chefs, restaurateurs, food producers and purveyors, and equipment vendors. Membership is open to students and working professionals.

National Association for the Specialty Food Trade, Inc.
120 Wall Street, 27th floor
New York, NY 10005-4001
Tel: (212) 482-6440
FAX: (212) 482-6459

This professional organization represents manufacturers, brokers, and importers of specialty foods. It manages the yearly Fancy Food Shows in New York, Chicago, and San Francisco to showcase their members' products and publishes *NASFT Showcase* magazine.

U.S. Pastry Alliance
3349 Somerset Trace
Marietta, GA 30087
Tel: (888) 272-7879
FAX: (770) 980-9573
Internet: www.uspastry.org
E-mail: Maison1@CompuServe.com

This professional organization of pastry cooks and chefs was founded in 1994 by master pastry chef Gilles Renusson to advance the professional status of those in the pastry and confectionery field. The U.S. Pastry Alliance is a clearing house of information on schools, jobs in the industry, competitions, trade shows, and resources. The Alliance organizes a yearly educational conference. Membership is open to students and apprentices as well as working professionals.

CHOCOLATE SCHOOLS

L'Academie de Cuisine
  Professional programs
  16006 Industrial Drive
  Gaithersburg, MD 20877
  Tel: (800) 445-1959, (301) 670-8670
  FAX: (301) 670-0450
  E-mail: lacademe@erols.com

  Avocational programs
  5021 Wilson Lane
  Bethesda, MD 20814
  Tel: (800) 445-1959, (301) 986-9490
  FAX: (301) 652-7970
  Internet: www.lacademie.com
  E-mail: lacademie1@aol.com

Within the six-month professional pastry arts program classes are taught on the art of chocolate. Avocational classes include decorating with chocolate, chocolate cakes, introduction to chocolate techniques, which focuses on fillings, tempering, dipping, and storage, care, and handling, and intermediate chocolate techniques.

Amy Malone School of Cake Decorating
4212 Camino Alegre
La Mesa, CA 91941
Tel: (619) 660-1900
E-mail: amymalone@aol.com

A variety of classes are offered in the fall and winter months on chocolate desserts, simplified candy making, and chocolate artistry, including how to make chocolate flowers and decorations.

Ecole Gastronomique Bellouet Conseil
48, rue de Sevres
75007 Paris, France
Tel: (011 33 1) 40.56.91.20
FAX: (011 33 1) 45.66.48.61
Director: Jöel Bellouet

The school offers several two- and three-day intensive, hands-on courses in chocolate, which include making several types of fillings for elegant pralines and bonbons, tempering and enrobing, decoration, showpieces and centerpieces, holiday specialties, and presentation. Other courses are offered in small cakes, large cakes, petit fours, plated desserts, and pulled and blown sugar work.

Les Chocolates Bernard Dufoux

32 et 40, rue Centrale
71800 La Clayette, France
Tel: (011 33 03) 85.28.08.10
FAX: (011 33 03) 85.26.83.56

Master chocolate maker Bernard Dufoux offers four-hour demonstration classes on the first Wednesday of each month from 2 to 6 P.M. He teaches the art of making truffles, palets d'or, and other candies including dipping and finishing, as well as making marzipan roses. Included is a video presentation on the history of chocolate. The class fee is 300 French francs. He also offers a day-long course for groups that includes lunch. These classes are limited to twenty people and cost 400 French francs per person.

Cacao Barry Training Center

Barry Callebaut U.S.A., Inc.
Gourmet Department
1500 Suckle Highway
Pennsauken, NJ 08110
Tel: (800) 836-2626, (609) 663-2260
FAX: (609) 665-0474

This school is for professionals only and offers classes in continuing education for pastry chefs and confectioners who use Barry Callebaut chocolate products. Pascal Janvier, master chocolatier and pastry chef and Gourmet Department technical manager teaches three- and five-day specialty participation courses on French candies, contemporary French cakes, creative petits fours, French gourmet selection, plated desserts, ice cream and sorbets, Valentine's Day, and les grands classiques. The emphasis in all classes in on technique. The three-day courses cost $395 and the five-day course is $590.

California Culinary Academy
625 Polk Street
San Francisco, CA 94102
Tel: (800) 229-2433, ext. 241, (415) 771-3536
FAX: (415) 771-2108

The baking and pastry certificate course includes a class on confectionery techniques, which delves in-depth into creating high-quality chocolate pralines and bonbons and tempering and dipping. Chocolate is also covered in classes on cakes, tortes, and decorating techniques, French pastries and buffet presentations, and showpiece techniques. Chocolate courses are also offered through the continuing education program.

Le Cordon Bleu Ecole de Cuisine et de Pâtisserie
8, rue Leon Dehomme
75015 Paris, France
Tel: (011 33 1) 53.68.22.50
FAX: (011 33 1) 48.56.03.96

114 Marylebone Lane
London W1M 6HH, England
Tel: (011 44 171) 935-3503, (0800) 980-3503 (toll free in the United Kingdom)
FAX: (011 44 171) 935-7621
Internet: www.cordonbleu.net
E-mail: information@cordonbleu.co.uk

1390 Prince of Wales Drive
Ottawa, Ontario K2C 3N5, Canada
Tel: (613) 224-8603
FAX: (613) 224-9966

ROOB-1, 28-13 Sarugaku-CHO
Shibuya-ka, Tokyo, 150, Japan
Tel: (011 81 3) 54.89.01.41
FAX: (011 81 3) 54.89.01.45

250 Blaxland Road Ryde
Sydney, NSW 2112, Australia
Tel: (011 61 29) 808-8307
FAX: (011 61 29) 809-3346

Le Cordon Bleu Corporate Office
404 Airport Executive Park
Nanuet, NY 10952
Tel: (800) 457-2433, (914) 426-7400
FAX: (914) 426-0104

Daily demonstrations at all locations include a variety of in-depth classes on chocolate pastries, desserts, and confections, covering such topics as introduction to chocolate work, tempering, dipping, and molding. Gourmet courses for the interested amateur include a variety of chocolate classes as well as seasonal courses. Within the pastry diploma program there are three levels of full-time classes; beginning includes an introduction to chocolate work, intermediate covers more in-depth chocolate work, and superior level spends a third of course time on chocolate work exploring its many facets. The techniques covered include tempering, sculpture and display, hand-dipping and filled molded chocolates, and chocolate techniques, including combe and molded boxes and flowers. Private instruction is also available.

The Culinary Institute of America
433 Albany Post Road
Hyde Park, NY 12538-1499
Tel: (800) 285-4627 (admissions), (914) 452-9600
   (800) 888-7850 (continuing education)
FAX: (914) 452-8629
Internet: www.ciachef.edu/cia.html

Courses are offered leading to either an associate or bachelor's degree in culinary arts. Within these programs students who specialize in baking and pastry arts take a variety of courses, some of which emphasize chocolate.

Culinary Institute of America at Greystone
2555 Main Street
St. Helena, CA 94574
Tel: (800) 333-9242, (707) 967-1100
FAX: (707) 967-2412

Classes are offered on chocolate fundamentals, one-week, three-week, and six-week baking and pastry fundamentals, baking and pastry arts certificate, European pastries, and plated desserts.

Draeger's Culinary Center
1010 University Drive
Menlo Park, CA 94025
Tel: (650) 685-3704
FAX: (650) 685-3728

The school teaches avocational courses in two locations that include a variety of chocolate desserts, pastries, and confections. Many classes are offered seasonally.

The French Culinary Institute
462 Broadway
New York, NY 10013-2618
Tel: (212) 219-8890
FAX: (212) 219-9292

Within the pastry arts program or as a short course, chocolate creations is a fifty-hour course covering tempering, molding, chocolate decorations, candies, fillings, chocolate techniques including spraying, piping, and decorative chocolate showpieces.

French Pastry School
    1153 West Grand
    Chicago, IL 60622
    Tel: (312) 243-3808
    FAX: (312) 243-1430
    E-mail: jpfeif0927@aol.com

Jacquy Pfeiffer and Sebastian Canonne, award-winning pastry chefs, teach specialty courses on chocolate candy making and confectionery, chocolate decoration, wedding cakes, ice creams and sorbets, sugar decorations, and a course on competition preparation in their state-of-the-art school. Each session is three days long and is limited to eight hands-on students. Each session is $450 and includes all equipment used.

Grand Rapids Community College
    Hospitality Education
    151 Fountain N.E.
    Grand Rapids, MI 49503-3295
    Tel: (616) 771-3690
    FAX: (616) 771-3698

Chocolate classes are offered in the two-year AAS degree program in baking and pastry arts. Classes are both demonstration and hands-on. A 240-hour externship during the summer semester helps students refine their skills in a work situation. Chocolate classes are also offered in continuing education seminars throughout the year.

International School of Confectionery Arts
9209 Gaither Road
Gaithersburg, MD 20877
Tel: (301) 963-9077
FAX: (301) 869-7669
E-mail: esnotter@aol.com

Courses are offered to amateurs and professionals on chocolate decoration, mold making techniques, contemporary chocolate techniques, preparation for international competitions, and Swiss candy making.

International School of Decor and Confectionery Art
St. Martin Str. 38
81541 Munich, Germany
Tel: (011 49 89) 69.56.36
FAX: (011 49 89) 69.56.73
Tel. in USA: (714) 544-1048
Internet: www.sweetart.de
E-mail: office@sweetart.de

Continuing education courses are offered to working professionals. Classes include the art of chocolate showpieces, the art of fine pralines, gourmet dessert creations, petits fours and cookies, and the art of French cakes and design. Courses are also offered in Hawaii and Mexico City. All classes are hands-on and are kept to a maximum of eight participants. Robert Oppeneder, a highly creative and successful Austrian pastry chef, founded the school to increase standards of excellence in the confectionery field and provide support for competitions and exhibitions.

Johnson & Wales University

8 Abbott Park Place
Providence, RI 02903
Tel: (800) 342-5598, (401) 598-1000
FAX: (401) 598-4712
Internet: www.jwu.edu

The university offers a two-year associate in applied science degree and a four-year program for a bachelor of science, each with a specialty in baking and pastry arts. During these programs students take a variety of courses including chocolate and sugar artistry and showpieces, which emphasize pralines and chocolates, tempering, molding, centerpieces, candies, artistry and chocolate and sugar, cocoa painting, and chocolate modeling and spraying.

Ecole Lenôtre

Boîte Postale 6
40, rue Pierre Curie
78373 Plaisir Cedex, France
Tel: (011 33 1) 30.81.46.34/46.35
FAX: (011 33 1) 30.54.73.70

At this leading French school for gastronomy there are several specialty chocolate classes including introduction to chocolate hand dipping, the realm of ancient candy making, chocolate sculpture, Bonbons, Liqueurs, and machine coating. The class titled Chocolate No. 3 covers a new look on chocolate bonbons, discovering strong and generous tastes and bold top-of-the-line flavors, and prestigious shapes and presentations. The class titled Entrements/Cakes No. 3 covers chocolate artistry, blending of flavors, and advanced techniques. Most classes are four and a half days for a total of thirty-six hours. They are taught in French with full English translation and are primarily hands-on, with some demonstration.

McCall's School of Cake Decoration Inc.
3810 Bloor Street West
Etobicoke, Ontario M9B 6C2, Canada
Tel: (416) 231-8040
FAX: (416) 231-9956
Internet: www.mccalls-cakes.com
E-mail: decorate@mccalls-cakes.com

Pure chocolate techniques is a five-day full-time course that includes tempering, dipping, starch molding, hollow molding, truffles, and other centers such as nougats, marzipan, and fondants. Cocoa painting techniques includes transfers, patterns, and surface preparation.

New England Culinary Institute
250 Main Street
Montpelier, VT 05602-9720
Tel: (802) 223-6324
FAX: (802) 223-0634

Continuing education classes include the chocolate lover's dessert making weekend. The two-year culinary arts program includes hands-on chocolate and candy-making classes.

New School for Social Research
Culinary Arts Division
100 Greenwich Avenue
New York, NY 10011
Executive director: Gary A. Goldberg
Tel: (212) 229-5690, (212) 255-4141 for waiting list
FAX: (212) 229-5648

The school offers classes on chocolate tempering and molding and making hand-molded chocolate roses, bags, boxes, ruffles, curls, and other decorations, truffles, clusters, and hand-dipped fruits, new chocolate desserts, and modeling chocolate. Classes are taught by Lisa Montenegro, Linda Dann,

Daniel Rosati, and Stephen Schmidt. Sessions meet at various times throughout the year. Also offered is a professional level master class in baking that spans fifteen weeks and covers many topics, including chocolate work.

Pacific Institute of Culinary Arts
    1505 West Second Avenue
    Vancouver, British Columbia V6H 3Y4, Canada
    Tel: (800) 416-4040, (604) 734-4488
    FAX: (604) 734-4408
    Internet: www.picularts.bc.ca
    E-mail: admissiona@picularts.bc.ca

A six-month course in baking and pastry arts includes chocolate work. Ninety percent of training time is hands-on, which includes twelve weeks of product preparation for the Institute restaurant. After completion of the program, a one-week industry practicum is required.

Peter Kump's School of Culinary Arts
    307 East 92nd Street
    New York, NY 10128
    Tel: (800) 522-4610, (212)410-4601
    FAX: (212) 348-6360

Avocational programs include chocolate 1-2, a series of classes teaching how to prepare chocolate confections, decorations, and desserts, and how to temper and mold chocolate. Professional chocolate techniques are taught within the pastry and baking arts career program.

Richardson Researches
23449 Foley Street
Hayward, CA 94545
Tel: (510) 785-1350
FAX: (510) 785-6857
Internet: www.richres.com
E-mail: info@richres.com

Chocolate technology focuses on the theoretical and practical knowledge of chocolate and chocolate technology and continental chocolates emphasizes the techniques of making delicious, unique, gourmet confections. These classes are aimed at those who aspire to be or are professionals working in the field.

Richemont Bakery and Confectionery School
Rigistrasse 28
6006 Lucerne, Switzerland
Tel: (011 41 41) 419.03.30
FAX: (011 41 41) 419.03.40
E-mail: wboesch@swissbaker.ch

Avenue Général-Guisan 48
1009 Pully, Switzerland
Tel: (011 41 21) 728.46.75
FAX: (011 41 21) 729-48.32

One-day to two-week courses for continuing professional education are taught in modern, state-of-the art facilities. Hands-on courses are offered on chocolate pralines and specialties, which include tempering and molding, chocolate pastries, cakes, and desserts, cocoa painting, and chocolate sculpture.

Ritz-Escoffier Ecole de Gastronomie Française
15 Place Vendome
75001 Paris, France
Tel: (011 33 1) 43.16.30.50 / 43.16.31.49
FAX: (011 33 1) 43.16.31.50

Within the twelve-week art of French pastry diploma program courses are taught on chocolate and confectionery and all about chocolate. Chocolate is also used in many of the other pastry courses. All courses emphasize technique. Guest instructors, such as Robert Linxe, teach a variety of chocolate classes.

Seasons of My Heart
Rancho Aurora
A.P. Postal 42, Admon 3
Oaxaca 68101, Mexico
Tel: (011 52 951) 87726, (011 52 954) 83115
FAX: (011 52 951) 87726
E-mail: seasons@antequera.com

The principal emphasis in this school is on native and pre-Hispanic foods. Classes are offered in week-long, four-day weekend, and day formats. Sweets and chocolate classes feature visits to chocolate mills, candy sellers, and local markets, as well as hands-on cooking. Several theme courses are offered throughout the year such as Dia de Muertos and Seven Days for Seven Moles. Special classes can be arranged to study chocolate in-depth.

Southeastern Community College
116 Concert Street
Keokuk, IA 52632
Tel: (319) 524-4716

Sharon Burdick, American confections historian, leads classes in making classic American fudge in a variety of unique flavors and fancy shapes. Included is a history of American confections.

Squires Kitchen International School of Cake Decorating
Squires House
3 Waverley Lane
Farnham, Surrey GU9 8BB, England
Tel: (011 44 0) 1252 734304
FAX: (011 44 0) 1252 714714

Certificates are issued for students who complete a variety of classes on chocolate including tempering, molding, dipping, piping, and candies. A professional class is also offered.

La Varenne Ecole de Cuisine
Château du Fëy
89300 Villecien, France
Tel: (011 33) 86.63.18.34
FAX: (011 33) 86.63.10.33
E-mail: lavarenne@compuserve.com

P.O. Box 25574
Washington, DC 20007
Tel: (800) 537-6486, (202) 337-0073
FAX: (703) 823-5438

One-week, intensive, hands-on course in French pastry includes chocolate work. Classes are limited to fifteen students and are held in a sixteenth-century country estate in the Burgundy region of France. Students live and study on the estate. All classes are taught by talented French chefs and are conducted in French with simultaneous English translation.

CHOCOLATE ON THE WORLD WIDE WEB

"Chocolate is a serious thing."

—Deanna Troi from *Star Trek: The Next Generation*

Chocolate can be found all over the Web. Some sites are primarily informational, others allow you to order chocolate, and some have recipes. Many sites are rather spectacular with a lot of pictures, while others are mostly text.

I have selected what I consider to be the most important chocolate sites on the Web. These are sites that have been on the web for a while and have a good deal of educational information as well as product information. Included are chocolate manufacturers, chocolate confectioners, associations and clubs, and a few personal sites. I tried to stay away from sites that are strongly commercial and that did not seem to be updated on a regular basis. (Note that several Web sites are listed for specific companies in the section on "Where to Find the Best Chocolate in the World," page 245, and "Chocolate Manufacturers," page 287.) Also, the World Wide Web is always in transition, so if you get a dead end from any of the Web addresses listed below, my apologies. In addition, the World Wide Web is growing very, very rapidly and new sites are springing up daily. To find these new sites the best bet is to use one of your browser's search engines like Yahoo or Infoseek.

One final word of advice is that you might want to set a time limit on your visit to the Web sites I selected. Some of them seem to go on and on and on, especially if you follow all the links.

Happy surfing.

American Cocoa Research Institute: www.candyusa.org/who_acri.html

This Web site gives background information about the American Cocoa Research Institute including their mission statement, as well as an e-mail link to contact them. Included at the bottom of their page are several links to Web pages that have information about candy, including chocolate candy. If you try the Stats link you will find another link to How America Loves Chocolate. The Sweet Truth link take you to another interesting link to Chocolate Facts and Fallacies. There is also a link to the Chocolate Manufacturers Association at this site. All of the links from this site are very interesting and educational.

Cadbury: www.cadbury.co.uk

Comprehensive is the best word to describe this Web site. A menu is provided that links you to Cadbury Events, Facts, Recipes, Cadbury World, Resources of Education, What's New, FAQ (Frequently Asked Questions), Recruitment, Links, and Cadbury's Boost (name of one of their candy bars) Yamaha motorcycle racing team. The Cadbury World link sends you to a page that provides information and more links related to Cadbury World (see "Chocolate Museums, Attractions, Theme Parks, and Factory Tours," page 197). The Recipes link has some great chocolate recipes and the Resources for Education has some great ideas and curriculum for teachers and students. Pictures are used throughout this site, which means it loads a little slow but it's worth the wait.

Caffarel Chocolate: www.caffarel.com

You need to go to the bottom of the first page and click on the British flag or it's all Italian at this Web site. Caffarel has a long and rich history and they are eager to tell you about it through their Our 170 Years Old History link. Other internal links give you information about their products and organization. Although this is a small site, there are several neat graphics and vintage pictures.

Chocoholic.com: www.chocoholic.com

The first thing that struck me about this site was its appearance. It's nice and clean without a lot of fancy graphics and text. It's also very simple to navigate. Chocoholic is a commercial site that offers a variety of chocolates from several different sources. The site offers some interesting features such as a brief introduction to each chocolate they sell and a way to get the exact type of chocolate you want by clicking on one of their candy selections like dairy-free or marzipan. They even have a Chocolate of the Month Club to join and a free Reminder Service to e-mail you so that you don't forget someone's special day.

Chocolates à la carte: www.chocolates-ala-carte.com

This Web site starts off with a home page that is definitely award-winning. It's slightly heavy on the graphics so it loads slowly but it's worth the wait, especially for the pictures, which are fabulous. The site is easy to navigate with links to information about Chocolate à la carte including their Retail Products and newsletter, *Chocolations*. There are also links to some recipes and a Professionals Only link that requires a password, which can be obtained for free. This link gives more in-depth information about their products including prices and an internal search engine.

Chocolate Ibarra: chocoibarra.com.mx/ic.htm

This Web site is packed with information about the history of chocolate, which stands to reason given that Ibarra is a Mexican company. Internal links are provided to Chocolate Ibarra's history, Chocolate Ibarra market, products, and distributors. The Products page provides a link to some good nutritional information for Ibarra chocolates. There is one internal link at this site that I thought was rather interesting. At the bottom of the home page (the first page you come to) there is a link called "From Mexico . . ." Try it and learn the word for chocolate in fifteen languages. Several external links to Chocolate Around the World are also provided at this site.

The Chocolate Lovers' Page: chocolate.emanon.net

Try not to get overwhelmed with this site because it's packed. You might say everything about chocolate is in this site somewhere or an external link has been provided to where the information can be found. There is even an internal search engine to search the site by keyword. The Shops link takes you to a page that lists well over a hundred chocolate shops where you can buy chocolate online. There is even a place to sign up to be notified when major updates occur at the site. It is easy to see that the people responsible for this site are serious about what they are doing—just check out the Credits link.

The Chocolate Society: www.chocolate.co.uk/about.htm

The mission of this site is to promote the very best chocolates of the world and sell some of them in the process. Through this site you can order my personal favorite, Valrhona chocolates. Some of the packaging that is used is handmade. Actually, in addition to selling the best chocolate, there is quite a lot of chocolate information offered. You can definitely broaden your chocolate vocabulary at this site. Find out what *guanaja, caraibe*, and *jivara* are. One more note about this site. Through their home page link you can find information about Eurochocolate (International Chocolate Exhibition and Festival) held every year in Perugia, Italy.

Chocolove: www.chocolove.com

Chocolove's Web site is pretty straightforward with one rather interesting twist—they provide a link to some love poems. Each time you click on Random Love Poems, that's right, you get a different love poem. They have other internal links including Our Line of Premium Belgian Chocolates, and the Chocolove Newsletter. If you click on "Our Line . . ." you will find a detailed description of each of their products. Links are also provided to stores where you can buy Chocolove. There is even an e-mail link directly to Chocolove's president.

Cloister's Chocolate Review Page: www.hhhh.org/cloister/chocolate

This Web site provides some great information on what they consider to be the best chocolates in the world. Numerous chocolates from several different companies such as Valrhona, Lindt, and Ghirardelli are reviewed and some great background information on these and many other chocolate manufactures are provided. Chocolates are ranked based on the personal preference of the reviewer, with Callebaut's Bittersweet taking first place. And I have to agree Callebaut produces some great chocolate. Links are also provided to other chocolate-related sites.

Ethel M Chocolate Factory: www.ethelm.com

Ethel M Chocolates Web site gets right to the point with several beautiful pictures of their chocolates on the home page of their site. The pictures are actually internal links to various other pages that primarily provide information on what Ethel M sells and how you can order it. One link sends you to a page where you can design your own box of chocolate candies. Other button links take you to pages where you can find information regarding shipping info, shop location, and factory tour. It's very easy to get around this site—all you need to do is click on a piece of chocolate candy.

Godiva Chocolates: www.godiva.com

Godiva Chocolates is one of the most elaborate and beautiful chocolate sites that I discovered. Shopping (including kosher products), store locations, recipes, and much, much more can be found. There are even a sweepstakes and a soap opera, really. There is so much at this site that a site map (outline) is provided for you to use to find your way around. Actually, there are a lot of good menu bars to use to link between the various topics. There are detailed pictures throughout the site so it loads a little slow but it's definitely worth a visit, if only to see some beautiful chocolates. Set aside a little time for this site.

Green & Black's Chocolates: www.earthfoods.co.uk/gbs/home.html

When Green & Black's says organic they mean it. This site offers some good information regarding what organic chocolate is as well as where to find Green & Black's chocolates in the United States. A breakdown regarding the contents of their Dark, Milk, Mint, and, my favorite, Maya Gold (which is made with small amounts of orange and spices), is provided. External links connect to a host of environmentally conscious sites. It is very easy to see that the people at Green & Black's are passionate about their product.

Hershey Chocolate North America:
www.hersheys.com/hcna/index.html

This is a power-packed Web site with everything including a hundred-plus chocolate recipes through the link to Hershey's Online Cookbook. Several other internal links are provided that take you to pages and pages of information about Hershey's chocolates including all of their great chocolate treats (my personal favorite is Reese's peanut butter cups). There is some good nutritional information given at this site as well as a lot of fun stuff. Try the Fun Facts link to find out the size of the largest-ever Hershey's Kiss. The Fun Link takes you to a page that has some great links to numerous external sites oriented mostly toward young people.

M & M's Studios (Mars, Inc.): www.m-ms.com/index2.html

Fun, fun, fun is the best way to describe this site. The color, neat little pictures, and movement on the home page tells you that you are in for an interesting visit. What Mars (the makers of M & M's) has done is create an interactive site that lets you play with the M & M's Studios characters. You navigate your way around exploring all kinds of fun and educational things including The Bakery where you will find some recipes using M & M's. This is pretty much a kids' site that you don't want to miss.

Nestlé Chocolate & Confectionery:
www.nestle.com/brands/html/b5.html

Nestle's chocolate Web site is part of a much larger Web site that covers all of Nestlé's products. The chocolate site starts out by discussing the history of chocolate and how Nestlé came to be so prominent in the field of chocolate and confectionery. The most popular Nestlé's chocolate confections like their Crunch, Kit Kat, Rolo, and Polo are all pictured with links to bigger pictures of each. Some of the bigger confection pictures have links to other external sites. Try clicking on the word *Italy* on the Baci page. Overall this is a very slick site with a lot of internal site links directed at marketing Nestlé's products.

Slitti Handmade Chocolates:
www.italway.it/aziende/slitti/index1.html
If you are looking for some chocolate artwork you must visit this Web site. Links are provided to pages that have information regarding Slitti's history, products, specialties, and artistic compositions. The Artistic Compositions link has some absolutely beautiful chocolate creations by Andrea Slitti. Address, telephone, fax, and an e-mail link are also given.

WHERE TO FIND THE BEST CHOCOLATE IN THE WORLD

"Life is like a box of chocolates because you never know what you'll get."
—**Forrest Gump in the movie *Forrest Gump***

I have searched far and wide for the best chocolate. The following list is the result of my efforts. I feel very confident that everyone will find confections to their liking among the shops listed here. Many of these shops will mail order their products and I have stated this under those listings. Call, write, fax, or e-mail for a catalog. Better yet, if they have a Web site, visit it to see what they have to offer. If you don't know the Web site address, use your browser's search engine to find them on the Internet.

Each chocolate is ranked, based on my personal tastes. My experience in the field does give me a fair amount of objectivity; however tastes do differ. The factors that I took into consideration are appearance, aroma, flavor, texture, aftertaste, freshness of other ingredients, and quality of couverture.

The chocolates are ranked based on the following system of asterisks:

blank = average
* = good
** = excellent
*** = superb

Britain spends the most per year on chocolate, $5.3 billion.

It was reported in 1997 that the average consumer in the United Kingdom spends $99.11 a year on chocolate. It is the largest consumer of chocolate in Europe.

**Ackerman's Chocolates Ltd.

63 Pratt Street
London NW1 0BY, England
Tel: (011 44 171) 482-3731
FAX: (011 44 171) 482-4651

Ackerman's was awarded a Royal Warrant by the Queen Mother in 1969. They make a wide variety of truffles, wafer thins, pralines, and chocolates in many flavors using top-quality couvertures. They also make several seasonal specialties and novelties such as rabbits, chickens, Easter eggs, Valentine hearts, and snowmen. Their chocolate champagne bottle filled with truffles is a signature item.

**Altmann & Kuhne

Graben 30
1010 Vienna, Austria
Tel: (011 43 1) 53 30 927

This company is best known for their exquisite miniature chocolates made and dipped entirely by hand and beautifully packed in miniature chests of drawers and chests. The company has been making these specialties for over eighty years.

Sales of chocolate candy in the United States are at an all-time high of $12 billion annually and growing steadily.

*Andre's Swiss Confiserie
1026 South Brentwood Boulevard
St. Louis, MO 63117
Tel: (314) 727-9928
FAX: (314) 727-0635

Ulrich T. Wagner makes handcrafted pralines and candies in the classic Swiss style using top-quality ingredients.

**Au Palet d'Or
136 Boulevard de la Rochelle
55000 Bar-Le-Duc, France
Tel: (011 33 3) 29.79.08.32

Here you will find exquisite handmade bonbons, pralines, truffles, and pastries using premium quality ingredients. Carré lait has a gianduia hazelnut ganache enrobed with milk chocolate, meker is made with a raspberry ganache filling enrobed with dark chocolate, gâteau symphonie is composed of layers of mousse made with Caribe chocolate, hazelnut croquant, and coffee buttercream. André Cordel and his shop have been voted one of the ten best chocolatiers in France by the Club des Croqueurs de Chocolat, a group of seriously dedicated chocolate enthusiasts.

**Michel Belin

4, rue du Docteur-Camboulives
81000 Albi, France
Tel: (011 33 563) 63.38.95.33, 63.54.18.46

Michel Belin makes premium-quality chocolate pralines, truffles, bonbons, and pastries on the premises with only the very best ingredients. Almond gianduia is made with roasted almonds, palet orgeat has a dark chocolate filling infused with almonds, petit matin has a filling of milk chocolate and chicory, and santal is a dark chocolate ganache with spices. Belin has been voted one of the ten best chocolatiers in France by the Club des Croqueurs de Chocolat, a group of seriously dedicated chocolate enthusiasts.

**Bendicks of Mayfair

Moorside Road
Winchester, Hampshire 023 7SA, England
Tel: (011 44 1962) 844800
FAX: (011 44 1962) 841547

Available at four stores in London, at major department stores throughout the United Kingdom, and by mail order.

Holders of a Royal Warrant granted in 1962, Bendicks is well-known for their Bittermint chocolates, a mint fondant center made from pure peppermint oil enrobed with bitter chocolate. Bittermints are traditionally served at the end of a substantial meal, but are delicious anytime. Bendicks also makes several other mint-flavored chocolates including mint crisp, Mayfair mint, Victorian peppermint creams, and creme de menthe in addition to chocolate fudge, caramels, and chocolate-dipped fruit fondants. Sporting & Military mildly bitter plain chocolate is another of the company's well-known confections.

***Bernachon

42, Cours Franklin-Roosevelt
69006 Lyon, France
Tel: (011 33 04) 78.24.37.98
FAX: (011 33 04) 78.52.67.77

Ballotins of assorted chocolates, boxes of truffles, cubes of palets d'or, and assorted house chocolates are available by mail-order.

The Bernachons are best known for their exquisite handmade truffles and candies using top-quality ingredients and chocolate made in-house with their own formula from the world's finest cacao beans. Some of the chocolates they are famous for are palet d'or—crème fraîche and dark chocolate decorated with gold leaf; palet moka—the same as palet d'or but flavored with coffee; pacha—a chocolate praline flavored with old rum; truffles; and nougatine—a blend of crushed roasted almonds and caramel enrobed with chocolate. The Bernachons also make over thirty varieties of chocolate bars. All pralines and truffles are packed in beautiful boxes especially designed for each particular item.

***Les Chocolates Bernard Dufoux

32 et 40, rue Centrale
71800 La Clayette, France
Tel: (011 33 03) 85.28.08.10
FAX: (011 33 03) 85.26.83.56

All items are available through mail order.

Dufoux makes exquisite handmade truffles and pralines using Valrhona couvertures made from Venezuelan and Caribbean cacao. The palet d'or has a chocolate mousse filling using 61 percent cocoa and le chocophile uses 70 percent cocoa in the mousse filling. He makes several other delectable candies with names such as Bigorneau (hazelnut paste on a nougatine base), Moustache (almond marzipan with pistachio), and Totolais (orange and raisin filling). Some of his other chocolates have unusual flavors such as blackberry, mint, and black currant. His masterpiece is a trompe l'oeil foie gras and a stunning confection dubbed Le Conquistador, in homage to the fifteenth-century Spanish discoverers of cacao. It is a round cylinder of pure bittersweet chocolate filled with praline, caramel, pistachios, candied orange peel, rum-infused raisins, hazelnuts, and almonds, enrobed in dark chocolate and served with a crème anglaise sauce flavored with vanilla, coffee, or fresh mint and accompanied with fresh orange slices.

**Black Hound

170 Second Avenue   The Mall at Short Hills,
New York, NY 10003   New Jersey
Tel: (212) 979-9505   Tel: (201) 467-2800

All items are available through mail order.

Black Hound makes a variety of chocolate truffles and confections in small batches by hand, using only the best-quality natural ingredients. Black Hound products reflect a passion for unique flavor combinations, extraordinary taste, and artful presentation. The company is known for its elegant, understated packaging such as Shaker-style wood boxes and wax-sealed tin containers.

*Bodega Fudge and Chocolates

34255 Pacific Coast Highway, #106
Dana Point, CA 92629
Tel: (888) 326-3342 (toll free), (714) 489-0708
FAX: (714) 487-1537
Internet: www.drbodega.com
E-mail: info@drbodega.com

All items are available by mail order and in specialty food stores nationwide.

"Nothing but the finest. Nothing but the best. No exceptions. This they will remember."

Winner of numerous national and international confectionery awards, this small family company makes handmade fudge in a variety of flavors including traditional (with or without nuts), bittersweet, butter vanilla, caramel, fudgescotti (made with chunks of biscotti) low-fat, and rocky road. English toffee, truffles, hot fudge sauce, and chocolate-dipped shortbread are also made with care and top-quality ingredients. Holiday baskets and gift packs are made to order. Bodega Fudge and Chocolates has been recognized as a top chocolatier and recommended in many local and national publications.

**Bridgewater Chocolate

P.O. Box 131
27 Main Street South
Bridgewater, CT 06752
Tel: (800) 888-8742, (860) 350-5887
FAX: (860) 350-6582

All items are available by mail order.

Bridgewater prides itself on producing handmade chocolates the old-fashioned way. They specialize in caramels, toffees, and nuts coated in luscious top-quality chocolate to create a simple yet elegant line of first-rate confections. All items are prepared fresh daily with top-quality ingredients and no preservatives. Company owner and chocolatier Erik Landegren of Stockholm, Sweden, has developed recipes that reflect quality and purity. The company uses its own blend of the finest imported Belgian chocolate to hand-dip their oversize confections, which have received recognition from connoisseurs throughout the United States.

***L. A. Burdick Chocolates
P.O. Box 63
Main Street
Walpole, NH 03608
Tel: (800) 229-2419
FAX: (603) 756-4326

All items are available by mail order.

Rated number one by Consumer Reports in 1996, Burdick Chocolates are most famous for their handmade chocolate mice with toasted almond ears and silk tails. Burdick also makes exquisite, sophisticated European-style pralines and chocolates entirely by hand using Valrhona chocolate and the very best-quality fresh ingredients. No extracts, concentrates, or flavorings are used. The chocolates are smaller than most, about two-bite size. They are made to order and shipped soon thereafter. The presentation is superb. The chocolates arrive packed in redwood boxes, tied with silk ribbon, and stamped with sealing wax and the letter "B." Burdick's are my favorite domestic chocolates. They are truly superb.

**Candidas Chocolatier
2435 Highway PB
Verona, WI 53593
Tel: (800) 845-1554, (608) 845-1545

All items are available through mail order.

Started in 1994, Markus Candidas is American-born of Swiss parents and is Swiss trained. He makes handmade European-style chocolates with artistry, experience, and attention to detail using the freshest and finest quality ingredients. His specialties include champagne truffles and gianduia.

*Charbonnel et Walker
One, The Royal Arcade
28 Old Bond Street
London W1X 4BT, England
Tel: (011 44 171) 491-0939
FAX: (011 44 171) 495-6279

Established in 1875 as Britain's master chocolatiers, the shop holds a Royal Warrant as sole chocolate supplier to Queen Elizabeth. They make a large variety of exquisite truffles and molded chocolates and are well known for their after-dinner mints, bittermints. Also available is Chocolate Charbonnel for preparing drinking chocolate, in original and mocha flavors. The packaging is artful and original. Each box is accompanied by a small pamphlet with drawings of the shapes and explanations of the fillings and flavors of the chocolates, so mistakes can be avoided in choosing.

***Michel Chaudun
149, rue de l'Université
75007 Paris, France
Tel: (011 33 1) 47.53.74.40

Chaudun creates unusual sculptures in chocolate and is well-known for his exquisite pralines, truffles, and bonbons made with subtle flavors. All of his chocolates are enrobed, not molded. He uses the very best French chocolate couvertures made from the world's finest cacao beans. Chaudun was voted one of the ten best chocolatiers in France in 1994 by the Club des Croqueurs de Chocolat, a group of dedicated chocolate enthusiasts.

**Chocolate Arts
2037 West 4th Avenue
Vancouver, British Columbia, V6J 1N3 Canada
Tel: (604) 739-0475
FAX: (604) 739-6847

Mail order available.

Master chocolatier Greg Hook creates the highest-quality chocolates on an artisan scale. His chocolates are handcrafted daily in small batches using only the finest ingredients available, many of which are organically grown. Belgian Callebaut chocolate is used to create these specialties. Greg is extremely concerned about freshness and passionate about quality. He has a particular love for produce and uses many fruits and berries in his chocolates. Each box of chocolates is accompanied by an accordion-folded legend with pictures and descriptions of the different chocolates. Many seasonal specialties are also available.

**Chocolaterie Bernard Callebaut
1313 1st Street S.E.
Calgary, Alberta T2G 5L1, Canada
Tel: (800) 661-8367, (403) 265-5777
FAX: (403) 265-7738

Bernard Callebaut has shops in several locations throughout Canada in Vancouver, Richmond, Banff, Edmonton, Saskatoon, Winnipeg, and Toronto. There are also shops in Scottsdale, Arizona, Kirkland, Washington, Palm Desert and La Jolla, California.

A descendant of the family who owned the Callebaut Chocolate Factory in Wieze, Belgium, from 1911 to 1980, Bernard Callebaut came to Canada in 1982 to produce fine-quality handcrafted pralines and candies in the European style. Over seventy different types of centers are made using only the freshest and finest-quality ingredients, without any artificial additives or preservatives. Emphasis is on seasonal flavors. Exquisite packaging adds to the appeal.

**Chocolat Nouveau
265 Airport Road
Oceanside, CA 92054
Tel: (760) 757-6832
FAX: (760) 757-4891

Mail order available.

Chocolate Nouveau specializes in fine-quality pralines and truffles using Callebaut Belgian chocolate and other top-quality ingredients. Their elegant packaging is very innovative using natural rice paper and other handmade papers, special craft wraps, and seasonal raw silk flowers. The chocolates can be found in fine retail locations, including major upscale department stores and fine hotels throughout the United States. Expansion plans include a larger location where a tour of the chocolate-making facilities will be available along with sample tasting and shopping at the factory store.

***Chocolats Le Français
269 South Milwaukee Avenue
Wheeling, IL 60090
Tel: (847) 541-1317
FAX: (847) 541-7489

All items are available through mail order.

A limited, but exquisite, selection of premium-quality handmade chocolates and pralines is available.

**Christian Constant

26, rue du Bac   37, rue d'Assas
75007 Paris, France   75006 Paris, France
Tel: (011 33 1) 47.03.30.00   Tel: (011 33 1) 45.48.45.51

Christain Constant makes excellent-quality pralines and bonbons with exotic and unique ganache centers using flavors such as teas, spices, flower oils, and Tahitian vanilla. The chocolates are packaged in exquisite boxes. Christian Constant was voted one of the ten best chocolatiers in France by the Club des Croqueurs de Chocolat, a group of dedicated chocolate enthusiasts.

*Cocoa Mill Chocolate Company

115 West Nelson Street
Lexington, VA 24450
Tel: (800) 421-6220, (540) 464-8400
FAX: (540) 464-8468

All items available through mail order.

This company hand makes European-style truffles in a variety of flavors such as Grand Marnier, hazelnut, raspberry, and cappuccino using only premium natural ingredients. Snappers, a sophisticated version of Turtles using pecans, house-made caramel, and rich milk chocolate is a house specialty, as is dipped crystallized ginger and shortbread. Cocoa Mill is also known for their wine-filled and hot pepper jelly chocolates. Any of their confections can be packed in a chocolate heart box.

**Daskalides Chocolatier
860 Sand Pine Drive NE
St. Petersburg, FL 33703
Tel: (800) 615-7177,
    (813) 521-3008
FAX: (888) 275-9110
    (toll free) (813) 522-8070
Internet: www.daskalides.com
E-mail: daska@gte.net

Daskalides nv
Einde Were 47
B-9000 Gent, Belgium
Tel: (011 32 9) 225.35.57
FAX: (011 32 9) 224.01.78

Available at retail shops in most Western European countries, Morocco, Japan, Israel, South Africa, and Canada. Also available by mail order.

The company offers a large variety of premium-quality European-style pralines and bonbons made from Belgian chocolate and other premium ingredients. Orders are shipped via two-day delivery carefully packed in a Styrofoam container so they arrive in prime condition.

**Death By Chocolate
For a True Taste SINsation
91 Tamaki Drive, Mission Bay
Auckland, New Zealand
Tel: (011 64 9) 521-4783

Corporate Headquarters:
Level 15, BNZ Tower
125 Queen Street
Auckland, New Zealand 1015
Tel: (011 64 9) 376-6820
FAX: (011 64 9) 302-1174

This lovely cafe serves decadent chocolate desserts and pastries made on the premises using top-quality ingredients.

*Debauve & Gallais

30, rue des Saint-Pères
75007 Paris, France
Tel: (011 33 1) 45.48.54.67

Debauve & Gallais make a large variety of excellent-quality chocolates and pralines, including some considered to be historical because of their flavors.

***DeBondt Chocolates

Via Turati 22
56125 Pisa, Italy
Tel/FAX: (011 39 50) 501-896

Mail order available.

Dutch-trained pastry chef Paul DeBondt and Italian artist Cecilia Iacobelli teamed up to create elegant, exquisite chocolates using only the finest and freshest ingredients, which are chosen carefully. They make a variety of superb pralines and chocolates that truly melt in the mouth. The chocolate gems are presented in striking modern-style boxes with clean, uncluttered lines, reflecting the style of the chocolates.

**de Granvelle Belgian Chocolatier

347 Madison Avenue
New York, NY 10017
Tel: (800) 923-5448, (212) 953-8888
FAX: (212) 953-7095
Internet: www.degranvelle.com
E-mail: granvell@inch.com

Shops in Brussels, London, Paris, Rome, and Tokyo. All confections available by mail order.

Here you will find premium-quality pralines, truffles, and bonbons made from pure, natural ingredients with no preservatives, inspired by recipes of the eighteenth-century Baron de Granvelle who was well known for his sumptuous banquets with fabulous chocolate desserts. Over a hundred different pralines are produced in strictly controlled conditions. Most of the candies are molded rather than dipped. Attractive, exclusive packaging completes the overall image and design of these highly rated chocolates.

**Deleans
20, rue Cérès
51100 Reims, France
Tel: (011 33 03) 26.47.46.35

This artisanal chocolatier produces top-quality handmade chocolates and pralines in small quantities for sale on the premises, using the best available ingredients. Couverture is blended in-house using French and Belgian materials. The house specialty is Nelusko, cherries macerated for three years in cognac and dipped in chocolate. Deleans also makes several ganache-filled chocolates and pralines with almonds and hazelnuts.

**Ch. Demel & Sohne
14 Kohlmarkt
A1010 Vienna, Austria
Tel: (011 43 1) 533.55.16
Internet: www.demel.at/english/start_english.htm

In this renowned pastry shop you will find a wide assortment of classic and old-world chocolate pastries and bonbons, including the world-famous Sachertorte, made on the premises, using premium-quality ingredients. The pastries are displayed on beautiful platters arranged artfully on multilayered marble and glass counters. Demel's makes its own chocolate bonbons and has a variety of unique and specialized packaging.

*Dilettante Chocolates

2300 East Cherry	416 Broadway Avenue East
Seattle, WA 98122	Seattle, WA 98102
Tel: (800) 482-0281,	Tel: (206) 329-6463
(206) 328-1530	
FAX: (206) 328-1553	
Internet: www.onlygourmet.com	

Two other locations in Seattle. Most items are available by mail order.

Based on formulas of the grandfather of the company's president and choco-latier, whose brother-in-law was chocolatier by appointment to Tsar Nicholas II, Dilettante makes European artisanal truffles and pralines with "more flavor than sweetness." Ephemere and champagne truffles Romanov are the most popular truffles. Chocolate sauces, dragées, solid chocolate bars, and a few chocolate-enrobed marzipan specialties are also very popu-lar. A variety of seasonal and elegant packaging enhances the fine-quality chocolates. A few select chocolate European-style cakes and pastries, as well as truffle ice cream are served in the shops.

***Richard H. Donnelly Fine Chocolates

1509 Mission Street
Santa Cruz, CA 95060
Tel: (408) 458-4214
FAX: (408) 425-0678
Internet: www.donnellychocolates.com
E-mail: Richard@donnellychocolates.com

All items are available through mail order.

Richard Donnelly makes elegant, top-quality handmade truffles and pralines using European chocolate and techniques with unique and distinct fillings such as pistachio marzipan, hazelnut, and macadamia nut. He also makes a variety of 12-ounce candy bars with sophisticated flavors and unique Japanese-style wrapping papers. Double-dipped chocolate macadamia nuts, chocolate coffee beans, and a life-size chocolate champagne bottle filled with chocolates are other house specialties. Donnelly chocolates are also available at a few select locations in northern California, Boston, Massachusetts, Ann Arbor, Michigan, and Durham, North Carolina.

**Durand

5, quai Chateaubriand
35000 Rennes, France
Tel: (011 33 299) 99.78.10.00

Durand makes exquisite artisanal pralines, truffles, bonbons, and pastries with premium-quality ingredients. Guyane has a filling of milk chocolate, cinnamon, and sun-dried bourbon vanilla; orange is made with ganache scented with fresh orange zest; bergamote has a ganache filling of milk chocolate infused with tea and enrobed with Guayaquil couverture; and avenline is a divine cake made with three different chocolate ganaches layered with chocolate cake, and garnished with caramelized almonds. Joel Durand was chosen as one of the ten best chocolatiers in France by the Club des Croqueurs de Chocolat, a group of seriously dedicated chocolate enthusiasts.

*Escriba

Gran Via, 546
08011 Barcelona, Spain
Tel: (011 34 3) 454.75.35/29
FAX: (011 34 3) 454.69.12

Antonio Escriba is a third-generation chocolatier and a true chocolate artist. He is known throughout the world as a chocolate magician. Escriba has won numerous awards consistently throughout Europe for his chocolate sculptures. He has lectured on his art to other professionals at conferences worldwide. Escriba makes a variety of chocolate pastries and bonbons and many special-order items using only premium-quality ingredients.

Ethel M Chocolates
One Sunset Way
Henderson, NV 89014
Tel: (702) 458-8864
FAX: (702) 451-8379
Mail order: (800) 438-4356
Internet: www.ethelm.com
All items are available by mail order.

Shops are located at a variety of locations throughout Nevada and the United States.

The company makes a large variety of quality gourmet chocolates using top-quality ingredients with no preservatives.

*Fannie May
P.O. Box 6939
Chicago, IL 60680-6939
Tel: (800) 333-3629
FAX: (800) 600-3629
Internet: www.fanniemaycandies.com

Many shops throughout the United States. All items are available by mail order.

A large variety of candies and bonbons available in both milk and dark chocolate using good-quality chocolate. There are many seasonal specialties and variety packages to choose from. You can also choose you own assortment. A big emphasis is placed on gifts.

***Fauchon
26-28-30, place de la Madeleine
75008 Paris, France
Tel: (011 33 1) 47.42.60.11

Fauchon makes exquisite pralines, truffles, bonbons, pastries, and desserts with Valrhona chocolate and other top-quality ingredients. Until recently Pierre Hermé was the guiding hand of the patisserie and chocolate section of this famed food shop. He is known for his original creations and adaptations of the great classic recipes. Some of the house praline specialties include palet d'or, malakoff with layers of praline, gianduia, milk chocolate, and toasted almonds, and carré framboise with raspberry-infused ganache. Rive Gauche and Marigny are two of the special chocolate cakes made in-house. Pierre Hermé was voted one of the ten best chocolatiers in France in 1994 by the Club des Croqueurs de Chocolat, a group of dedicated chocolate enthusiasts.

*Fenton & Lee Chocolatiers
35 East 8th Avenue
P.O. Box 3244
Eugene, OR 97403
Tel: (800) 336-8661, (541) 343-7629
FAX: (541) 343-6385
Internet: www.chocoholics.com

All items available by mail order.

Owner Janele Smith makes preservative- and chemical-free chocolate wafers in espresso, ginger tea, and hazelnut flavors. The espresso wafers won the NASFT Best Confection trophy in 1992. The company also makes assorted truffles and chocolates packed in boxes wrapped in handmade natural-dyed papers tied with twine and an embossed seal. In 1997 Honorable Mention for packaging was awarded at the Fancy Food & Confection Show. Seasonal molded chocolates include a chocolate caramel silk filled Easter egg and Yule log, which is available in the Williams-Sonoma holiday catalog.

**Fouquet

22, rue Françoise 1er	36, rue Laffitte
75008 Paris, France	75009 Paris, France
Tel: (011 33 1) 47.23.30.36	Tel: (011 33 1) 47.70.85.00
FAX: (011 33 1) 47.23.30.56	FAX: (011 33 1) 47.70.35.52

Artisanal chocolates made daily with traditional methods and craftsmanship using fresh, top-quality products and chocolate made with cacao beans from Central America and Central Africa. The company is particularly noted for its pralines and crystallized ginger enrobed with dark chocolate. All chocolates are packed in ballotins wrapped with their signature chocolate-brown paper with white writing and tied with a satin ribbon.

**Fran's Chocolates

2805 East Madison Street (retail location)
Seattle, WA 98122
1300 East Pike Street (Laboratoire du Chocolat)
Seattle, WA 98122
Tel: (800) 422-3726, (206) 322-0233
FAX: (206) 322-0452
Internet: www.franschocolates.com

All items are available through mail order.

Winner of several awards and honors from the National Association of the Specialty Food Trade (NASFT), Fran Bieglow makes intensely flavored, elegant chocolates with the finest and freshest ingredients. Her GoldBar and GoldBites, made with soft butter caramel and nuts coated with Callebaut Belgian chocolate couverture, and dark chocolate truffles have been lauded as exquisite adult candy bars. The signature assortment of chocolate truffles are presented in elegant rectangular and round boxes, wrapped with grosgrain ribbon. The company also makes premium chocolate bars with pure Venezuelan chocolate.

*Grand Avenue Chocolates
1011 A Detroit Avenue
Concord, CA 94518
Tel: (800) 798-4322, (510) 798-4231
FAX: (510) 798-4387

Mail order available.

Creator of Ebirds, The Perfect Peppermint Chocolate Cookie, using top-quality ingredients. The company also creates and prepares fine custom-made chocolates, including designing one-of-a-kind molds. Both wholesale and retail orders are welcome.

*Haigh's Chocolates
154 Greenhill Road
Parkside (Adelaide), South Australia 5063
Tel: (011 61 8) 8271 3770
FAX: (011 61 8) 8373 0528

The oldest chocolate maker in Australia, Haigh's has been producing quality chocolates since 1915. The company makes its own chocolate from raw cacao beans. Shiraz truffles made with Australian wine are their finest specialty. Haigh's makes a wide variety of truffles and assorted chocolates.

**Harbor Sweets
85 Leavitt Street
Salem, MA 01970-5546
Tel: (800) 243-2115, (508) 745-7648
FAX: (508) 741-7811

Available at outlets throughout the United States and by mail order.

Harbor Sweets is best known for whimsical handcrafted gift chocolates made with premium-quality ingredients, without preservatives, in a variety of specialty shapes. Sweet Sloops, Marblehead Mints, Sand Dollars, Sweet Shells, Harbor Lights, The Robert L. Stohecker Assorted Rabbits, and Dark Horse Chocolates are trademarks and some of the company's specialties. Sugar-free chocolates shaped as sea horses and sand dollars are made with Maltitol. All the candies are packed in various sizes from a hostess pack of eight pieces to a grand gift of seventy-six pieces, to the hundred-piece show-case assortment. Gold boxes with white ribbons and colored bands are the signature packaging.

**Hauser Chocolatier

137 Greenwood Avenue
Bethel, CT 06801
Tel: (800) 542-8737,
    (203) 794-1861
FAX: (203) 792-1153

190 Main Street
Westport, CT 06880-3234

All items available by mail order.

Hailing from Switzerland, Rudi Hauser is the winner of several awards of excellence for his truffles du jour, Swiss-style soft creamy centers made with the finest chocolate, fresh dairy cream, sweet butter, and natural flavors. The company makes over fifteen different truffles, as well as a variety of other European-style assorted chocolates, which are attractively packaged. Dessert sauces, chocolate linzertorte, chocolate liqueur cups, and chocolate-covered almonds and hazelnuts are other delicious items offered by the company.

*Helen Grace Chocolates
General Offices
2369 East Pacifica Place
Rancho Dominguez, CA 90220
Tel: (800) 367-4240, (310) 638-8400
FAX: (310) 635-0143

Seven other retail locations in Long Beach, Torrance, Brea, Cerritos, Lynwood, Newport Beach, and Huntington Beach, California. Mail order is available.

Helen Grace Chocolates makes a wide variety of candies using excellent-quality ingredients, such as fudge, English toffee, truffles, and assorted chocolates. They blend their own couverture with a combination of Callebaut and Guittard. Specialty and seasonal items and packaging are offered, as well as a variety of candy bars. Many novelty pieces such as anniversary and birthday cards, champagne bottles, animals, and chocolate letters and numbers are available. Personalized favor boxes for use at special occasions such as weddings or business parties can be ordered with choices from a wide range of colors and art. The company also supplies other retail outlets with their wholesale products and works closely with schools and organizations for fund-raising, providing quantity discounts where appropriate.

CHOCOLATE CONSUMPTION PER PERSON PER COUNTRY

1.	United Kingdom	30.0 pounds
2.	Switzerland	21.1 pounds
3.	Germany	19.48 pounds
4.	Austria	18.1 pounds
5.	Norway	18.0 pounds
6.	Ireland	17.6 pounds
7.	Belgium	16.76 pounds
8.	Denmark	15.38 pounds
9.	France	14.7 pounds
10.	Sweden	12.0 pounds
11.	U.S.A.	11.5 pounds
12.	Netherlands	10.1 pounds
13.	Finland	8.0 pounds
14.	Italy	6.8 pounds
15.	Spain	3.31 pounds

Britain spends the most per year on chocolate, $5.3 billion.

***Jean-Paul Hevin

3, rue Vavin
75006 Paris, France
Tel: (011 33 1) 43.54.09.85

16, avenue de la Motte-Picqeut
75007 Paris, France
Tel: (011 33 1) 45.51.77.48

Exquisite handmade truffles and candies using top-quality ingredients and Valrhona chocolate. Pralines and bonbons of note are Caribe, Trinidad with lemon-infused ganache, vanilla, and le petit boule with a caramelized ganache filling. One of his specialties is a unique truffle made with both white and dark chocolate and a blend of Camembert, Roquefort, and goat cheese. Hevin also makes exquisite chocolate pastries and cakes. He is best known for pyramide, a chocolate-almond-pistachio cake layered with bittersweet ganache; Guayaquil, a chocolate-almond cake layered with cocoa mousse; and Caracas, a chocolate-almond cake layered with dark chocolate mousse flavored with orange zest. Hevin was voted second-best chocolatier in France (after Robert Linxe) in 1994 by the Club des Croqueurs de Chocolat, a dedicated group of chocolate enthusiasts.

House of Brussels Chocolates
208-750 Terminal Avenue
Vancouver, British Columbia V6A 2M5, Canada
Tel: (800) 661-1524, (604) 687-1524
FAX: (604) 687-0142

Nine other locations throughout British Columbia. Products are also available worldwide at several other locations.

European-style molded truffles and pralines using premium-quality ingredients. The signature product is the hedgehog, a specialty candy in the shape of a hedgehog with a distinctive blend of pure hazelnut butter on the inside and the finest European chocolate on the outside. Other specialties include maple chocolates and maple creams, which are shaped like maple leaves and made with pure maple syrup, macadamia chocolates have a filling of macadamia nuts that are roasted in maple syrup then blended with white or milk chocolate and molded into maple leaf shapes. Other candies with the maple leaf shape are hazelnut cream chocolates, macadamia cream chocolates, hazelnut maples, and macadamia maples.

Jerbeau Chocolate
1080 Avenida Ascanso
Camarillo, CA 93012
Tel: (800) 755-3723
FAX: (805) 484-2477

Mail order only.

Jerbeau makes European-style premium-quality chocolates and pralines, using top-quality ingredients. The company blends their own couverture chocolate. Jerbeau makes some of their truffles in a unique triangular shape and they come in a wide variety of flavors. Seasonal specialties such as solid molded chocolate rabbits and eggs are also available. The chocolates are exquisitely packaged in a variety of eye-catching shapes and assortments. Jerbeau sells to retail outlets and to individual consumers.

*Karl Bissinger French Confections
4742 McPherson Avenue
St. Louis, MO 63108
Tel: (314) 534-2400
FAX: (314) 534-2419

Mail order only: (800) 325-8881, (314) 367-9750

Bissinger makes a variety of excellent-quality European-style chocolates and pralines. The company is famous for their fondant-coated, chocolate-covered fresh Oregon raspberries that are picked, coated, and packaged within a few hours then shipped directly to customers. These are available for only a three-week period in the summer during the peak of the growing season.

*La Cabosse d'Or Chocolaterie
973, Ozias Leduc
Otterburn Park, Quebec J3G 4S6, Canada
Tel: (800) 784-6937, (514) 464-6937
FAX: (514) 464-9933
Internet: www.cabissedir.qc.ca

All items are available by mail order.

The company makes a variety of European-style pralines in many flavors such as coffee, almond, raspberry, orange, and fresh cream. Chocolates are primarily molded in many shapes, although a few specialties are hand-dipped. Seasonal specialties are also available.

**La Fontaine au Chocolat (Michel Cluziel)

201, rue Saint Honoré
75001 Paris, France
Tel: (011 33 1) 42.44.11.66
FAX: (011 33 1) 42.44.11.60

Avenue de Conches
Le Roncenay
27240 Danville, France
Tel: (011 33 2) 32.35.60.00
FAX: (011 33 2) 32.34.83.63

Michel Cluziel is one of the few remaining family-owned small companies specializing in the manufacture of premium-quality chocolates with extremely high cocoa butter content from the world's finest cacao beans. Dark chocolates contain 72 percent and 85 percent cocoa butter, and a bar made with roasted cacao beans contains 99 percent. The company's milk chocolate has a cocoa butter content of 50 percent, the highest in the world. They produce a wide range of assorted bonbons and pralines as well as several bars. Sophisticated red and black packaging is their trademark. Besides their own named line, which is available in their own shop and through several high-end pastry and confectionery shops, the company also manufactures for top hotels such as the Relais & Chateaux group, department stores in Munich and Berlin, and airlines such as British Airways and Japan Airlines.

Lake Champlain Chocolates

431 Pine Street
Burlington, VT 05401
Tel: (800) 465-5909
FAX: (802) 864-1806

60 Church Street
Burlington, VT 05401
Tel: (802) 862-5185

All items are available through mail order.

Handcrafted European-style praline and candies using top-quality ingredients and highlighting ingredients native to Vermont such as maple syrup.

***La Maison Du Chocolat

225, rue du Fauborg Saint-
Honoré
75008 Paris, France
Tel: (011 33 1) 42.27.39.44
FAX: (011 33 1) 47.64.03.75

25 East 73rd Street
New York, NY 10021
Tel: (212) 744-7117

Many items are available by mail order.

Robert Linxe makes exquisite classic and unique handmade chocolates and
pralines using chocolate made in-house from the world's finest cacao beans.
Ganache is the house specialty and many of the chocolates contain ganache
centers with a variety of flavors such as lemon, mocha, raspberry, and mint.
Sleek, elegant chocolate-brown boxes tied with brown woven ribbon,
inspired by Hermés, completes the presentation.

**Laudrée

16, rue Royale
75008 Paris, France
Tel: (011 33 1) 42.60.21.79

This elegant tea salon makes the best classic French chocolate macaroons
in town, filled with chocolate ganache.

**Confiserie Lauenstein

Lauensteiner Strasse 42
96337 Ludwigsstadt, Germany
Tel: (011 49 9263) 944-0
FAX: (011 49 9263) 944-44

The company has been making handcrafted premium-quality truffles and
pralines without any preservatives or additives for over thirty years.
Seasonal specialties such as Easter eggs and several Christmas assortments
are also offered. Simple yet elegant packaging, including wooden gift boxes
complete the presentation. The company also produces pralines and truffles
under the brand name Maxim's de Paris.

***Lenôtre
44, rue du Bac
75007 Paris, France
Tel: (011 33 1) 42.22.39.39

Seven other locations in Paris.

Lenôtre has set the standard for quality in the world of desserts, pastries, and confections. The company makes a wide variety of excellent-quality chocolates and pralines using top-quality ingredients and chocolate. Many of the world's best pastry chefs and chocolatiers learned their art from Lenôtre, who was voted one of the ten best chocolatiers in France in 1994 by the Club des Croqueurs de Chocolat, a group of dedicated chocolate enthusiasts.

***Le Roux Chocolatier et Caramelier
18, rue de Port-Maria
56170 Quiberon, France
Tel: (011 33 2) 97.50.06.83
FAX: (011 33 2) 97.30.57.94

Mail order available.

Le Roux makes premium artisanal pralines, bonbons, and truffles made with the best-quality ingredients. Henri and Lorraine Le Roux are renowned not only for their chocolates, but for their unique salted butter caramels. Some of the house specialties are bonbons made with green tea, nougatine gianduia, criollo ganache blended with ginger-flavored marzipan. Each beautifully wrapped box of pralines and chocolates is tied with a chocolate-brown ribbon that holds a small booklet, which has a drawing of each chocolate and an explanation of its composition. Henri Le Roux is considered a modern master and an extremely innovative creator with chocolate. He grew up in the pastry and confectionery business and trained in Switzerland, which is evident his technical skill. Le Roux has been chosen as one of the ten best chocolatiers in France by the Club des Croqueurs de Chocolat, a group of seriously dedicated chocolate enthusiasts.

**Lisa Lerner Chocolates
2984 San Pablo Avenue
Berkeley, CA 94702
Tel: (510) 843-5445
FAX: (510) 843-0221

Mail order is available.

Lisa Lerner studied the art of confectionery in Switzerland and was head baker at Cocolat in Berkeley before opening her own business in 1979. This company has a serious commitment to using only the very best-quality ingredients to produce their signature truffles and Villettes, thin crisp tuile cookies coated with chocolate. The company custom blends their own couverture, often using as much as 70 percent cocoa solids in some of their confections. They work with individuals and caterers to create a wide variety of custom confections for any occasion. Lisa Lerner Chocolates are available at several retail sources in the San Francisco area including Peaberry's Coffee & Tea, Peet's Coffee & Tea, Draeger's, Neiman-Marcus, and the Oakville grocery, and at Arazzo Market Cafe in Rancho Santa Fe, California.

***Confections by Michael Recchiuti
2565 Third Street, #336
San Francisco, CA 94107
Tel: (800) 500-3396, (415) 826-2868
FAX: (415) 826-2868
E-mail: confecbymr@aol.com

Mail order available.

Passionate chocolatier Michael Recchiuti creates some of the most unusual and outstanding chocolates to be found. They arrive in striking yet understated custom-designed packaging announcing that you have received something very special. A card enclosed with the box describes each different confection (eight to a quarter pound), how to taste them, and how to store them for maximum flavor retention. There are three different boxed collections available or you can create your own. Michael uses a variety of premium quality chocolate couvertures—Scharffen Berger, El Rey, Valrhona, and Felchlin—to create his jewellike confections. Other ingredients are the very best available. Custom-designed chocolates are also available. The chocolates can be found in a handful of retail outlets in San Francisco or at Formaggio Kitchen in Cambridge, Massachusetts. Michael also supplies his confections to several caterers, prestigious restaurants, and resorts. Chocolate bars made from the couvertures Michael uses and chocolate sauces are forthcoming new items.

**Minerva Street Chocolates
 1053 Olivia
 Ann Arbor, MI 48104
 Tel: (313) 996-4090
 FAX: (313) 665-0753
 E-mail: JudyW1234@aol.com
 All items available by mail order.
Several flavors of hand-dipped chocolate truffles using top-quality ingredients. Owner Judy Weinblatt has developed her recipes over many years of trial and error. Her confections have received recognition in many major magazines and she appeared on David Letterman's show to make her specialties.

**Neuhaus

Boutique at Saks Fifth Avenue
New York, NY 10017

2 Secatoag Avenue
Port Washington, NY 11050
Tel: (516) 883-7400
FAX: (516) 883-7429

25 Galerie de la Reine
1000 Brussels, Belgium
Tel: (011 32 2) 512-6359
FAX: (011 32 2) 640-8275

1 Boulevard de Waterloo
1050 Brussels, Belgium
Tel: (011 32 2) 514-1965

Many other locations throughout Brussels and the world.

Neuhaus makes top-quality pralines and chocolates known for their subtle, rich flavors. They are prepared with only the finest and freshest ingredients, including Callebaut couverture that is conched for seventy-two to eighty hours to create the smoothest, most palatable chocolate.

**Payard Patisserie & Bistro

1032 Lexington Avenue
New York, NY 10021
Tel: (212) 717-5252
FAX: (212) 717-0986

Mail order is available.

Françoise Payard, pastry chef, and Daniel Bouloud, owner of Restaurant Daniel, have teamed up to delight New York with a casual yet elegant setting for some of the most sumptuous chocolates and pastries to be found. A full range of chocolate and fruit pastries and cakes are available as well as a variety of exquisite handmade chocolates such as palet d'or, praline wafers, nut clusters, and a selection of truffles. Seasonal specialties such as Santas molded in family heirloom molds and chocolate-dipped Cape gooseberries are available.

**Peyrano
Corso Moncalieri, 47
10133 Turin, Italy
Tel: (011 39 11) 660.22.02
FAX: (011 39 11) 660.21.31

This company makes top-quality pralines and chocolates. They make their own couverture in-house with the world's finest cacao beans from Venezuela, Ecuador, Trinidad, and Sumatra. Peyrano is world famous for bicherin paste, a mixture of dark chocolate, cocoa, honey, and hazelnuts. It is sold in pots and is used in place of sugar to sweeten coffee. Gianduia and candies made with gianduia is a house specialty.

*Perugina
520 Madison Avenue
New York, NY 10022
Tel: (800) 272-0500, (212) 668-2490
FAX: (212) 750-9225

All items are available through mail order.

Best known for their Baci candies, chocolate domes wrapped in silver foil covered with blue stars, Perugina also makes a delectable assortment of elegant and distinctive chocolate pralines and bars, including seasonal specialties.

Perugina chocolate bars and Baci candies are available at many specialty food and gift shops throughout the world and by mail order.

*Pinehill Fudge Collection at Historic Pinehill B & B
400 Mix Street (at Jackson)
Oregon, IL 61061
Tel: (815) 732-2061

All items are available by mail order.

Sharon Burdick makes more than thirty exotic flavors of rich, handmade, historic American fudge in seasonal and whimsical shapes.

**Pralines Leonidas
41-43 Boulevard Jules Graindor   485 Madison Avenue
B-1070-Brussels, Belgium   New York, NY 10022
Tel: (011 32 2) 522.19.57   Tel: (800) 900-2462,
                                    (212) 980-2608
                                    FAX: (212) 980-2609

Several other locations in California, Connecticut, Washington, DC, Atlanta, Chicago, Massachusetts, Michigan, North Carolina, Ohio, Tennessee, Texas, and Virginia.

This company makes a large variety of high-quality pralines and chocolates created in Belgium and flown in fresh weekly.

Purdy's Chocolates
2777 Kingsway
Vancouver, British Columbia V5R 5H7, Canada
Tel: (800) 778-7397, (604) 454-2777
FAX: (800) 529-1166, (604) 454-2701
E-mail: choklit@purdys.com

Many items available by mail order.

The hedgehog, a European-style chocolate hazelnut truffle made with Belgian milk chocolate is Purdy's signature candy. The company also makes a variety of truffles and other chocolate candies.

*Puyricard

Quartier Beaufort
13090 Aix-en-Provence, France
Tel: (011 33 442) 42.96.11.21

7, rue Rifle-Rafle
13100 Aix-en-Provence, France
Tel: (011 33 442) 42.21.13.26

Several other locations in Arles, Avignon, Marseille, Nice, Paris, and Toulon.

Also available by mail order in the United States. Contact:

930 Valley View Drive
Healdsburg, CA 95448
Tel: (707) 431-0233
FAX: (707) 433-7143

The company makes handmade French chocolates in the Belgian tradition using only the freshest ingredients and flavorings. A variety of assorted boxed arrangements are available.

**Richart Design et Chocolate

258, boulevard Saint-Germain
75007 Paris, France
Tel: (011 33 1) 45.55.66.00

36, avenue Wagram
75008 Paris, France
Tel: (011 33 1) 45.74.94.00

1, rue du Plat
69002 Lyon, France
Tel: (011 33 04) 72.37.38.55

7 East 55th Street
New York, NY 10022
Tel: (800) 742-4278 (RICH-ART),
(212) 371-9369

All items available through mail order.

Unique hand-crafted boutique chocolates made in a large variety of shapes, such as bite-size squares and hearts. Various designs are imprinted on the surface of the chocolates with silk screens. The chocolates are extremely artfully arranged and packaged. Many spices and essences are used to flavor chocolate made to resemble small tiles. Richart creates over eighty flavors that establish a fine balance among the ingredients. They consider each piece of chocolate to be a tiny jewel. Their chocolates are true works of art.

Rocky Mountain Chocolate Factory
222 South Main Street
P.O. Box 2761
Breckenridge, CO 80424
Tel: (888) 275-7623, (970) 453-2094
FAX: (970) 453-4694
Internet: www.imagepage.com/rmcfbrk

Stores in many states and mail-order catalog available.

The company makes a variety of American-style chocolate candies including fudge and chocolate caramel-coated apples. Many seasonal and gift items are offered in the stores and the catalogs.

**Rococo
321 King's Road
London SW3 5EP, England
Tel: (011 44 171) 352-5857
FAX: (011 44 171) 352-7360

Mail order is available.

Art school graduate Chantal Coady makes excellent European-style truffles, bonbons, and specialty bars using Valrhona chocolate and top-quality ingredients. Some of her candies have unusual flavors such as lavender, juniper, thyme, and tea. This tiny, delightful shop, established in 1983, is always crowded with chocolate devotees.

**Sara Jayne's Truffles
517 Old York Road
London SW18 1TF, England
Tel: (011 44 181) 874-8500
FAX: (011 44 181) 874-8575

Handmade chocolate truffles using only the best French and English couverture chocolates with high cocoa butter content, double Devon cream, and love. A variety of unique flavors are available including ginger spice, lapsang souchong, Earl Grey, and pistachio.

*Joseph Schmidt Confections

665 22nd Street
San Francisco, CA 94107
Tel: (800) 327-4740, (415) 695-7700
FAX: (415) 695-1867

Also available in several shops and department stores throughout the United States.

The company is best known for its egg-shaped large truffles and unique sculptural designs in top-quality chocolate. Joseph Schmidt also produces a number of seasonal specialty items.

*See's

P.O. Box S
Culver City, CA 90231-0018
Tel: (800) 347-7337
FAX: (800) 930-7337

Two hundred store locations throughout the western United States. All items available by mail order.

For over seventy-five years See's has been making close to a hundred different candies and bonbons available in both milk and dark chocolate using good-quality chocolate. There are many seasonal specialties and popular novelties to choose from. You can also choose your own assortment. A big emphasis is placed on gifts and packaging.

***Slitti

Via Francesca Sud, 240
51030 Cintolese
Monsummano Terme (PT), Italy
Tel/FAX: (011 39 572) 640.240
Internet: www.italway.it/aziende/slitti/

Andrea Slitti is recognized as a modern master of chocolate sculpture and other chocolate creations. His chocolate sculptures are available by special order. He is well known for his "rusty" chocolate tools, dusted with cocoa powder. Other specialties include chocolate-covered coffee beans, barolo cinato (flavored wine) chocolate, roasted almonds, and oven-popped rice coated with chocolate. Andrea Slitti uses top-quality ingredients and personally oversees all aspects of his operation. All chocolates are handmade in small quantities. Some of Slitti's pralines can be found in a few select shops in London (Fortnum & Mason), New York, the Netherlands, and Spain.

Special Edition Continental Chocolates

Honeyholes Lane
Dunholme, Lincolnshire LN2 3SU, England
Tel: (011 44 1673) 860616

Also available by mail order.

Special Edition makes handmade molded and filled chocolates and truffles including after-dinner mints, replicas of the Lincoln imp (a carving in Lincoln Cathedral), drunken butterfly, liqueur-filled chocolates using only top-quality name-brand spirits, Diamond Nine Red Arrow milk chocolate and dark chocolate bars.

***Sprüngli**

Bahnhofstrasse 21
8022 Zurich, Switzerland
Tel: (011 41 1) 211-5777
FAX: (011 41 1) 211-3435

Eleven locations within Zurich and at the airport. Mail-order world-wide service is available.

Sprüngli is well known for its artisanal chocolates, pralines, truffles, and pastries made in-house with premium-quality ingredients. One of the most popular tearooms-confiseries in Zurich, Sprüngli consistently makes excellent truffles du jour, champagne truffles, and a wide variety of other bonbons and pastries.

*Sweet Inspiration Fine Chocolate

6 Bay Street
P.O. Box 1014
Sag Harbor, NY 11963
Tel: (800) 722-0773, (516) 725-7400
FAX: (516) 725-5600

E-mail: cocoloveyu@aol.com

This mail-order only company makes some of the most interesting chocolates available. Assorted truffles in a variety of flavors such as grand orange, hazelnut, espresso, and raspberry, truffle-filled Swiss chocolate cigars, and four wishes—four gold-foil wrapped chocolate triangles embossed with the words *Love, Longevity, Abundance,* and *Peace* are some of the specialties. All come in attractive packaging festooned with ribbons and bows. Custom chocolates and custom arrangements for all occasions are available.

**Teuscher Chocolates of Switzerland

620 Fifth Avenue at
Rockefeller Center
New York, NY 10020
Tel: (212) 246-4416

Madison Avenue at 61st Street
New York, NY 10021
Tel: (212) 751-8482

Other store locations in Buenos Aires, Dubai, Geneva, Frankfurt, Houston, Los Angeles, San Francisco, Singapore, Tokyo, Toronto, and Zurich.

Best known for their marvelous champagne truffles, Teuscher makes over a hundred varieties of truffles and pralines using the world's purest, finest, and freshest natural ingredients with no preservatives.

*Tom & Sally's Handmade Chocolates, Péché Luxury Chocolates

6 Harmony Place
Brattleboro, VT 05301
Tel: (800) 827-0800,
  (802) 254-4200
FAX: (802) 254-5518
E-mail: tomandsallys.com

55 Elliot Street
Brattleboro, VT 05301
Tel: (802) 258-3065

Also available through mail order.

Winners of eight national awards for their handcrafted chocolates, Tom & Sally's has received acclaim in many publications and broadcast media, as well. Tom & Sally create fine-quality, handmade, European-style candies and pralines with no preservatives, using top-quality Belgian and French chocolate. They have a broad range of specialties from the most formal European-style chocolates to novelty items.

**Weiss
8, rue du Général-Foy
42000 Saint Etienne, France
Tel: (011 33 77) 77.32.41.80

Other locations in Lyon and Paris.

Weiss makes premium-quality pralines, bonbons, truffles, and chocolate bars with the best-quality ingredients. Weiss also produces couverture for use by other chocolatiers. Consistency and quality are the hallmarks at Weiss. Seductive packaging contributes to the overall presentation of the superb-tasting chocolates.

**Wittamer
6 Place du Grand Sablon
Brussels, Belgium
Tel: (011 32 2) 512.37.42, 512.84.51
FAX: (011 31 2) 512.52.09

The company will ship their chocolates worldwide via overnight express.

Exquisite chocolates and truffles handcrafted on the premises from premium-quality ingredients and original recipes. Wittamer is considered by many to make the best chocolates in Belgium. They are passionate about quality control and purposely limit the number of offerings so they can produce very perfect chocolates. Henri-Paul, the family chocolatier has won numerous prizes for his original creations and has been made a member of Relais Desserts, a prestigious organization that recognizes the world's finest desserts. Included with mail-order shipments is a small booklet describing how to best store the chocolates and how long the different types will keep.

CHOCOLATE MANUFACTURERS

These are the companies that process chocolate and chocolate products from the raw cacao bean to the final products. They supply most of the world's candy makers and confectioners with bulk chocolate and cocoa, which is used to make candies, bars, and many confections. Some of these manufacturers also make their own label candies, bars, and other confections from their bulk chocolate products.

ADM Cocoa

300 First Stamford Place
Stamford, CT 06902
Tel: (203) 351-9600
FAX: (203) 351-9625

160 Oakland Street
Mansfield, MA 02048
Tel: (508) 261-8900
FAX: (508) 261-8921

12500 West Carmen Avenue
Milwaukee, WI 53225-6199
Tel: (414) 358-5700
FAX: (414) 358-5880

Offices also in Canada, France, Germany, The Netherlands, and Singapore.

The world's largest producer of cocoa-related products, the company manufactures chocolate couvertures made to exact specifications for particular industrial clients in block or liquid form, compound coatings, baking chips, chunks, batons, and disks and a variety of cocoa powders, ranging from vibrant reds to dark browns with different fat contents and degrees of alkalization.

Barry Callebaut USA, Inc.

1500 Scukle Highway
Pennsauken, NJ 08110
Tel: (800) 836-2626, (609) 663-2260
FAX: (609) 665-0474

Offices throughout the world in Europe, Asia, the Middle East, South Africa, and South America.

The world's leader in cocoa processing with nineteen factories worldwide. This company, formed in 1997 by a merger of Cacao Barry and Callebaut, currently processes approximately 15 percent of the worldwide cacao bean crop and manufacturers two distinct lines of chocolate and chocolate products under both these names. Callebaut produces premium-quality couvertures, cocoa liquor, cocoa butter, cocoa powder, chocolate coatings, chocolate and nut pastes, gianduias and nut pastes, and chocolate flavorings for use by the industry. The Cacao Barry line includes premium-quality couvertures, cocoa powder, cocoa butter, cocoa paste, and chocolate decorations for use by both the industry and the consumer. Many of the company's products are available through distributors and at the retail level in private label packaging in a variety of shops that carry high-end, imported food and culinary equipment.

Belcolade Chocolate
 U.S. Headquarters
 8030 National Highway
 Pennsauken, NJ 08109
 Tel: (800) 654-0036, (609) 665-1650
 FAX: (609) 428-2939, (609) 665-0005

This Belgian company specializes in the manufacture of a large variety of high-quality couverture chocolate for molding and enrobing. Over the company's more than ten years of operation they have developed a unique total quality control system to ensure consistent high quality. Belcolade also produces cocoa, chocolate sticks and grains for use in fillings, and chocolate shavings, as well as praliné, a blend of hazelnuts and sugar for use as a filling for confections and pastries.

The Bloomer Chocolate Company

1101 Bloomer Drive
P.O. Box 45
East Greenville, PA 18401
Tel: (800) 825-8181,
   (215) 679-4472
FAX: (215) 679-4196

600 West Kinzie Street
Chicago, IL 60610-3977
Tel: (800) 621-1606,
   (312) 226-7700
FAX: (312) 226-4141

1515 Pacific Street
Union City, CA 94587
Tel: (800) 533-4301,
   (510) 471-4300
FAX: (510) 471-3756

Manufacturer of a full line of chocolate products including couverture, compound coatings, and chocolate chips. Bloomer is the only U.S. manufacturer of Dutch-processed cocoas available in a wide color and flavor spectrum. The company supplies the dairy, baking, and confectionery industries.

Caffarel

Via Gianavello, 41
1062 Luserna San Giovanni (TO), Italy
Tel: (011 39 121) 900344
FAX: (011 39 121) 901853
Internet: www.piw.it/caffarel
E-mail: caffarel@pw.it

Manufacturer of the popular confection, Gianduia 1865, and chocolate and confectionery specialties including a wide variety of milk and bittersweet chocolates with smooth creams and crunchy hazelnuts using superior-quality ingredients. Original and novelty packaging complete the overall presentation. Caffarel also makes gianduia couverture chocolate.

Carma Chocolate AG

Neugutstrasse 58
8600 Dubendorf, Switzerland
Tel: (011 41 1) 821.06.44
Distributed in the United States by Albert Uster Imports, Inc.
Tel: (800) 231-8154

Manufacturer of high-quality couvertures, gianduias, and confectionery products for the industry.

Chocolat Alprose S.A.

via Rompada
P.O. Box 147
CH 6987 Caslano-Lugano, Switzerland
Tel: (011 41 91) 71666
FAX: (011 41 91) 715185

Manufacturer of a wide variety of confectionery and chocolate products including chocolate dragées and pralines. The company markets its products under several trade names such as Alpes d'Or, Alpia Swiss, and Goldina.

Chocolats Camille Bloch S.A.

CH-2608 Courtelary, Switzerland
Tel: (011 41 39) 44.17.17
FAX: (011 41 39) 44.12.43
Internet: www.cbsa.ch

The company's motto is: "One single aim: to give pleasure."

This company is a medium-size manufacturer of high-quality chocolate couverture and a full line of chocolate bars and pralines for the consumer, including Ragusa—toasted hazelnut–filled bar; Kirsch-li—kirsch liqueur filling; Cognac—cognac-filled bar; Torino—almond-filled milk chocolate bars; and Les Delicieux—boxed assortments of fine bonbons and pralines.

El Rey America, Inc., a division of Chocolates El Rey C.A. of Venezuela
P. O. Box 853
Fredericksburg, TX 78624
Tel: (800) 357-3999 (orders only), (210) 997-2200
FAX: (210) 997-2417

Manufacturers of premium-quality chocolate couverture made from 100 percent Venezuelan cacao, available to the industry and consumers through several retail outlets throughout the United States. El Rey makes Carenero Superior from beans grown in the Barlovento central region of Venezuela, known for its complex flavor notes of fruit, flower, spice, and nut. The line comes in three varieties: Gran Saman Extra (70 percent cocoa), Bucare Bittersweet (58.5 percent cocoa), and Caoba Dark Milk (41 percent cocoa). From heirloom cacao grown in the Paria Peninsula the company also produces ICOA white chocolate made with undeodorized cocoa butter, which allows a fuller, more rounded flavor to come through. This chocolate takes its name from the legendary Indian maiden worshiped by the native parianos as the goddess of rivers and lakes. Also from a rich and robust cacao grown in the Paria Peninsula comes the Rio Caribe line of couvertures.

Max Felchlin, Inc.
Bahnhofstrasse 63
CH-6431 Schwyz, Switzerland
Tel: (011 41 41) 819.65.75
FAX: (011 41 41) 819.65.70
E-mail: export felchlin.com

Distributed by Swiss Chalet Fine Foods in Houston, Texas, Santa Fe Springs, California, and Miami, Florida; Mid-West Imports in Chicago, Illinois; The Peterson Co. in Auburn, Washington; Walker Foods, Inc. in Springfield, New Jersey; and E. A. Tosi and Sons Co., Inc., in Braintree, Massachusetts.

This company manufactures high-quality chocolates, couvertures, and pastry products, such as gianduia, fillings, glazes, and truffle shells for the industry.

Gerkens Cacao
Veerdijk 82
1531 Wormer, The Netherlands
Tel: (011 31 75) 629.32.93
FAX: (011 31 75) 621.25.71

Manufacturer of high-quality cocoa, chocolate, and cocoa butter for the food and confectionery industries, Gerkens is the world's largest processor of cacao beans.

Ghirardelli Chocolate Company
1111 139th Avenue West
San Leandro, CA 94578
Tel: (510) 697-4427

Manufacturers of a wide variety of chocolate products including sweet ground chocolate and cocoa, unsweetened, bittersweet, semisweet, and sweet chocolate baking bars, semisweet chocolate chips, milk chocolate baking bars and chips, and premium unsweetened (natural) cocoa. Ghirardelli products are found in grocery stores throughout the United States.

Green & Black's
P.O. Box 1937
London W11 1ZU, England
Tel: (011 44 171) 243-0562
FAX: (011 44 171) 229-7031
Internet: www.earthfoods.co.uk
Available in the United States through Terra Verde in New York.
Tel: (212) 925-4533
FAX: (212) 925-4540

Green & Black's manufactures high-quality organically grown chocolate. The company philosophy is one of fair trade and works directly with the growers and owners of the cacao beans to ensure quality, organically grown beans. By paying a premium for the cacao beans the farmers are able to continue to grow and produce high-quality organic cacao, to sustain the rain forest, and to live a better life. Green & Black's has consistently won awards for their high-quality products, which contain at least 70 percent cocoa solids. All other ingredients used to produce Green & Black's chocolate bars are also organic, so no hormones, pesticides, or herbicides are in the product. The main products are Maya Gold, a unique dark chocolate bar with 55 percent cocoa solids, orange and spices; dark chocolate, containing 70 percent cocoa solids made exclusively with organic forastero beans from the mountain highlands of Togo; milk chocolate with a cocoa solids content of 34 percent; mint chocolate made from dark chocolate with a strong mint filling; and hazelnut and currant dark chocolate. The company also makes organic chocolate ice cream and hot chocolate.

Guittard Chocolate Company
   10 Guittard Road
   P.O. Box 4308
   Burlingame, CA 94010
   Tel: (800) 468-2462, (415) 697-4427
   FAX: (415) 692-2761
   Internet: www.guitard.com
   E-mail: sales@guittard.com

Manufacturers of a full line of chocolates, couvertures, pastel coatings, confectionery coatings, chocolate decoratifs, natural and Dutch-processed cocoa powder, sweet ground chocolate powder, sweet ground chocolate flavored syrup, and sweet ground white satin syrup for the industry. They also work with companies to custom blend products to exact specifications.

Hawaiian Vintage Chocolate Company
   4614 Kileuea Avenue, Suite 435
   Honolulu, HI 96816
   Tel: (800) 345-1543 (from U.S. mainland), (800) 429-6246,
      (808) 735-8494
   FAX: (808) 735-9640

The first cacao successfully grown and manufactured in the United States, Hawaiian Vintage produces premium-quality couverture chocolate from cacao beans grown in a single year's harvest and from single estates. Different environmental conditions produce different flavor notes. Dry seasons bring out the floral, fruit character and wet seasons enrich and deepen the chocolate heart. Available in coin-size pistoles in bittersweet and white varieties.

Hershey Foods Corporation
P.O. Box 810
Hershey, PA 17033-0810
Tel: (717) 534-4200
FAX: (717) 534-8666
Internet: www.800hershey.com/
E-mail: pr@hersheys.com

Manufacturer of a wide variety of chocolate and chocolate products including couvertures and confectionery coatings for the industry, chocolate chips, cocoa powder, and a myriad of candy bars and candies for the consumer.

Hershey Chocolate U.S.A. is the largest single user of almonds in the United States.

The main storage facility in Hershey, Pennsylvania, holds more than 90 million pounds of cacao beans, enough for about 5.5 billion Hershey's candy bars.

The Hershey Chocolate U.S.A. plant in Pennsylvania uses enough milk to supply everyone in a city the size of Philadelphia. Approximately 1.5 million pounds (700,000 quarts) of milk are used daily.

Jacobs Suchard Figaro A.S.
Racianska 44
832 42 Bratislava, Slovakia
Tel: (011 42 7) 504-3111
FAX: (011 42 7) 525-7152

Manufacturer of high-quality chocolate and cocoa products, including couvertures and a wide variety of bars, pralines, and bonbons, marzipan, and other confectionery products.

Kessko
Kessler & Comp. GmbH. & Co. KG
P.O. Box 30 07 53-57
53187 Bonn (Beuel), Germany
Tel: (011 49 228) 400 00-0
FAX: (011 49 228) 400 00 77

Manufacturer of high-quality semifinished cocoa and chocolate products and other pastry and confectionery specialties for the pastry and confectionery industries.

Lindt & Sprüngli
Seestrasse 204
CH-8002 Kilchberg, Switzerland
Tel: (011 41 1) 716.22.33
FAX: (011 41 1) 715.39.85

Lindt & Sprüngli (USA), Inc.
One Fine Chocolate Place
Stratham, NH 03885
Tel: (603) 778-8100
FAX: (603) 778-3102

Manufacturer of top-quality chocolate couvertures and a wide variety of filled chocolate bars that are well known worldwide.

Nestlé Chocolate
  800 North Brand Boulevard
  Glendale, CA 91203
  Tel: (800) 368-5594, (818) 549-6000
  FAX: (818) 549-6952

Manufacturer of a wide variety of chocolate couvertures and confectionery coatings and sugar-free coatings, including Peter's Chocolate with several types of dark, milk, and white chocolates for the industry; natural cocoa powder, Dutch-processed cocoa powder, and a large selection of candy bars for the consumer are also produced.

According to *The Worldwide Cocoa Trade*, published by Nestlé S.A., the world's largest chocolate manufacturers in order of production are:

Nestlé	Switzerland
Jacobs-Suchard	Switzerland
Mars	United States
Hershey	United States
Cadbury Schweppes	United Kingdom
Ferrero	Italy

The Omanhene Cocoa Bean Company
P.O. Box 22
Milwaukee, WI 53201-0022
Tel: (800) 588-2462 (orders), (414) 332-6252
FAX: (414) 332-5237
Internet: www.omanhene.com
E-mail: omanhene@execpc.com
Products can also be ordered from Fancy Food Gourmet catalog.
Tel: (800) 576-3548

Manufacturer of the only chocolate and cocoa grown and processed in Ghana in a joint venture between the Ghanaian government and a U.S. businessman. The company currently produces a dark milk chocolate and a hot cocoa drink.

Organic Commodity Project, Inc.
160 Second Street
Cambridge, MA 02142
Tel: (617) 661-1100
FAX: (627) 661-0100
E-mail: ocp@shore.net

The world's largest manufacturer of premium-quality organic bulk chocolate, couvertures, chocolate chips, cocoa powder, and cocoa butter. All of the products are certified kosher. The company also makes private label chocolate products and does product development and ingredient sourcing. The company works closely with the cocoa-producing organizations representing the growers to maintain and ensure high quality, organically grown cacao beans. This method of sustainable agriculture makes sure the workers receive a living wage so they can continue to grow the cacao beans organically.

Paris Gourmet Patisfrance
161 East Union Avenue
East Rutherford, NJ 07073
Tel: (800) 727-9791, (201) 939-5656
FAX: (201) 939-5613

Manufacturer of premium-quality dark, milk, and white chocolate couverture, confectionery coatings, chocolate decorations, chocolate glazes, cocoa powder, and other pastry ingredients for use by the industry.

Rademaker BV

P.O. Box 58268
1040 HG Amsterdam, The
Netherlands
Internet: www.rademakerbv.com
E-mail: info@rademakerbv.com

Oceanenweg 1
1047 BA Amsterdam, The
Netherlands
Tel: (011 31 0) 20-4070500
FAX: (011 31 0) 20-4976454

Manufacturer of high-quality chocolate couverture, bars, and tablets including plain, dark, milk, and white chocolate, chocolate sticks, filled candies such as Paso Doble, and sugar-free chocolates and candies.

Scharffen Berger Chocolate Maker
250 South Maple Avenue E & F
South San Francisco, CA 94080
Tel: (800) 930-4528, (650) 866-3300
FAX: (650) 855-3301
Internet: www.scharffen-berger.com
E-mail: bean2bar@aol.com

The company was founded in 1996 by Robert Steinberg and former champagne maker John Scharffenberger because of their love of fine chocolate. They are creating a superior American-made chocolate by following the classic European tradition of manufacturing chocolate in small batches using vintage equipment and hand-selected cacao beans from the world's finest plantations. Products include a 3 kilo box holding two 1.5 kilo bars bittersweet chocolate with 70 percent cocoa and 62 percent cocoa and 1.5 kilo bars of the same chocolate presented in a cigar box. Three-ounce bars are also available. Home Chef Bars are 275 grams of pure dark chocolate available in 70 percent bittersweet and 99 percent unsweetened. These are scored into two-ounce portions. The company supplies both wholesale accounts and retail customers and mail order is available.

Chocolate shower and bath gel is made by the San Francisco Soap Company in Petaluma, CA 94975-0428.

Chocolate crème body wash with cocoa butter is made by St. Ives Company as part of their line of botanicals. The luxury body wash is blended with a mixture of botanicals such as cucumber extract and chamomile with the addition of vitamins A, E, and D. The pH-balanced formula is available in supermarkets and drugstores throughout the United States. It is for external use only, not for consumption.

Valrhona

26600 Tain-L'Hermitage, France
Tel: (011 33 475) 75.07.90.90
FAX: (011 33 475) 75.08.05.17

Manufacturer of premium-quality chocolate couvertures considered by many to be the world's finest. Valrhona produces grand cru chocolates made from single-origin cacao beans. Dark chocolates are Guanaja, which contains 70 percent South American cocoa with low sugar content; Pur Caribe is 66 percent cocoa made from Caribbean trinitario cacao beans; Manjari is 64 percent cocoa from Indian Ocean criollo beans. The line of milk chocolates consists of Guanaja Lactee with 41 percent cocoa and very low sugar content; Jivara Lactee with 40 percent cocoa, brown sugar, and malt; and Equatorial Lactee, which is a light milky couverture with 35 percent cocoa.

Wilbur Chocolate Company

48 North Broad Street
Lititz, PA 17543
Tel: (717) 626-3249

Wilbur manufactures a full line of chocolate and cocoa powder for use by the industry as well as the well-known candy, Wilbur Buds, small chocolate drops similar to Kisses.

Chocolate truffle soaps look good enough to eat. Made from pure vegetable oil, these soaps are shaped and wrapped to look like European truffles, and they smell like the real thing all the way to the center. Six individually wrapped candy look-alikes are packaged in a box made from natural fibers. The variety includes two each of chocolate crème de menthe, chocolate citrus, and chocolate toffee crunch. Included in the box is a diagram of the fillings, just like a real box of chocolates. Order by mail from:

Food Stuffs Mail Order, LLC
245 Eighth Avenue, Suite 133
New York, NY 10011
Tel: (888) 377-8337 (toll free)

$\mathscr{W}$HOLESALE CANDY AND CONFECTIONERY MANUFACTURERS

"Chocolate is my life and candy is my business."
—Alfred Kane (Sugar) in the movie *Chocolate Fever*

This is a small list of some of the companies that use the bulk chocolate products from chocolate manufacturers to make chocolate candies, bars, and confections. These products are distributed by wholesalers to retail outlets where they can be bought by the public. In some cases these products can be ordered directly from the producer.

Chocolove
P.O. Box 19526
Boulder, CO 80308
Tel: (888) 246-2656, (303) 786-7888
FAX: (303) 440-8850
Internet: www.chocolove.com

Manufacturer of premium-quality Belgian chocolate bars in a variety of flavors with high cocoa content. The line includes six different bars: pure milk chocolate, 33 percent cocoa; milk chocolate with cacao beans, 40 percent;

pure dark chocolate, 55 percent; dark chocolate with cacao beans, 60 percent; rich dark chocolate, 65 percent; and strong dark chocolate, 70 percent. In addition, Chocolove produces some bars exclusively for the Williams-Sonoma stores, including milk chocolate with hazelnut and dark chocolate with almonds and cherries. The packaging is designed to look like a love letter and classic love poems are printed inside each wrapper, making a romantic and appealing statement.

Cloud Nine, Inc.
  300 Observer Highway, Third Floor
  Hoboken, NJ 07030
  Tel: (201) 216-0382
  FAX: (201) 216-0383
  E-mail: cloud9choc@aol.com

Maker of premium-quality all-natural Cloud Nine chocolate bars in a wide variety of flavors. Tropical Source is the company's label for dairy-free chocolate bars in several flavors. A new line of certified organic, refined sugar-free chocolate bars is also produced under the Tropical Source label.

Elite Industries Ltd.
  P.O. Box 19
  Ramat Gan, Israel
  Tel: (011 972 3) 37.54.11.11
  FAX: (011 972 3) 37.51.41.87
  Additional offices in the United States, the United Kingdom, France, Poland, and Romania.

A large producer of food products, the company manufacturers a wide variety of cocoa, chocolate candies and bars, including several brands under license from their manufacturers. These products are sold through wholesale distributors and are available on the retail level worldwide.

Endangered Species Chocolate Company
809 South Pacific Highway
Talent, OR 97540
Tel: (800) 293-0160, (541) 535-2170
FAX: (541) 535-4270
Internet: www.chocolatebar.com
E-Mail: especies@chocolatebar.com

"Chocolate that makes a world of difference."

Maker of high-quality 3-ounce chocolate bars in a wide variety of flavors and combinations blending premium-quality Belgian chocolate with other naturally and organically grown ingredients. The bars are wrapped in recycled paper, using soy-based inks. Each of the wrappers for the sixteen different bars highlight an endangered species such as dolphins, elephants, tigers, baby harp seals, orcas, and polar bears. The company donates 10 percent of its profits to non-profit groups dedicated to preserving endangered species and the environment.

Grand Finale
25067 Viking Street
Hayward, CA 94545
Tel: (510) 293-6887
FAX: (510) 293-6887
E-mail: grndfinale@aol.com

Maker and wholesale distributor of milk chocolate and dark chocolate bars with caramel-pecan and caramel-almond filling and premium-quality chocolate sauce. Tiger Paws are extra-large combinations of layered whole nuts, creamy caramel, and rich Belgian chocolate, topped with the signature Grand Finale chocolate medallion.

Helen Grace Chocolates
General Offices
2369 East Pacifica Place
Rancho Dominguez, CA 90220
Tel: (800) 367-4240, (310) 638-8400
FAX: (310) 635-0143

Helen Grace Chocolates makes a wide variety of candies using excellent-quality ingredients, such as fudge, English toffee, truffles, and assorted chocolates. Specialty and seasonal items and packaging are offered, as well as a variety of candy bars. Many novelty pieces such as anniversary and birthday cards, champagne bottles, animals, and chocolate letters and numbers are available. Personalized favor boxes for use at special occasions such as weddings or business parties can be ordered with choices from a wide range of colors and art. The company supplies retail outlets with their wholesale products and works closely with schools and organizations for fund-raising, providing quantity discounts where appropriate.

Kara Chocolates
418 South 1325 West
P.O. Box 1962
Orem, UT 84058
Tel: (800) 284-5272, (801) 224-9500
FAX: (801) 224-9588

Manufacturer of sugar-free chocolate truffles and bars. The company also manufacturers the same products for private labels.

Newman's Own Organics
P.O. Box 2098
Aptos, CA 95001
Tel: (408) 685-2866
FAX: (408) 685-2261

Manufacturer of organic chocolate bars in five flavor variations: sweet dark chocolate, milk chocolate, milk chocolate with rice crisps, espresso sweet dark chocolate, and sweet dark chocolate with orange oil. Organically grown ingredients used include cacao from the rain forests in the Talamanca region on the Atlantic coast of Costa Rica, vanilla from the Pacific coast of Costa Rica and Veracruz, Mexico, and sugar from a variety of sources including Mauritius.

Rapunzel Pure Organics
122 Smith Road
Kinderhook, NY 12106
Tel: (800) 207-2814
FAX: (518) 758-6493
Internet: www.rapunzel.com
E-mail: info@rapunzel.com

Manufacturers of certified pure organic Swiss chocolate products including bars in eight flavors, ladybug design truffles, bulk bittersweet dairy-free chocolate, rain forest cocoa powder, and chocolate hazelnut and chocolate peanut spreads. The company has a fair trade policy and buys for a minimum guaranteed price from growers who must meet stringent standards for growing the cacao, as well as for the living and working conditions of their workers.

Russell Stover Candies, Inc.
1000 Walnut Street
Kansas City, MO 64106
Tel: (816) 842-9240
FAX: (816) 842-5593

Russell Stover is the largest U.S. producer of boxed chocolates. They manufacture myriad seasonal specialties, shapes, and novelty items, and license the images of such icons as Barbie, Batman, Bugs Bunny, Elvis, Snoopy, and Superman. Their products are in the seventy company-owned stores and in drug and discount shops throughout the United States, Canada, Australia, and Hong Kong. The company also manufacturers the Whitman's brands.

ℐOURCES FOR CHOCOLATE

"I never met a chocolate I didn't like."

—Deanna Troi in *Star Trek: The Next Generation*

Listed here are mail-order sources for home cooks and suppliers for professionals for chocolate, chocolate products, and other ingredients for making desserts, candies, and confections.

For Home Cooks

Fern Cliff House
P.O. Box 177
Tremont City, OH 45372
Tel: (513) 390-6420

Mail-order source for Nestlé and Merckens chocolates and chips, and candy molds, papers, and boxes.

Gourmail

   126A Pleasant Valley, #401

   Methuen, MA 01844

   Tel: (800) 366-5900, ext. 96

   FAX: (508) 624-4717

Mail-order source for Cacao Barry, Callebaut, Valrhona, and Nestlé's Peters chocolates.

King Arthur Flour Baker's Catalog

   P.O. Box 876

   Norwich, VT 05055-0876

   Tel: (800) 777-4434

Mail-order source for ingredients including flavorings, extracts, nuts, nut pastes, crystallized ginger, candied fruits and peels, fruit purees, Merckens, Van Leer, Peter's, and El Rey chocolates, and Bensdorp, Merckens, and Van Leer cocoa powders.

Maison Glass

   P.O. Box 317H

   Scarsdale, NY 10583-8817

   Tel: (800) 822-5564, (914) 725-1662

   FAX: (914) 725-1663

   E-mail: maisonglass@juno.com

Mail-order source for Valrhona, Cacao Barry, and Callebaut chocolates, vanilla beans, praline paste, and other ingredients.

McCalls
3810 Bloor Street West
Etobicoke, Ontario M9B 6C2, Canada
Tel: (416) 231-8040
FAX: (800) 541-3415, (416) 231-9956

Store and mail-order catalog for Callebaut and Tobler chocolates, Merckens and Van Leer compound coatings, candy-making supplies including a large variety of molds, dipping tools, cutters, pastry bags and tips, candy papers, and packaging.

New York Cake & Baking Distributor
56 West 22nd Street
New York, NY 10010
Tel: (800) 942-2539, (212) 675-2253
FAX: (212) 657-7009

Store and mail-order source for Van Leer chocolate, confectionery coatings, and cocoa powder, Callebaut chocolate, and Valrhona chocolate and cocoa powder.

Paradigm Foodworks, Inc.
5775 S.W. Jean Road, 106A
Lake Oswego, OR 97035
Tel: (800) 234-0250, (503) 636-4880
FAX: (503) 636-4886

Mail-order source for Guittard, Merckens, Nestlés, and Lindt couvertures, baking chocolates, and cocoa powder.

Sweet Celebrations
P.O. Box 39426
Edina, MN 55439-0426
Tel: (800) 328-6722
FAX: (612) 943-1688

Mail-order catalog for Cacao Barry, Callebaut, and Lindt chocolates, molds, equipment, and chocolate books.

Williams-Sonoma
Mail Order Department
P.O. Box 7456
San Francisco, CA 94120-7456
Tel: (800) 541-2233, (415) 421-4242
FAX: (415) 421-5253

Stores throughout the country and a mail-order catalog for a variety of chocolate and cocoas including Cacao Barry, Callebaut, Lindt, Michel Cluziel, Pernigotti, and Valrhona.

For Professionals

Albert Uster Imports, Inc.
9211 Gaither Road
Gaithersburg, MD 20877-1419
Tel: (800) 231-8154, (301) 258-7350 (East Coast),
(510) 569-0280 (West Coast)
FAX: (301) 948-2601

Carma chocolates, glazes, decorations, flavoring and modeling pastes, De Zaan cocoa powder, Laderach chocolate candy shells, cups, candies and truffles, Bombasei chocolate transfer sheets and decorations, and a variety of nuts and other pastry ingredients and tools.

Classic Gourmet
David Kee
4820 Clark Howell Highway, Suite C-7
Atlanta, GA 30349
Tel: (800) 235-6763, (404) 767-7655
FAX: (404) 767-6567

Patisfrance couvertures, glazes, and coatings, Cacao Barry couverture in pistoles and blocks, modeling chocolates, coatings, bars, and decorations, El Rey couvertures, Callebaut couverture blocks and disks, cocoa powder, cocoa butter, Dobla, Van Der Meer, and Mona Lisa chocolate shells, Maison Robert truffles and pralines, Auer wafer decorations, marzipan decorations, a variety of chocolate shavings, curls, cigarettes, decorations, and labels, flavoring pastes, chocolate transfer sheets, and a full range of pastry ingredients, paper products, and equipment.

Chocolates à la Carte
  13190 Telfair Avenue
  Sylmar, CA 91342
  Tel: (800) 818-2462, (818) 364-6777
  FAX: (818) 364-8303
  Internet: www.chocolates-ala-carte.com

Producers of chocolate containers such as cups, shells, swans, boxes, bags, and over five hundred other seasonal and signature designs for use by the industry. They are the industry resource for chocolate designs that can be imprinted with company logos and other artwork and work closely with their customers to produce custom designs. The company also manufactures its own line of signature truffles and pralines from Valrhona chocolate.

Continental Food Corporation
  1701 East 123rd Street
  Olathe, KA 66061
  Tel: (800) 345-1543, (913) 829-2293
  FAX: (800) 345-1544, (913) 829-2497

Distributor of Callebaut coating and couvertures, Hawaiian Vintage Chocolate, Schokinag couvertures, Cacao Barry coatings, couvertures, and cocoa powders, Valrhona grand cru chocolates, chocolate decorations, chocolate transfer sheets, crystallized flowers, Astor chocolate cups, Mona Lisa chocolate cups, gum paste flowers, Hauser chocolate cups and shells, and assorted finished truffles and pralines, pastry and tartlet shells, fruit glazes and purees, Dreidoppel flavor compounds and pastes, almond paste, marzipan, nut flours and nuts, vanilla beans and extracts, Cacao Barry polycarbonate chocolate molds, cardboard cake circles, paper candy cups, glassine doilies, paper pastry cups and petit-four cups, and truffle boxes.

Daprano & Company
203 East Harris Street
South San Francisco, CA 94880
Tel: (800) 722-6333
FAX: (415) 588-4996

Importer and distributor of Caffarel chocolates, bonbons, and novelties.

De Choix Specialty Foods Co.

58-25 52nd Avenue
Woodside, NY 11377
Tel: (800) 332-4649
   (1-800-DECHOIX)
FAX: (718) 335-9150

1055-29 Quesada Avenue
San Francisco, CA 94124
Tel: (800) 841-5499
FAX: (415) 822-3390

Importer and distributor of Belgian Callebaut chocolate and Italian Fabbri nut pastes, fruit flavorings, syrups, and fruits in syrups for pastry and gelato production.

G. Detou
58, rue Tiquetonne
75002 Paris, France
Tel: (011 33 1) 42.36.54.67
FAX: (011 33 1) 40.39.08.04

Pastry and confectionery ingredients including chocolate couvertures.

Gosanko Chocolate Art
13611 26th Place South
Seattle, WA 98168
Tel: (800) 584-7790, (253) 839-1147
FAX: (253) 839-1954

Gus Gosanko sculpts unique one-of-a-kind molds for solid chocolate logos, promotional items, and other customized chocolate designs made to your specifications from premium-quality chocolate.

Great Lakes Gourmet
Food Service Company
12130 Greenfield Road
Detroit, MI 48227
Tel: (800) 625-4591, (313) 270-4433
FAX: (313) 270-4570

Distributor of Schokinag chocolate couverture and chips, Driedoppel fruit and aroma pastes, Patisfrance chocolate and pastry ingredients, Callebaut chocolate couverture, Cacao Barry chocolate couverture, Guittard coating chocolate, Valrhona couverture, custom chocolate logos, sugar petal royal icing and pastillage flowers, acetate sheets and skroll sheet templates, Mona Lisa chocolate shells and cups, sweet Swiss chocolate plaques, Astor's chocolate cups and shells, decorations, points, shavings, and curls, and vanilla beans and extracts.

International Foods and Confections, Inc.
4040 Nine-McFarlkand Drive, Suite 1100
Alpharetta, GA 30201
Tel: (888) 432-2462 (toll free), (770) 667-9198
FAX: (770) 343-8458
Internet: www.chocovic.es
E-mail: ifc@mindspring.com

Sole United States importers for Chocovic chocolates produced in Spain. Their Origin Unico dark chocolate couvertures are made from single-origin fine grade cocoas. Included are Ocumare, produced from 100 percent Venezuelan criollo cacao beans; Guaranda made from 100 percent Ecuadorian forastero cacao beans; and Guyave made from 100 percent Grenadian trinitario cacao beans. They also produce blended couvertures and compound coatings for use by the confectionery industry.

Paris Gourmet Patisfrance
161 East Union Avenue
East Rutherford, NJ 07073
Tel: (800) 727-9791, (201) 939-5656
FAX: (201) 939-5613

Manufacturer of premium-quality Patisfrance dark, milk, and white chocolate couverture, confectionery coatings, chocolate decorations, chocolate glazes, cocoa powder, chocolate transfer sheets, and other pastry ingredients such as glazes and gels, fruit fillings and specialty fruits, candied fruits and decorations, Van Der Meer chocolates, fondants, gelatin, and almond paste and nuts products for use by the industry. Patisfrance products are available through several wholesale distributors throughout the United States.

Quinza Specialty Foods, Inc.
375 Oyster Point Boulevard, #2
South San Francisco, CA 94080
Tel: (800) 396-2872, (415) 589-1230
FAX: (415) 589-1038

Offices also in Vancouver, Edmonton, Toronto, New York, and Miami.

Wholesale supplier of a large variety of Callebaut chocolate couvertures in large blocks, calets, or liquor, Guittard ground chocolate, cocoa, couvertures, compound coatings, and chocolate syrups, pistachio and hazelnut nut pastes, marzipan, truffle shells, Nederland Dutch cocoa, and other confectionery and pastry ingredients.

Ritter Courivaud
17, Northfield Estate
Beresford Avenue
Wembly, Middlesex
England HA0 1GJ
Tel: (011 44 181) 903-7177
FAX: (011 44 181) 900-1215

Importer and distributor of specialty ingredients for pastry and confectionery, including nuts, dried fruits, spices, flavorings, oils, chocolates, and cocoa powders, such as Cacao Barry.

Rykoff-Sexton, Inc./U.S. Foodservice, Inc.
613 Baltimore Drive
East Mountain Corporate Center
Wilkes-Barre, PA 18702-7944
Tel: (717) 831-7500
FAX: (717) 819-4220

Distribution centers and distributors in most states throughout the United States.

Distributor of a variety of brands of premium-quality chocolate and couvertures including Cacao Barry, Callebaut, El Rey, Guittard, Ambrosia, and Ghirardelli. In addition the company also carries other pastry and confectionery ingredients and equipment.

Swiss Chalet Fine Foods, Inc.
8956 Sorensen Avenue
Santa Fe Springs, CA 90670-2639
Tel: (800) 359-4226, (562) 946-6816
FAX: (562) 946-6084

Wholesale distributor of Max Felchlin Swiss chocolate couvertures, fillings such as Pralinosa and Nutosa, gianduias, chocolate glazes, and other pastry ingredients.

Town and Country Chocolates
52 Oxford Road
Uxbridge, Middlesex
England UB9 4DH
Tel: (011 44 1895) 256166
FAX: (011 44 1895) 257700

Supplier of ingredients including a variety of couverture chocolates, compound coatings, pre-molded shells, marzipan, gold leaf, and flavorings.

Valrhona Chocolates
> Bernard J. Duclos, Executive Vice President and COO
> 1901 Avenue of the Stars, Suite 1800
> Los Angeles, CA 90067
> Tel: (310) 277-0401
> FAX: (310) 277-7304

Wholesale supplier and distributor of Valrhona chocolate.

Van Rex Gourmet Foods, Inc.
> 2055 East 51st Street
> Vernon, CA 90058
> Tel: (800) 970-9952, (213) 581-7999
> Pager: (702) 678-8076

Wholesale distributor of Valrhona, Cacao Barry, Callebaut, Schokinag, and Patisfrance chocolates and cocoas, Astor and Carma chocolate cups and shavings, Pernigotti, Ferrero Rochers, Lindt, and Toblerone bars, Van Der Meer chocolate forms, chocolate transfer sheets, a variety of nuts and other pastry ingredients.

SOURCES FOR CHOCOLATE EQUIPMENT, TOOLS, AND UTENSILS

American Chocolate Mould Company, Inc.
3194 Lawson Boulevard
Oceanside, NY 11572
Tel: (516) 766-1414
FAX: (516) 766-1485

Chocolate tempering machines for home and small-scale commercial use, using digital technology. Suppliers of European chocolate molds, enrobers, temperers, wrapping machines, and foil to the confectionery industry.

Beryl's Cake Decorating Equipment
P.O. Box 1584
North Springfield, VA 22151
Tel: (800) 448-2749, (703) 256-6951
FAX: (703) 750-3779
Internet: www.beryls.com
E-mail: beryls@beryls.com

Mail-order catalog source for cutters, marzipan tools, baking pans, cake rounds, rolling pins, art and pastry brushes, cake stands, stencils, chocolate transfer sheets, pastry bags and tips, books, marzipan, chocolate, and cocoa butter.

Bridge Kitchenware
214 East 52nd Street
New York, NY 10022
Tel: (800) 274-3435 ext. 3 (orders only), (212) 838-1901 ext. 3 (New York only), (212) 838-6746 ext. 5 (information and customer service)
Internet: www.bridgekitchenware.com

This store and catalog offers a large variety of European chocolate and pastry equipment including scales, knives, pans, molds, flan rings, tart pans, petit-four molds, chocolate dipping tools, marzipan sculpting sets, rolling pins, pastry brushes, pastry bags and tips, whisks, cake turntables, testers, and scorers, measuring devices, thermometers, ice-cream scoops, ladles, rubber spatulas, doilies, parchment paper, stencils, and paper candy cups.

CK Products
310 Racquet Drive
Fort Wayne, IN 46825
Tel: (219) 484-2517
FAX: (800) 837-2686

Wholesale source for candy-making supplies and packaging.

A slice of Double Chocolate Fudge Cake, a wedge of Devil's Food Checkerboard, or a whole Chocolate Heart Cake are whimsical metal containers perfect for stashing valuables such as chocolate truffles. They are available by mail order from:

Loose Ends
P.O. Box 20310
Keizer, OR 97307
Tel: (503) 390-7457
FAX: (503) 390-4724
E-mail: losend@teleport.com

Chandré LLC
14 Catharine Street
Poughkeepsie, NY 12601
Tel: (800) 324-6252
FAX: (914) 473-8004

Manufacturer of the Sinsation Chocolate Maker, a computer-controlled chocolate tempering system that takes the guesswork out of tempering. It is revolutionary because the temperatures for the different types of chocolate are preset at the factory. Simply push the correct buttons, walk away, and come back to perfectly tempered chocolate ready for dipping, molding, and decorating.

Chef's Catalog
 3215 Commercial Avenue
 Northbrook, IL 60062-1900
 Tel: (800) 338-3232
 FAX: (800) 967-3291

Mail-order source for a variety of equipment for both the professional and the home cook. Timers, thermometers, electric mixers, rubber spatulas, pastry bags and tips, scales, ice-cream makers and scoops, pastry brushes, measuring utensils, and bakeware are some of the many items available.

Continental Chefs Supplies
 Unit 4c, South Hetton Industrial Estate
 South Hetton Co.
 Durham, England DH6 2UZ
 Tel: (011 44 191) 526-4107
 FAX: (011 44 191) 526-8399

Supplier of specialty equipment, such as chocolate molds, knives, cutters, stencils, baking pans, and a variety of pastry products.

Cooper Instrument Corporation
 33 Reeds Gap Road
 Middlefield, CT 06455-0450
 Tel: (800) 835-5011, (860) 347-2256
 FAX: (860) 347-5135

Manufacturer of food service thermometers, including digital thermometers and those for candy, ovens, refrigerators, freezers, instant-read, and for chocolate work. Available at retail outlets nationwide.

Creeds (Southern Limited)
New Street
Waddesdon, Aylesbury
Buckinghamshire, England HP 18 OLR
Tel: (011 44 1296) 654849
FAX: (011 44 1296) 658443

Suppliers of equipment, pastry bags, dipping forks, and molds to the baking and confectionery trade.

David Mellor
4 Sloane Square
London SW 1W 8EE, England
Tel: (011 44 171) 730-4259
FAX: (011 44 171) 730-7240

Store and mail-order source for professional equipment including various molds, cutters, spatulas, thermometers, pastry bags and tips, and other decorating tools.

E. Dehellerin
18-20, rue Coquillière
75001 Paris, France
Tel: (011 33 1) 42.36.53.13
FAX: (011 33 1) 45.08.86.83

Store for professional equipment including various molds, cutters, spatulas, thermometers, pastry bags and tips, and other decorating tools.

Divertimenti

45-47 Wigmore Street
London W1H 9LE, England
Tel: (011 44 71) 935-0689

Store for professional equipment including various molds, cutters, candy papers, boxes, spatulas, thermometers, pastry bags and tips, and other decorating tools.

East Coast Mold Mfg.

69A Nancy Street
West Babylon, NY 11704
Tel: (800) 933-9533, (516) 253-2397
FAX: (516) 253-2399

Manufacturers and suppliers to the retail trade of a large variety of plastic candy molds and other candy supplies, such as packaging, doilies, ribbons, candy cups, dipping tools, decorating bags and tubes.

Hilliard's Chocolate System

275 East Center Street
West Bridgewater, MA 02379
Tel: (800) 258-1300, (508) 587-3666
FAX: (508) 587-3735

Chocolate tempering machines for home and commercial use that process from 10 to 100 pounds, enrobing machines and cooling tunnels, stringers (decorators), cooling cabinets, and a variety of utensils for candy making including chocolate thermometers, spatulas, scrapers, brushes, and specialized dipping forks.

J. B. Prince Company, Inc.
36 East 31st Street
New York, NY 10016
Tel: (212) 863-3553
FAX: (212) 683-4488

Store and mail-order source for professional chefs' equipment and tools, many imported from Europe. A large variety of baking pans, chocolate molds, fiberglass Flexipans, pastry brushes, cloth and plastic pastry bags and tips, rolling pins, scales, thermometers, fondant funnels, chocolate cutters and dipping tools, ACMC chocolate tempering machine, professional chocolate molds, electric and manual chocolate shavers, confectionery cutter, metal and plastic spatulas, knives, and cake stands. Books and chefs uniforms are also available.

Keylink Limited
Blackburn Road
Rotherham, England S61 2DR
Tel: (011 44 1709) 550206
FAX: (011 44 1709) 556857

Suppliers of a wide variety of equipment and tools, several couverture chocolates, cocoa powder, boxes, and packaging.

King Arthur Flour Baker's Catalog
P.O. Box 876
Norwich, VT 05055-0876
Tel: (800) 777-4434

Mail-order source for baking pans, pastry brushes, measuring equipment, and scales.

Kitchen Glamour
39049 Webb Court
Westland, MI 48185-7606
Tel: (800) 641-1252
FAX: (313) 641-1240

Four retail locations throughout Michigan and mail-order catalog source for baking pans, electric stand mixers, thermometers, parchment paper, cutters, knives, rubber spatulas, rolling pins, timers, measuring utensils, scales, whisks, chocolate, and cocoa powder.

Kolb Bäckereimaschinen AG
Hauptstrassem 51
9463 Oberriet, Switzerland
Tel: (011 41 71) 78 22 55

A variety of professional culinary equipment including molds, cutters, dipping tools, pastry bags and tips, and spatulas.

La Cuisine
323 Cameron Street
Alexandria, VA 22314-3219
Tel: (800) 521-1176 (also for Canada), (703) 836-4435
FAX: (703) 836-8925
Internet: www.vmcs.com/lacuisine
E-mail: lacuisine@worldnet.att.net

Store and mail-order source for a large variety of equipment including molds, cutters, scales, measuring equipment, pastry bags and tips, and books. Catalog fee is $5, refundable with first purchase.

Lamalle Kitchenware
36 West 25th Street
New York, NY 10010
Tel: (800) 660-0750, (212) 242-0750
FAX: (212) 645-2996
Internet: www.lamalle.com

Store and mail-order source for chocolate dipping tools, thermometers, measuring equipment, cutters, pastry bags and tips, and pastry brushes.

McCalls
3810 Bloor Street West
Etobicoke, Ontario M9B 6C2, Canada
Tel: (416) 231-8040
FAX: (800) 541-3415, (416) 231-9956

Store and mail-order catalog of chocolate and candy-making supplies including a large variety of molds, dipping tools, cutters, pastry bags and tips, candy papers, and packaging.

M. Fish Limited
7, Faraday Close
Oakwood Business Park
Clacton on Sea
Essex, England CO15 4TR
Tel: (011 44 125) 475964
FAX: (011 44 125) 221125

Supplier of specialty boxes, including those made to order.

Matfer Kitchen and Bakery Supplies

6249 Stagg Street

Van Nuys, CA 91406

Tel: (800) 766-0333,

(818) 782-0792

FAX: (818) 782-0799

9, rue du Tapis Vert

93260 Les Lilas, France

Tel: (011 33 1) 43.62.60.40

FAX: (011 33 1) 43.62.50.82

Mail-order source for the professional French-manufactured Matfer line of baking and pastry equipment including molds, cake pans, baking sheets and mats, pastry brushes, offset and flexible blade spatulas, cutters, rolling pins, thermometers, scales, measuring equipment, whisks, chocolate dipping tools, stencils, ribbons, pastry bags and tips, decorating stands, display racks, knives, cookware, timers, ice-cream scoops, and baker's scrapers.

MORA

13, rue Montmartre

75001 Paris, France

Tel: (011 33 1) 45.08.19.24

Professional chocolate equipment including molds, cutters, dipping tools, pastry bags and tips, and spatulas.

New York Cake & Baking Distributor

56 West 22nd Street

New York, NY 10010

Tel: (800) 942-2539, (212) 675-2253

FAX: (212) 657-7009

Supplies include candy papers, boxes, and inserts, foil squares, cellophane bags, molds, dipping tools, chocolate chippers and shavers, and cutters.

Parrish's Cake Decorating Supplies, Inc.
225 West 146th Street
Gardena, CA 90248-1803
Tel: (800) 736-8443, (310) 324-2253
FAX: (310) 324-8277

Store and mail-order source for chocolate molds, brushes, candy papers, screens, pastry bags and tips, and spatulas.

Qualitá Paper Products
2737 South Croddy Way, Suite I
Santa Ana, CA 92704
Tel: (714) 540-0994
FAX: (714) 540-1077

Wholesale supplier of self-standing paper baking molds, paper candy cups and baking cups, cake boards and circles, cake boxes, cardboard pastry trays, doilies, candy boxes, and hard-bottom polypropylene candy bags. Custom printing is available.

Quinza Specialty Foods, Inc.
375 Oyster Point Boulevard, #2
South San Francisco, CA 94080
Tel: (800) 396-2872, (415) 589-1230
FAX: (415) 589-1038

Offices also in Vancouver, Edmonton, Toronto, New York, and Miami.

Wholesale supplier of chocolate tempering machines including the Chocotec 60 and 20 tabletop temperer, and the ACMC tabletop temperer.

Spectrum Ascona, Inc.
1305 Fraser Street, Suite D-1
Bellingham, WA 98226
Tel: (800) 356-1473, (360) 647-0877
FAX: (360) 734-8106

Wholesale specialty packaging consultants and purveyors of a wide variety of chocolate and candy packaging including soft- and hard-bottom cellophane bags and ribbons, boxes, bags, paper and aluminum candy cups, and shrink-wrap systems.

Sur La Table
1765 Sixth Avenue South
Seattle, WA 93134-1608
Tel: (800) 243-0852

Stores in Washington and California and mail-order source for baking pans, measuring tools, scales, knives, molds, cutters, pastry brushes, pastry bags and tips, whisks, ice-cream makers, ice-cream scoops and serving dishes, rolling pins, marble boards, rubber spatulas, and mixing bowls.

Surprise Packages
Specialty Boxes
Box 9
Bridgeport, PA 19405
Tel: (800) 711-3650, (610) 277-2300
FAX: (610) 275-1644

Wholesale supplier for a large variety of specialty boxes, ribbons, poly-cello bags, crinkle grass, and tissue paper.

Sweet Celebrations
P.O. Box 39426
Edina, MN 55439-0426
Tel: (800) 328-6722, (612) 943-1508
FAX: (612) 943-1688

Mail-order catalog for chocolate molds, a large variety of candy cups, dipping tools, decorating bags and tubes, doilies, ribbons, boxes, and chocolate books.

Today's Chef
413 Broadway
Bayonne, NJ 07002
Tel: (800) 989-1984, (201) 436-5082
FAX: (201) 436-9095

Mail-order and retail shop for a large variety of professional chocolate confectionery and pastry tools, equipment, and supplies including spatulas, baking pans, brushes, cake and chocolate molds, design transfer sheets, multiple disk cutters, flexipans, gold leaf, cake pans, tart pans, cookie and tart cutting sheets, pastry and decorative cutters, pastry bags and tips, spatulas, whisks, mixing bowls, rolling pins and cutting rollers, thermometers, sieves, ice-cream scoops, marzipan modeling tools, dipping forks, confectionery rulers, chocolate tempering machines, and books.

Tomric Plastics
136 Broadway
Buffalo, NY 14203
Tel: (716) 854-6050
FAX: (716) 854-7363

Manufacturer of over five hundred plastic chocolate molds, Tomric also makes custom molds to order. The company also carries imported and domestic chocolate dipping tools, tempering machines, a hollow spinning machine, and other candy-making equipment, as well as flavoring oils and a variety of boxes. A mail-order catalog is available.

Albert Uster Imports, Inc.
9211 Gaither Road
Gaithersburg, MD 20877-1419
Tel: (800) 231-8154; (301) 258-7350 (East Coast),
(510) 569-0280 (West Coast)
FAX: (301) 948-2601

Wholesale source for a variety of professional chocolate, including Carma, and high-quality pastry tools and equipment.

Vantage House
72 High Street
Brighton, East Sussex
England BN2 1RP

Supplier of equipment for confectionery including chocolate melting machines, tempering and enrobing machines.

Williams-Sonoma
Mail Order Department
P.O. Box 7456
San Francisco, CA 94120-7456
Tel: (800) 541-2233, (415) 421-4242
FAX: (415) 421-5253

Stores throughout the country and a mail-order catalog for a variety of chocolate equipment including molds, cutters, candy papers, boxes, pastry bags and tips, and spatulas.

Wilton Enterprises, Inc.
2240 West 75th Street
Woodridge, IL 60517
Tel: (603) 963-7100
FAX: (603) 963-7299, 963-7177
Internet: www.wilton.com
E-mail: zjunkin@wilton.com (Director of Consumer Affairs)

Mail-order catalog source for a large variety of chocolate candy-making and baking equipment including molds, dipping tools, baking pans, specialty and character pans, pastry bags and tips. Wilton products are available in many department and specialty stores throughout the United States.

Appendix

International Cocoa Cooperations Organizations

CAOBISCO: Association of Chocolate, Biscuit and Confectionery Industries of the EEC examines all projects and decisions of the Common Market relating to the economics of the European chocolate manufacturing industry. Within this organization is the Chambre Syndicale Nationale des Chocolatier that works closely with international financial bodies and food research and development organizations.

OICCC: International Cocoa, Chocolate, and Confectionery Organization, an association of seventeen countries representing their cocoa, chocolate, confectionery, and sugar industries. The aim of this organization is to encourage scientific research and development in its industries.

AFCC: Association Française du Commerce des Cacaos (French Cocoa Trading Association), formed in 1935, is an international group of professionals responsible for regulating the buying and selling terms of cacao beans and cacao by-products in France and internationally. The group is also entrusted with promoting research into improving the quality and quantity of cacao bean production and encourages the growth in consumption of cacao-based products. It also promotes cooperation between the various branches of the trade.

Caloric Content Per Ounce of Various Types of Chocolate

Unsweetened chocolate 143
Bittersweet chocolate   135
Sweet chocolate 149
Milk chocolate 147
Milk chocolate with almonds   150
Cocoa—high fat powder 84
Cocoa—low fat powder 53

Publications

These are the few publications that concentrate on chocolate and the confectionery trade.

CHOCOLATIER

Aimed at dedicated amateur gourmet chocolate lovers.

Published six times a year. Subscription $23.95 for one year.

Subscription services: **P.O. Box 333**
Mt. Morris, IL 61054
Phone: (815) 734-1109

Editorial offices: **45 West 34th Street, Suite 600**
New York, NY 10001
Phone: (212) 239-0855

PASTRY ART & DESIGN

Aimed at the professional pastry chef and confectioner.
Published bimonthly. Subscription $30 for one year.

Subscription services: **P.O. Box 333**
Mt. Morris, IL 61054
Phone: (815) 734-1109

Editorial offices: **45 West 34th Street, Suite 600**
New York, NY 10001
Phone: (212) 239-0855

CANDY INDUSTRY (TRADE ONLY)

The Magazine of Management and Technology

A trade publication covering all facets of the candy and confectionery industry. Subscription $39 for one year in the United States, $49 for one year in Canada and Mexico.

Editorial offices: **7500 Old Oak Boulevard**
Cleveland, OH 44130-3369
Phone: (216) 243-8100
FAX: (216) 891-2733

Chocolate in Literature

This is an eclectic list in no particular order of some of my favorite novels and books that mention or feature chocolate.

Le Bon Usage du The, du Caffe et du Chocolat by Mr. De Blegny, one of the doctors to Louis XIV. Seventeenth century.
This early work discusses the uses for chocolate during the time when it was in vogue at the French court.

Traités nouveaux et curieux du Café, du Thé et du Chocolat by Philippe Sylvestre Dufour. Paris, 1685.
The author describes the way chocolate is prepared with vanilla and how it is served in Mesoamerica.

A Tale of Two Cities by Charles Dickens. London, 1859.
In this classic novel Dickens describes chocolate drinking as a privilege enjoyed only by the upper classes of society, unknown to the average person. The scene described depicts the character Monseigneur as he is waited upon by four footmen to prepare and serve his chocolate.

Bittersweet Journey by Enid Futterman. New York: Viking, 1998.
This novel tells the story of a woman named Charlotte who travels the world searching for emotional and gustatory satisfaction. In her search she visits renowned chocolate shops in Brussels, Paris, and Vienna where she becomes involved in unsatisfactory relationships that still leave her hungry. Upon her return home to Brooklyn, Charlotte discovers her true love, where he has been all along. This enchanting story is accompanied by beautiful and seductive photographs of chocolates. A few select chocolate recipes are offered at the end of the book.

Ulysses by James Joyce. New York: Random House, 1934.
The two central characters, Leopold Bloom and Stephen Dedalus, share a cup of cocoa in Bloom's kitchen during the only time they meet. The use of cocoa for this important meeting between two middle-class men demonstrates how cocoa has become part of the fabric of daily life.

Charlie and the Chocolate Factory by Roald Dahl. New York: Junior Deluxe Editions, Alfred A. Knopf, 1964.
The adventures of Charlie, a young boy who visits a very whimsical chocolate factory and ends up with more than a chocolate bar. The movie *Willy Wonka and the Chocolate Factory* was made from this book.

Chocolate Fever by Robert Kimmel Smith. New York: Dell
Publishing, 1972.
The story of Henry Green, a young boy who loved to eat chocolate more than
anything and more than anyone else in the world. He ate chocolate for every
meal and in every conceivable form. One day Henry came down with the
only known case of Chocolate Fever and made medical history. Henry's series
of wacky adventures involve a wild chase and a very unusual hijacking.

A Chocolate Moose for Dinner, written and illustrated by Fred
Gwynne. New York: Simon & Schuster, Inc., 1976.
A young girl pictures the things that her parents discuss, such as a chocolate moose, shoe trees, and toasting Daddy. The comical illustrations point
out some of the funny turns of the English language.

The Chocolate Touch by Patrick Skene Catlling. New York:
William Morrow & Company, 1979.
This is the story of John who acquires the magic ability to turn everything
he touches into chocolate, much like the Midas touch. Soon John's delight
turns to dismay as he discovers he might have too much of a good thing.

Chocolate Mouse by Harriet Herbst. San Francisco: Mercury
House, 1988.
This suspenseful love story takes place in Dublin, Ireland. Aggie O'Connell
is a widow in her forties when her young son, Timmy, is diagnosed with dia-
betes. Aggie fears it will be difficult for her to cope because of her own pow-
erful taste for chocolate. Aggie falls in love with detective O'Hare who
hunts down the terrorists who almost killed Timmy in a bombing.

Chocolate Dreams by Arnold Adoff. New York: Lothrop, Lee &
Shepard Books, 1989.
A book of poetry about chocolate for children, illustrated with whimsical
drawings of chocolate confections by Turi MacCombie.

Chocolate Chip Cookies by Karen Wagner. New York: Henry Holt
& Company, 1990.
An illustrated book that guides young children through the simple step-by-
step process to make delicious chocolate chip cookies.

Harold & Chester in Hot Fudge by James Howe. New York:
Morrow Junior Books, 1990.
Harold the dog narrates this story about himself and his friends Chester the
cat and Howie the dachshund puppy. They take off in search of Mr.
Monroe's missing pan of newly made fudge. They have many adventures
while searching for the fudge, including an encounter with Bunnicula, the
world-famous vampire rabbit and his three buddies.

Sweet Death Come Softly by Barbara Whitehead. New York: St.
Martin's Press, 1992.
A mystery tale about Pierre Fontaine, a charming Belgian chocolate maker,
who comes to York, England, to test his new top-secret recipe. Soon after
his arrival he disappears and his car is found abandoned. The police are not
sure if Pierre's disappearance is industrial espionage, kidnapping, or murder
and begin following clues to find out. The taste and smell of chocolate per-
vade the story.

Such Devoted Sisters by Eileen Goudge. New York: Viking, 1992.
A novel of two sisters who are chocolatiers and rivals for the affections of
the same man. This sweeping saga of love and betrayal offers an in-depth
look at the world of chocolate making, from plantations where cacao is
grown to the shops of haute Parisian chocolatiers.

Dying for Chocolate by Diane Mott Davidson. New York: Bantam
Books, 1992, paperback edition, 1993.
A lighthearted culinary mystery featuring the character Goldy Bear, an
inventive caterer, who becomes involved in several personal disasters.
Included are ten recipes for such yummy dishes as Lethal Layers, Strawberry
Super Pie, and Montessori Muffins.

Chocolate by Hershey: A Story About Milton S. Hershey by Betty
Burford. Minneapolis: Carolrhoda Books, Inc., 1994.
For young readers, this is a biographical look at Milton S. Hershey and how
he grew up loving candy and learned to make it at a young age. The book
recounts Hershey's climb from novice candy maker to successful entrepreneur.

London by Edward Rutherford. New York: Crown Publishers, Inc., 1997.

In this novel the author traces the history of London from pre-Roman times to the present. He describes Lady St. James in 1750 as she sips her morning cup of hot chocolate while wearing a silk robe after taking her bath.

Chocolate Movies and Videos

These are some of my favorite movies and videos about chocolate.

Movies

CHOCOLATE

1996 Estate Films, Inc.

NBD Television

Chocolate is traced from it origins in the Americas to current times. Pioneers in the manufacturing and selling of chocolate are highlighted in a colorful manner with lots of interesting facts and trivia. Why we like chocolate so much is the theme of this well-done video.

CHOCOLATE FEVER

1989 CBS, Inc.

Playhouse Video

This animated short video (25 minutes) is all fun. Little Henry Green likes to eat chocolate so much that he contracts Chocolate Fever. He goes to the hospital where they don't know what to do with poor Henry who keeps growing more and more chocolate spots. Through newfound friends Henry finds a cure, a very logical one. Recommended for adults and kids.

THE CHOCOLATE SOLDIER

1941 Metro-Goldwyn-Mayer, Inc.
MGM/UA Home Video

With music written by Oscar Straus and based on the Ferenc Molnár's play *The French Soldier*, this musical comedy is a cultural delight. The setting for much of the film is a stage made of candy where, appropriately, Nelson Eddy (Karl in the film) offers chocolates to his wife, opera singer Risë Stevens (Maria in the film). Karl tests Maria's fidelity by masquerading as a Russian noblemen.

THE CHOCOLATE WAR

1989 M.C.E.G. Productions, Inc.
M.C.E.G. Home Video

The annual chocolate sale at a boys' private school turns out to be a lesson in stamina and principles.

FORREST GUMP

1994 Paramount Pictures, Inc.
Paramount Home Video

Forrest Gump, played by Tom Hanks, likes to make a special gift of chocolate candy in this all-American film. He immortalizes the saying ". . . life is like a box of chocolates, you never know what you'll get."

THE SECRET AGENT

1936 Gaumont British Picture Corporation, Ltd.
Public Media Home Vision

Alfred Hitchcock has British secret agents Peter Lorre and John Gielgud touring, tasting, and being chased in a Swiss chocolate factory.

WHO IS KILLING THE GREAT CHEFS OF EUROPE?

1978 N.F. Gerla II Filmgesellschaft m.b.h.

Warner Home Video

Romance, comedy, and murder all mixed together make this film very, very entertaining. Jacqueline Bisset plays the pastry chef who makes the chocolate bombe that's both beautiful and explosive.

WILLY WONKA & THE CHOCOLATE FACTORY

1971 Wolper Pictures Ltd. and Quaker Oats Company

Warner Home Video

A story about a boy who visits a very whimsical chocolate factory and ends up with more than a chocolate bar.

Videos

CANDY & CHOCOLATE (COOKING AT THE ACADEMY)

International Video Network
2242 Camino Ramon
San Ramon, CA 94583
Tel: (800) 294-2577
ISBN: 1-56345-0240-0
Price: $14.99

Several scrumptious chocolate candies are presented in this 30-minute video. Chef Greg Tompkins, from the California Culinary Academy, walks you through each step to assure that you are successful. Here's your chance to learn how to make your own chocolate truffles with fillings such as orange and almond liqueurs.

CHOCOLATE DREAMS

Great Chefs Publishing
P.O. Box 56757
New Orleans, LA 70156
Tel: (800) 321-1499
ISBN: 0-929714-86-5
Price: $19.95

Eight mouth-watering chocolate desserts are prepared by award-winning chefs. Michael Romano makes marble fudge brownies and Jean-Luc Albin prepares one of my favorites, chocolate Grand Marnier cake. Techniques are stressed throughout. A recipe book is included.

CHOCOLATE EDITION

Great Chefs Publishing
P.O. Box 56757
New Orleans, LA 70156
Tel: (800) 321-1499
ISBN: 0-929714-80-6
Price: $19.95

Step-by-step instruction is given as twenty-one well-known chefs prepare their chocolate specialties from start to finish. These specialties include many recipes ranging from a chocolate roulade with bittersweet sauce and hazelnut filling to a macaroon mocha buttercream cake. The video comes with a recipe book.

CHOCOLATE PASSION

Great Chefs Publishing
P.O. Box 56757
New Orleans, LA 70156
Tel: (800) 321-1499
ISBN: 0-929714-67-9
Price: $19.95

Step-by-step instruction is given as eight famous chefs prepare their most popular chocolate desserts. These range from chocolate terrine to one of my very favorite desserts, white chocolate mousse cake with Frangelico cream and hazelnut praline sauce. A recipe book accompanies the video.

Chocolate in Visual Art

This is a compilation of some of the many paintings and graphic arts that concentrate on chocolate.

The Dresden Codex: Mayan (late pre-Conquest, approximately eighth century). The text states that cacao must be offered to the Rain God during New Year rites.

The Madrid Codex: Mayan (date uncertain), depicts Mayan gods bleeding over cacao. The text specifies the number of cacao beans to be offered to these gods.

The Codex Tudela from the late sixteenth century contains a watercolor of an Aztec woman pouring chocolate from her shoulder height to a vessel near her feet, which will make it foam.

An Aztec stone figure from the mid-fifteenth century depicts a man holding a cacao pod. (The Brooklyn Museum, Brooklyn, New York.)

A woodcut from the 1565 book, *La Historia del Mondo* by the Venetian author G. Benzoni, depicts a cacao tree and shows cacao beans spread out to dry.

A woodcut from the 1565 book, *La Historia del Mondo* by the Venetian author G. Benzoni, depicts Aztecs roasting cacao beans over a fire, pulverizing them to a paste on a metate, and pouring the drink made from these cacao beans.

The History of Mexico, a painting by Mexican artist Diego Rivera has a section showing offerings to Montezuma by other Aztecs. Cacao beans are included along with fruit, vanilla, and tobacco. (Palacio Nacional, Mexico City.)

The frontispiece of a Latin book from 1639 about chocolate shows the sea god Neptune being handed a box of chocolate so he can carry it across the sea from the New World to Europe.

An engraving from Philippe Dufour's seventeenth-century book, *Treatises on Coffee, Tea, and Chocolate*, shows chocolate being drunk along with coffee and tea by a native of each drink's country of origin. The molinet used to prepare chocolate is prominently displayed in the foreground.

Spanish artist Velázquez painted a portrait of the Spanish royal family in which Maria Teresa as a young girl took center stage.

A *Man Scraping Chocolate*, a painting by an anonymous Spanish artist, c.1680–1780, depicts a man crushing cacao nibs on a metate. (The North Carolina Museum of Art, Raleigh, North Carolina.)

Mademoiselle de Charolais, an early eighteenth-century portrait of Louise-Anne de Bourbon-Condé, dressed in a monk's habit to show her dedication to the Franciscan order, with a cup of chocolate. (Collection Château de Versailles, France.)

La Xocolatada, a Catalonian panel of glazed earthenware tiles, about 1720, depicting gentlemen preparing hot chocolate from small sticks of chocolate and serving the beverage to ladies. (Museum of Ceramics, Barcelona, Spain.)

Still Life: Chocolate Service, by Spanish artist Luis Menendez, 1776, depicts a copper chocolate pot with a molinet, large cups to hold the beverage, and tablets of chocolate used to prepare the drink. (Museo del Prado, Madrid, Spain.)

The Cup of Chocolate, an eighteenth-century painting by Jean-Baptiste Charpentier, depicts members of the French court, the family of the Duc de Penthièvre, who are enjoying their chocolate. (Collection Château de Versailles, France.)

The Cup of Chocolate, an eighteenth-century French painting by Nicolas Lancret, shows chocolate being served to a family and drunk in their garden. (The National Gallery, London, England.)

A *Valet Serving Chocolate*, an eighteenth-century red and black chalk drawing, heightened with white, on buff paper by François Boucher is a study for his painting *Le Dejuner*, which is in the collection of the Louvre in Paris. This drawing depicts chocolate being served by a valet to his master. (The Art Institute of Chicago.)

Le Déjeuner, by François Boucher, 1739, is a portrait of Boucher's family at breakfast, being served chocolate by their valet. (The Louvre, Paris, France.)

The Beautiful Chocolate Girl, by Swiss painter Jean-étienne Liotard, about 1743, depicts the chambermaid who brought his daily chocolate. This painting became the trademark for the Walter Baker Chocolate Company. (Gemaldegalerie, Alte Meister Staatliche Kunstsammlungen, Dresden, Germany.)

Breakfast, by Swiss painter Jean-étienne Liotard, 1754, depicts an upper-class young woman sitting in a chair while her serving woman brings her a cup of breakfast chocolate. (Alten Pinakothek, Munich, Germany.)

Fear, an engraving by mid-eighteenth-century French artist Noel Le Mire of an alluring woman in bed reaching for her morning cup of chocolate, who is obviously startled by an intruder or a noise. (Art Institute, Williamstown, Massachusetts.)

The Bath, by Swiss painter Sigmund Ferudenberger, late eighteenth century, depicts a maid bringing her morning cup of chocolate and a love letter to a woman in her bath. (The Metropolitan Museum of Art, New York.)

Breakfast, an eighteenth-century French engraving by Lépicié depicts a servant pouring chocolate from its pot. (The Metropolitan Museum of Art, New York.)

Still Life, by Antonio Pereda, 1652, depicts all the instruments for preparing and enjoying a chocolate beverage: the molinet, chocolate pot, chocolate drinking cups, a jug of water, sweetened chocolate in rolls, and sweet bread to accompany the drink. (The Hermitage Museum, St. Petersburg, Russia.)

A watercolor painted in 1787 by English artist Thomas Rowlandson depicts the inside of a chocolate house. (Museum of London.)

Friar Drinking Chocolate, 1891, a painting by Mexican artist Jose M. Oropeza, depicts a hooded friar smiling in anticipation as he brings a cup of chocolate to his lips to taste. (Museo Nacional de Historia, Mexico City.)

The Cup of Chocolate, by Mary Cassatt, 1897, is a pastel on paper mounted on canvas. (Terra Museum of American Art, Chicago, Illinois.)

Chocolate Grinder, No. 2, by French artist Marcel Duchamp, 1912, depicts his interpretation of an old-fashioned chocolate grinder that he observed in a confectioner's shop window in Rouen. (The Philadelphia Museum of Art, Philadelphia, Pennsylvania.)

Breakfast, by Spanish artist Juan Gris, 1914, depicts a set of chocolate cups and a chocolate pot on a kitchen table executed in mixed medium of crayon, oil, and paper. (The Museum of Modern Art, New York.)

Give Me Chocolate or Give Me Death, a poster published by Ten Speed Press. (Berkeley, California.)

A still life by seventeenth-century French painter Alexandre-François Desportes depicts a silver chocolate pot next to a sliver tray holding several cups for the hot chocolate, in a fanciful garden setting, surrounded by a heaping basket of fresh oranges, a green velvet cloth, a violin, a cello, and a book of music.

Denis Diederot's *Pictorial Encyclopedia of Trades and Industry* depicts an eighteenth-century French chocolate workshop, including a screw press and roller table.

Madame Brion by the eighteenth-century Flemish painter Jacques André Joseph Aved shows an average person, a bourgeoise, drinking chocolate.

Maria Theresa's breakfast service contains a chocolate pot made from gold vermeil and chocolate cups of Chinese porcelain mounted in gold. (The Kunsthistoriche Museum, Vienna, Austria.)

Louis XV's queen, Marie Leszcynska, owned a gold gilded chocolate pot. (Cliché des Musées Nationaux, Paris, France.)

A thirty-eight-foot tall chocolate sculpture of Germania standing inside a pavilion was made of thirty thousand pounds of chocolate by the Stollwerck chocolate company of Cologne, Germany for the 1893 World's Columbian Exposition in Chicago, Illinois.

Early twentieth-century chocolate posters by chocolate manufacturers such as Suchard, Tobler, Menier, Cailler, Kohler, Nestlé, Poulain, and Cadbury were used to advertise their products.

Czech artist Alphonse Mucha's art nouveau poster for Chocolat Idéal, which was produced by the Compagnie Française des Chocolates et des Thés.

Chocolat Suchard, a 1939 color lithograph by Alois Carigiet is a poster-type advertisement for Suchard chocolate.

Decorative chocolate boxes designed by Richard Cadbury in the late nineteenth century carried his original paintings of his children.

Chocolat de Montreux, date unknown, is a poster advertisement for the chocolate company. It depicts two children in a rural landscape. (The Art Institute of Chicago.)

The Garden Parasol, painted in 1910 by Frederick Carl Frieseke (collection the North Carolina Museum of Art, Raleigh, North Carolina) adorns 1997 boxes of Russell Stover candies produced for Mother's Day.

Ramon Roca of Confiteria Bomboneria Roca in Girona, Spain, (mid-twentieth century) hand-formed a chocolate reproduction of a twelfth-century tapestry in the cathedral of Girona, the oldest tapestry in the cathedral. He decorated the chocolate tapestry with pastry tips using colored chocolate.

The Statue of Liberty was sculpted in chocolate by Barcelona confectioner José Balcells Pallarés in 1984. The statue weighed 229 pounds and was eight and a half feet tall.

White House pastry chef Roland Mesnier sculpted a chocolate eagle atop the Presidential Seal, also in chocolate, for the 1997 inauguration of President Bill Clinton. Individual chocolate medals adorn the sculpture.

Bibliography

Bavoillot, Ghislaine, ed. *The Book of Chocolate*. New York: Flammarion, 1996.

Bernachon, Maurice, and Jean-Jacques Bernachon, translated and adapted by Rose Levy Beranbaum. *A Passion For Chocolate*. New York: William Morrow, 1989.

Bloom, Carole. *The Candy Cookbook*. San Francisco: Chronicle Books, 1995.

————. *Truffles, Candies, & Confections: Elegant Candymaking in the Home*. Freedom, Calif.: The Crossing Press, 1992, 1996.

Boynton, Sandra. *Chocolate: The Consuming Passion*. New York: Workman Publishing, 1982.

Brody, Lora. *Growing Up on the Chocolate Diet, A Memoir with Recipes*. Boston: Little, Brown, 1985.

Centre d'Etudes Pâtisserie Excel. *Les Chocolates en pâtisserie et confiserie*. Paris: Excel-Erti, 1957.

Coady, Chantal. *Chocolate: Food of the Gods*. San Francisco: Chronicle Books, 1993.

————. *The Chocolate Companion*. New York: Simon & Schuster, 1995.

Coe, Sophie D., and Michael D. Coe. *The True History of Chocolate*. New York: Thames and Hudson, 1996.

Colmenero de Ledesma, Antonio. *Chocolate: or, an Indian Drinke*. London: J. Oakes, 1652.

Constant, Christian. *Le Chocolat*. Paris: Nathan, 1988.

Desaulniers, Marcel. *Death by Chocolate*. New York: Rizzoli Books, 1992.

Divone, Judene. *Chocolate Moulds: A History & Encyclopedia*. Oakton, Va.: Oakton Hills Publications, 1987.

Fuller, Linda K., PhD. *Chocolate Fads, Folklore, & Fantasies: 1,000 + Chunks of Chocolate Information*. New York: The Haworth Press, 1994.

Gage, Thomas. *A New Survey of the West Indies, 1648*. New York: Robert M. McBride & Co., 1929.

Gonzalez, Elaine. *Chocolate Artistry*. Chicago: Contemporary Books, 1986.

Head, Brandon. *The Food of the Gods*. London: George Routledge & Sons Ltd., 1903.

Heatter, Maida. *Maida Heatter's Book of Great Chocolate Desserts*. New York: Alfred A. Knopf, 1980.

Historicus (Cadbury, Richard). *Cocoa: All About It*. London: Sampson Low, Marston and Company Ltd., 1896.

Lenôtre, Gaston, translated and adapted by Philip and Mary Hyman. *Lenôtre's Desserts and Pastries*. Woodbury, N.Y.: Barron's Educational Series, 1977.

————, translated and adapted by Philip and Mary Hyman. *Lenôtre's Ice Creams and Candies*. Woodbury, N.Y.: Barron's Educational Series, 1979.

Linxe, Robert. *La Maison du Chocolat*. Paris: Robert Laffont, 1992.

McFadden, Christine, and Christine France. *The Ultimate Encyclopedia of Chocolate*. London: Smithmark Publishers, 1997.

Medrich, Alice. *Cocolat: Extraordinary Chocolate Desserts*. New York: Warner Books, 1990.

————. *Chocolate and The Art of Low-Fat Baking.* New York: Warner Books, 1994.

Minifie, Bernard W. *Chocolate, Cocoa, and Confectionery: Science and Technology.* Third edition. New York: Van Nostrand Reinhold, 1989.

Morton, Marcia, and Frederic Morton. *Chocolate: An Illustrated History.* New York: Crown Publishers, Inc., 1988.

Norman, Jill. *Chocolate: The Chocolate Lover's Guide to Complete Indulgence.* London: Dorling Kindersley Ltd., 1990.

Ott, Jonathan. *The Cacahuatl Eater: Ruminations of an Unabashed Chocolate Addict.* Vashon, Wash.: Natural Products Co., 1985.

Paulli, Simon, translated by Dr. James. *A Treatise on Tobacco, Tea, Coffee, and Chocolate.* London: T. Osborne, 1846.

Perry, Sara. *The Chocolate Book.* San Francisco: Chronicle Books, 1992.

Rubin, Cynthia Elyce, ed. *Bread & Chocolate: Culinary Traditions of Switzerland.* New York: Writer's House, Inc., 1993.

Szogi, Alex, ed. *Chocolate: Food of the Gods.* Westport, Conn.: Greenwood Press, 1997.

Teubner, Christian. *The Chocolate Bible.* New York: Penguin Studio, 1997.

Walter Baker & Co., Ltd. *Description of the Educational Exhibit of Cocoa and Chocolate.* New York: The Barta Press, 1913.

Waterhouse, Debra. *Why Women Need Chocolate.* New York: Hyperion, 1995.

Wild, Antony. *The East India Company Book of Chocolate.* London: HarperCollins, 1995.

Willan, Anne. *Look & Cook Chocolate Desserts.* New York: Dorling Kindersley, Inc., 1992.

Wood, G. A. R., and R. A. Lass, *Cocoa.* Fourth edition. New York and London: Longman, Inc., 1985.

Young, Allen M. *The Chocolate Tree: A Natural History of Cacao.* Washington and London: Smithsonian Institution Press, 1994.

Index

F

Factory tours, museums,
attractions, and theme parks,
197–205
Fancy Food Show, 194
Fannie May, 262
Fantasies in Chocolate, 186
Fat, 165
Fauchon, 263
Felchlin, Max, 58, 292
Fenton & Lee Chocolatiers, 263
Fern Cliff House, 309
Ferrero, 59
Festivals, chocolate, 177–92
Fetzer Vineyards Red Wine &
Chocolate Spectacular, 182
Fiat Cremino, 59
5th Avenue, 59
Firehouse Art Center Chocolate
Festival, 183
M. Fish Limited, 329
Flavor, 154
Florentines, 59
Fondant chocolate, 59
Fondue, chocolate, 20–21
La Fontaine au Chocolat (Michel
Cluziel), 271
Forastero, 59–60, 144, 145
Fouquet, 264
Frango, 60
Frangomints, 60
Fran's Chocolates, 264
Frappé, chocolate, 21
French Chocolate Macaroons
(recipe), 24–25
French Culinary Institute, 228
French Pastry School, 229
Fry, J.S., & Sons, 60
Fudge, 60–61
Chocolate Nut (recipe), 61–62
hot, 70
Fudge, Hot, Sauce (recipe), 71
Futures, cocoa, 173–74

G

Ganache, 62–63
Squares, Lemon (recipe), 63–64
Ganache beurre, 64
Gâteau l'opéra, 64
G. Detou, 315
Gelato, chocolate, 21
Gerkens Cacao, 65, 293
German chocolate cake, 65
German's chocolate, 65
Ghirardelli Chocolate Company,
65, 293
Gianduia, 65–66, 148
Gianduia Chocolate Squares
(recipe), 66–67
Gianduiotti, 67
Glaze, chocolate, 21
Godiva Chocolates, 241
Goo Goo Cluster, 67
Gosanko Chocolate Art, 316
Gourmail, 310
Grace, Helen, Chocolates, 267, 306
Grand Avenue Chocolates, 265
Grand Finale, 305
Grand Rapids Community
College, 229
Great Lakes Gourmet, 316
Green & Black's, 67, 293–94
Web site, 241
Guayaquil, 68
Guittard Chocolate Company,
68, 294

H

Haigh's Chocolate Factory
Tours, 200
Haigh's Chocolates, 265
Handling chocolate, 158–60
Harbor Sweets, 266
Harry London Chocolate Factory
Tours, 200
Hauser Chocolatier, 266

V

Valrhona, 98, 301, 320
Van Houten, Coenraad, 98, 146
Vanilla bean, 98
Vanilla extract, 99, 155
Vanillin, 99
Van Rex Gourmet Foods, Inc., 320
Vantage House, 334
La Varenne Ecole de Cuisine, 236
Videos, 345–47
Viscosity, 99

W

Web sites, 237–43
Weiss, 285
West Coast Candy and Confections
    Expo, 194
Where to find chocolate, 245–85
White chocolate, 99–100, 147, 165
    Truffles, Swiss (recipe), 33–34

White's, 100
Wholesale candy and confectionery
    manufacturers, 303–8
Wilbur Chocolate Candy Americana
    Museum, 205
Wilbur Chocolate Company,
    100, 301
Williams-Sonoma, 312, 334
Wilton Enterprises, Inc., 335
Winnowing, 100
Wittamer, 285
World Pastry Cup, 214–15
World Wide Web, 237–43

X

Xocoatl, 100

Y

York, 100